"That adage—truth is stranger than fiction—does not begin to describe this fascinating book by Bard Lindeman. It is as interesting as a scientific detective story and as moving as any poignant novel I have read in recent years. I could not put it down."

—Ray Robinson, Articles Editor,
Good Housekeeping

"The whole story of the separate lives of the twins up to their discovery of each other's existence in adult years has the quality of a suspense novel. The book will receive much attention for the light it throws on the relative influences of heredity and environment, with much to be said for both sides."

—*Publishers' Weekly*

"**This is a fascinating true life story of the reunion of twins.** To me it has the ring of truth, for the close bond between twins described in the book corresponds to what I have observed in my clinical studies of twin pairs. The fascinating aspect is the strength of the twin bond in spite of the long separation between the two brothers."

—Dr. Edward D. Joseph, Psychoanalyst

THE TWINS WHO FOUND EACH OTHER
was originally published by William Morrow & Co., Inc.

The Twins

Who Found

Each Other

by Bard Lindeman

Introduction by Amram Scheinfeld

PUBLISHED BY **POCKET BOOKS** NEW YORK

For my wife

THE TWINS WHO FOUND EACH OTHER

William Morrow edition published October, 1969

Pocket Book edition published February, 1971

This *Pocket Book* edition includes every word
contained in the original, higher-priced edition. It is printed
from brand-new plates made from completely reset, clear, easy-to-read
type. *Pocket Book* editions are published by Pocket Books, a division
of Simon & Schuster, Inc., 630 Fifth Avenue, New York, N.Y. 10020.
Trademarks registered in the United States and other countries.

Standard Book Number: 671-77225-2.
Library of Congress Catalog Card Number: 76-85876.

Printed in the U.S.A.

INTRODUCTION

Among all the human subjects studied by geneticists, psychologists and other scientists with a view to throwing light on the inherent nature of human behavior, the most interesting may well have been identical twins who were separated in infancy and not brought together again until they were adults. The histories of such twins—only a few score have been recorded—have contributed greatly to our understanding of the relative influences of heredity and environment in making individuals what they are. Now, in the most recent of these case histories as reported by Bard Lindeman, we have perhaps the most thorough and perceptive account ever written about the lives of long-separated and then reunited twins. It is not only an engrossing narrative but a human document which will have special meaning for all who are personally or professionally concerned with twins and their problems.

The unusual story of these twins, Tony Milasi and Roger Brooks, comes at a time when various educators and psychologists have been stressing mainly the negative aspects of twinship and urging parents to rear them as differently as possible —never dressing them the same, separating them in school, and discouraging any undue closeness between them—lest their "ego identities" and "individualities" be threatened. But here, in this book, we have the story of young adult twins who believe that it was their very separation which had robbed them of something vitally important. They strove to find each other, and when their questing search finally brought them together, they felt that their lives had been made much richer, happier and more complete.

Another recent tendency among many social scientists has been to deprecate heredity and emphasize environment as almost the sole determinant of human intelligence and behavior patterns. On a broad scale, this has constructive value: Unquestionably, the major differences in behavior and achievement among *groups* of human beings can be attributed preponderantly to disparities in environment and conditioning. So, too, far more can be done immediately to upgrade human levels by environmental improvements than by any program for altering human heredity.

Yet this need not obscure the fact that between and among *individuals,* heredity may create important differences in mental and behavioral traits. Thus, since identical (*monozygotic*) twins have the same hereditary factors (being products of the same fertilized egg), those who have been long reared apart provide us with natural experimental material. We can then judge to what extent matching hereditary factors will assert themselves when exposed to different environments.

What happened, then, with Tony Milasi and Roger Brooks, who for their first two decades were reared so differently? Their religious, cultural, home, physical and psychological experiences were markedly disparate. As in many other cases of separated and reunited twins, they were brought together by the remarkable similarity in looks which caused people to confuse one with the other. The very fact that such resemblance in innumerable facial and bodily details could have developed by successive stages in distinctly different and widely separated environments offers evidence of the overwhelming effects of heredity on an individual's biological construction and functioning. But did the hereditary effects stop there? Could not the many biological similarities of the twins also extend to and influence their mental functioning and behavior? That they could and did is suggested by the detailed findings of the psychological tests made on them.

However, what may be most significant are not the twins'

psychological similarities, but some of the differences in their personalities and characters. In explanation, the author tells us that Tony was reared from birth in an Italian Catholic home, with the security offered by warm, affectionate, emotional foster parents and a host of loving relatives. In contrast, Roger was tossed about in institutions throughout his early childhood. He was physically and emotionally traumatized, and then reared haphazardly in a wholly atypical Jewish environment. These great disparities in conditioning should have led to extreme differences in the psychological traits of the two men. That, instead, these two emerged with virtually identical IQs and with many striking similarities in behavior and psychological responses might well suggest the strong influence of their identical heredity.

The author inevitably touches on the "mystic bond" believed to exist between identical twins, and perhaps between the twins in this account. No scientific proof yet exists for this presumed phenomenon, nor have extensive "extrasensory perception" tests of identical twins shown them to have exceptional "ESP" scores. There remains the theoretical possibility that if telepathic communication between human beings does exist, identical twins—with highly similar brain waves and brain functioning—would be particularly likely to have such sensitivity to each other's thoughts.

In any case, the strong desire of each twin to find the other should not be overlooked. In a world where the feeling of isolation, alienation and rejection is the cause of so much individual unhappiness and maladjustment, one should not minimize the opportunity—uniquely offered to identical twins—of being with another person so much like oneself, and whose destinies are inseparably linked with one's own.

One can be grateful to Tony and Roger, and to Mr. Lindeman, for enabling others to look into these two unusual lives, and to learn from them something of what might have happened to those of us who are singletons if we had been duplicated at birth and if each of our dual selves had been brought up apart in different environments.

AMRAM SCHEINFELD

New York. March 10, 1969

AUTHOR TO READER

Twins represent a biological rarity, a happening out of the ordinary. So impressive is this exception that it has left its mark on the imagination of men of every ethnic group in every epoch of history.

> —*Dr. Luigi Gedda, Rome University professor of medical genetics.*

The universal fascination of twins is an understandable phenomenon, for when two infants are born as human duplicates they provoke significant questions about all beings.

Moreover, in science's continuous assault upon the enigma: heredity versus environment, the identical twin has become an invaluable research instrument, because he and his partner begin life with identical genes. So there is between them a fixed control of the hereditary, or genetic, factors, and any differences that occur necessarily have their basis in environment. Conversely, all similarities, physical as well as those of personality and intelligence, must begin with their common hereditary contribution. Obviously then, the possibilities for study are limitless. One enthused researcher has called identical twins "our only living laboratory." Others have declared that worldwide twin studies have "significantly advanced the frontiers of genetics." This statement is unarguable, for through twin studies it has been proven there are hereditary elements in some forms of blindness, deafness, epilepsy, diabetes and polio; additionally, the first successful organ transplant was performed with an identical twin as the recipient of his brother's kidney, literally a lifesaving gift.

Now, though the use of twins in medical research is comparatively new, being less than one hundred years old, the fascination created by "look-alike" partners is nearly as old as the story of civilization. There is an entire literature of twin myths and lore dating from the Babylonian and Assyrian civilizations. The most famous of all twin legends is that of Romulus and Remus, sons of a Vestal Virgin, who in 753 B.C., on high ground close by the river Tiber, founded the city of Rome, affording it the claim to the title City of Twins.

Some early cultures regarded twins as magicians or gods of healing and saw them only in magnificent or heroic roles, such as Castor and Pollux, the fearless, inseparable brothers who, according to the Greek fable, became the Gemini or twin constellation. Other cultures, however, considered twins a threat. They believed that a curse or disease was responsible for the multiple birth and required one twin be sacrificed. If the twins were of opposite sex, it was the female who was murdered; a number of American Indian tribes put all second-born twins to death, holding that they were not real people, but carriers of bad fortune.

Other Indian nations, though, treated twins as favored children. They believed they were capable of supernatural acts and if not well pleased on earth would return to the heavens. Therefore, these twins were always set apart, made to dress alike in bright clothing and afforded special care.

Though motivated by superstition, the Indians were actually behaving in a natural and understandable way, for among civilized people the response to identical twins is almost always an enthusiastic one. As a result, twins have been made to feel unique and encouraged to believe they possess something that is interesting to others and, in some ways, superior.

The fascination with twins is reflected not just in myths and fables, but in all literature. There are enduring Greek and Roman dramas about twins and there are biblical twins: Jacob and Esau struggled within their mother's womb, arguing as to who was to be the first-born. And Shakespeare, a father of twins, made sport of twinship in *Twelfth Night* and *A Comedy of Errors*. Mark Twain, Alexandre Dumas, Thomas Mann, Aldous Huxley, Edgar Allan Poe and Thornton Wilder created fictional plots with twins; still further, there have been twins in opera, movie stories, stage plays, comic strips and several generations of American chidren grew up familiar with the derring-do of the Bobbsey Twins.

Yet, nowhere in all the millions of words written about twins is there a story, which for inscrutability, breadth of interest and dramatic realism, can match the account of the creation of identical or monozygotic, meaning one-egg, twins.

At first, there is a single fertilized egg. Life then begins as it does for any ordinary child, but some time between the first and tenth day after conception and for reasons that are beyond the ken of science, the egg separates. The forty-six chromosomes perform what has been described as "the dance of life." Each divides precisely in half, and now two eggs continue to grow in the womb. In each egg *all* the hereditary factors—forty-six chromosomes bearing an estimated fifty thousand genes—are going to be exactly alike. The result is the same person twice.

This miracle occurs approximately 3.5 times in every 1,000 births, and though a woman's age and previous childbearing experience affect her chances to bear *fraternal* twins, the worldwide incidence of identical twinning appears not to be affected by these factors. Oddly, fraternals are born most often to women between thirty-five and forty, and with the addition of each child to her family the possibilities of her having a multiple birth increase.

Moreover, it has been established that the likelihood of fraternal twinning becomes far greater if a woman has previously had twins and, to a lesser degree, is herself a twin. This of course suggests a hereditary basis for fraternal twinning. Although there is no evidence that identical twinning has any such background, there is speculation these tendencies exist.

Amram Scheinfeld, an inveterate twin investigator, has

said: "Whatever the facts may be about twinning inheritance, its workings are complex and any 'twinning' genes would come from bôth sides of a family."

Scheinfeld also wrote in his *Twins and Supertwins* that the appeal of infant twins is so overwhelming—particularly with women—that no mother of identical twins could possibly walk her babies along a busy sidewalk without being stopped by at least several admirers. Admittedly, a measure of this attraction is in the strong resemblance, and the second-born of all identicals is a human carbon of his partner. All their genetically determined features are alike; this is especially noticeable of the hands and fingers; the nose, ears, eyes, mouth, lips and chin; the teeth formations and jaw structure; the texture and whorl of the hair and even the number and the position of freckles. And according to the research of one medical investigator, the difference in the heart size of identical twins is less han one millimeter in diameter.

These uncommon partners have the same blood type and count, similar fingerprints, palm and footprints and generally tend to be alike in blood pressure, respiratory rate and, logically, their heartbeat. Equally incredible, there is an almost complete similarity in the structure of their bones. So close are they that frequently the X-rays of their hands and feet are interchangeable. Perhaps even more dramatic is medical science's evidence that though no singleton patient can receive a skin graft save from his own body, it is possible for monozygotic twins to exchange grafts.

Identical twins also have uncannily similar voices. In fact, in some cases they cannot recognize their own speech on tape, confusing it with that of their twin. Further, they have similar tastes, body odors and body chemicals and show their remarkable affinity in their smoking habits, like tolerance and appetite for foods and drink, particularly alcohol, and by similar sex drives.

So too do they age similarly, reaching puberty together and eventually developing facial wrinkles in the same areas at the same time. It is only natural, and understandable, that these twins confuse people. Even mothers of identicals have been momentarily fooled, and Sir Francis Galton, the pioneer geneticist, wrote of a case where a young girl began talking, or so she believed, with her sister. She was actually staring at her own mirrored image.

Researchers know, as well, that the IQs of identicals will be but a few points apart, generally much closer than those of fraternal twins and between siblings in the same family. Oftentimes this is so despite a wide disparity in the schooling and home environment of the twins, as for instance in the example of thirteen-year-old boys separated soon after birth. One became the adopted son of a medical doctor, his twin became the son of a laborer who was described as shiftless and unsuccessful. When tested, both boys were equally intelligent.

Experiments have shown further that monozygotics possess remarkably alike brain waves, giving support to a theory that their minds work similarly. These results have encouraged those few investigators who maintain that, in addition to their biological and physical ties, there is a psychic quality to the relationship between identical twins. How else, they ask, can one explain the times when a twin, even though far away, knows what his partner is doing or thinking? And how else can one account for the times when they unknowingly buy each other the same gift, or suffer similar accidents, or enlist in the military at almost the same time in different, and distant, cities?

In their autobiography *Double Exposure,* twins Gloria Vanderbilt and Thelma Lady Furness describe several parallel incidents. On a night during which her sister gave birth in England, Mrs. Vanderbilt, at home in New York City, complained of abdominal pains, and when she in turn became seriously ill with diphtheria, Lady Furness was forewarned by a sudden, seemingly inexplicable sore throat.

The sisters related there is between them "a strange sharing of each other's thoughts and feelings and while we differ in many ways, there is this common entity, this psychic bond. . . ."

This bond, where it exists, is a part of the total mystique that surrounds certain monozygotic partnerships and makes it credible to accept that *the closest of all human relationships is that between identical twins.* But this statement is not conjecture nor is it anyone's personal opinion. Rather, it is a scientific fact, clearly established through studies that have shown, as well, that the union between some identicals is so overwhelming that when they are apart they actually experience a sense of incompleteness.

There is, for example, the case of four-year-old English twins whom researchers called Bessie and Jessie. Because of Miss Jessie's having scarlet fever, she and her sister were separated. During her first days alone, Bessie never laughed. She smiled only infrequently, and her appetite was poor. Eventually, she retreated to her room and lay on the bed, lonely, confused, withdrawn.

"I want to sleep," she protested, "until my sister comes back from the hospital."

From her detailed observations of Bessie and Jessie and a small number of other twin pairs gathered in England at the Hampstead Nurseries during the years 1940-1945, psycho-analyst Dorothy Burlingham concluded: "Separation from the twin seems to have the same emotional value and produce the same reactions as separation from the mother."

As the twins grew older, Miss Burlingham found their reaction to separation was intensified and "approached a state of mourning." In support of this is an account of Jessie, again desperately lonely for her twin, gathering all her toys and quietly settling down before a mirror. "In this way, she was attempting to gain the companionship she was missing," Miss Burlingham wrote in her text *Twins*.

It is the companionship that so greatly contributes to the closeness between identicals, this communion which begins in the womb, matures all through life and has what many researchers contend is the power of a mystique.

When only sixteen months, little Jessie, sleeping alone, awoke in the middle of the night for no reason other than that her sister was crying in another room, one far out of her hearing range. At twenty-four months, the incident was repeated—only this night Jessie astounded her nurse by saying, "My Bessie crying."

"They understand each other when they are not understood by others," explained the British author. "They appear to perceive and answer to subtle and slight signs which are imperceptible to others and which give the impression their understanding goes beyond the realm of consciousness.

"It is true, the relationship goes through stormy periods but the need for the twin makes each partner adjust and the twin union therefore becomes the closest known tie between two individuals."

Indeed, so profound is this understanding that Miss Burlingham saw evidence between the twins of a contagion of feeling. "When either of them showed a strong emotion, the other caught it and then expressed it by identical behavior." So in spite of certain natural differences that developed as the two grew older, the almost constant process of emotional identification worked to keep the twins identical. The British scientist noted, "If one twin experienced a pleasure or pain, the other lived through the same experience in identification."

A twin himself, Thornton Wilder understood the mystique of identical twins and knew of the contagion of feeling. In *The Bridge of San Luis Rey,* he wrote of the twins Manuel and Esteban who sometimes spoke in a language intelligible only to themselves, a language that was "the symbol of their identity with one another." These two were so strongly simpatico that "all the world was remote and strange and hostile except one's brother."

When Manuel died, Esteban was distraught. It was as though a part of himself had died, and he was now deprived of any good reason for living. He tried to end his life by hanging. When he was saved, he fell to the floor, crying: "I am alone, alone, alone."

The scientific study of identical twins began when in 1875 Dr. Francis Galton, the founder of eugenics, correctly speculated that the "look-alike" twins were born of the same, divided egg. He at once recognized the great potential of the twins for studying the relative effects of heredity and environment, and though much of his early research was flawed, Sir Francis showed the way for others. Then, in the 1920s, several scientists grew dissatisfied with the too-similar environments in which twins were reared and decided to search out pairs who had been raised apart. They hoped to discover some with greatly dissimilar home lives, including differing parental controls, different schooling experiences and, perhaps, even different religious backgrounds. However, these cases occur infrequently, and even today the international literature on them is considered inadequate. Until recently, the most ambitious study of separated monozygotics was the classical American work *Twins—A Study of Heredity and Environment.* It was published in 1937 and reported on only nineteen pairs. The authors—Doctor H. H. Newmann and colleagues Dr. F. N. Freeman and Dr. K. J. Holzinger—spent ten years scouting twin pairs and preparing their work and then admitted that only in a few of the cases were the environmental differences thought to be great.

In 1962, the Newmann study was succeeded by the publication in London of James Shields' investigation into the personalities of forty-four pairs of separated twins, titled *Monozygotic Twins Brought Up Apart and Brought Up Together*. The thrust of this cautious work was that genetic factors must be regarded as playing an important part in the development of personality, while the causes of any differences "are multiple."

The author, a lecturer at the London Psychiatric Institute, concluded that with the majority of monozygotic pairs he examined "similarities were thought to be more outstanding than differences" and that in spite of any environmental differences the twins remained obstinately alike.

"It seems clear," Shields wrote, "that monozygotic twins frequently show important mental or behavioral similarities and their family environments can vary a lot without obscuring their basic personalities." The researcher cited similarities in voice, gait, vivacity, a common tendency toward caution, their attitudes toward each other and a similar sex life.

The earlier Newmann study offered a similar opinion. Although the overall analysis was weighted toward an environmental interpretation, Newmann himself was impressed "with the very great similarities after the twins had been exposed to environmental differences."

Still, neither of the research projects scored heavily on the side of heredity or environment. James Shields stated he was against taking sides "for it is the genes that are inherited, not finally formed physical characteristics . . . and there is no reason to assume that a trait cannot be effectively influenced by environmental factors."

In summary, Shields declared: "At our present stage of knowledge, much human behavior appears to be the result of individual unpredictability." Of course, genetics is a young science, and its application to human behavior is a recent development. So understandably, the authorities are most conservative in their interpretations, though disagreements among them are common. As an example, Ashley Montagu, the Princeton University anthropologist, faults those who give too much attention to the reportedly *remarkable* physical and psychological likenesses between identical twins, particularly those reared apart. He is skeptical of the findings of the Newmann study, and other smaller studies that followed it, because "when the cases are examined it is seen the differences in the environments were not really as great as superficially appeared to be." In his work *Human Heredity* Dr. Montagu wrote, "Whenever the environment of identicals is varied, we observe significant differences between them, and this is particularly true of those traits that are most subject to the influence of environment, namely psychological traits."

There is, however, one area of agreement among everyone active in the field: that is the call for more and more research. Almost as a plea, Shields writes:

"The study of monozygotics brought up apart must be judged of sufficient interest and importance for cases to be investigated and recorded in the literature whenever possible."

And others, equally concerned, have pointed out that such cases are increasingly more difficult to discover. Enlightened welfare policies, which assure greater financial aid to dependent children, coupled with the increased demand for twins to adopt, have meant there no longer are compelling reasons to separate twin pairs. Most adoption agencies today forbid the practice, regarding it as potentially unhealthy for both partners.

Amram Scheinfeld has declared, "Happily for twins, but regretfully for scientific study, the cases of those separated from infancy are becoming rare."

When in early December 1963 I first met the twins Tony Milasi and Roger Brooks, I had no thought that I was beginning an investigation into their personalities, a project that was to continue five years. Nor did I understand on this clear and cold winter's morning that their story belonged to the literature on separated monozygotics. But as we three worked together, fitting into place the scattered pieces of their lives, even to discovering the identity of their natural mother—a woman who, literally, is a stranger to them—I realized the uniqueness and merit of our study.

I read Shields and Newmann, Scheinfeld, Burlingham, Gedda and some others and learned that twin studies today are worldwide, with great research centers in England, Italy, Germany, Japan, Russia and Latin America. These studies all seek answers to the causes of disease, as well as reasons for certain human behavior. They range from the problem of nail biting to schizophrenia, and behind each inquiry is the question: "What part heredity, what part environment?" If one twin suffers with epilepsy or multiple sclerosis or leukemia, then what of his partner?

In time, I was committed to learning all that I possibly could of my subjects, of the forces of environment and heredity that helped mold them and of their mystique, this powerful need for each other.

This, I was finally to understand, was their very special property, and it transcended distance, time and whatever differences existed in their lives apart.

... all the world was remote and strange and hostile except one's brother.
—*Thornton Wilder.*

1

Roger

He can reach back and remember each detail. It began in Miami, Florida, on the night of September 28, 1962. This was Rosh Hashanah and, curiously, the only time in his life that Roger Brooks sang with the Temple Beth Shirah choir. He sang as a favor to his grandmother, who had said: "Please, do this for me, Roger, and God will one day reward you."

He didn't believe this, but he sang nonetheless; and after the service he and Ray Skop, the rabbi's son and his best friend, along with Ray's wife, drove south along U. S. Highway 1 looking for a restaurant. Alva Skop had complained of a headache and had wanted to go straight home. But Roger had insisted he was going to treat to coffee and cake, saying: "This is a night to celebrate."

It was a perfect fall night, warm with a soft onshore breeze cooling the land under a dark but cloudless sky. As they rode along, the three sitting up front in Roger's three-year-old Ford, they had no place in mind until Alva spotted the Pancake House. Roger turned off the highway and into the macadam parking lot, only then deciding to second-guess Alva Skop's suggestion.

"Pancakes at night? Who ever heard of eating pancakes at night?"

"Oh, Brooks," Alva said, "you're such a square."

"I don't even like pancakes in the morning," Roger said.

"Have a Danish then," Alva said. "Take the prune. It suits your personality."

As they sipped their coffee and Alva ate her order of pancakes, the three friends became aware that one of the white-jacketed busboys was staring at Roger.

"Maybe," Alva suggested, "he knows you don't like pancakes."

Ray said, "Ignore him. He'll give up."

The busboy didn't give up. Instead, he moved toward their table, his eyes still on Roger. When he reached the table, he asked: "Tony? Aren't you Tony Milasi?"

"No," Roger answered, shaking his head. "No, sorry."

"You're not Tony Milasi?" the busboy asked a second time.

"No. My name is Roger Brooks."

"I could have sworn you were Tony. I mean, you look exactly like him."

Obviously excited, the busboy continued: "I just left Tony in Buffalo, New York. It was about three weeks ago."

Roger was embarrassed, still he didn't want to be rude. "I knew you had me confused with someone you knew. I'm sorry—"

"Are you sure you're not Tony?" the youth interrupted. "You have the same voice. That's how I noticed you. I heard you talking to your friends. By the way, my name is Mark Frattalone."

Roger was aware that now people were looking over at them. He wanted to be away from this awkward little scene, yet he also felt a compulsion to ask this Mark Frattalone some questions.

"How old," he heard himself saying, "is your friend, this Tony Milasi?"

"About twenty-one, maybe twenty-two," answered the busboy. "We worked together, both of us selling for the Great Books Company. Tony has a good job with them."

Roger was twenty-four then, only he had no intention of admitting to Frattalone that he was apparently older than Tony Milasi. For even as he insisted that this was a case of mistaken identity he was secretly hoping that the busboy's story about his look-alike was accurate.

"You're almost the same size as Tony," Frattalone said, continuing to study Roger. "You've got the same shape head, too. And another thing, you both hold a coffee cup the same way. I was watching you. You grip it around the side, the same as Tony does."

Roger nodded, listening closely but adding nothing to the busboy's monologue. He absently took a cigarette from the pack in his shirt pocket and held it between his teeth. Frattalone immediately pointed to the cigarette.

"Tony does that," he said, his voice rising. "Tony does that —just like you."

Roger turned to Ray Skop. From the look on his face, Roger judged that his good friend now shared his own thought, that maybe this emotional young busboy did indeed have the very information that Roger had sought for so long.

"Mark," Roger said, it's late and I have to drive my friends home. I'd like to meet you tomorrow, though. I have an interesting story to tell you. I think you're going to like it."

They had set ten thirty the next morning as the hour to meet, and Mark Frattalone was on time. Roger already had been waiting in the Pancake House ten minutes. He ordered coffee for Mark and himself and then began.

"The story I want to tell you," he said, "is that I have a twin, a brother I've never seen. That is, we were born in Binghamton, in upstate New York, and separated when we were only a few weeks old. We were adopted and raised by two different families. I was in an orphans' home first, then a foster home and finally brought here, to Miami, when I was six years old. My adoptive mother, Mildred Brooks, is the one who brought me up.

"Ten years ago, I learned for the first time about my twin. Ever since then, I've wanted to find him, but I don't know where to start. I don't know his name or where he's living or anything. Do you know that I'm not even sure we look alike, that we're identicals?"

"Oh, that's him," Mark said quickly. "Tony Milasi, he's your twin."

"I don't know," Roger said. "I suppose it is possible. But

what do you know about Tony? Do you know where he was born and when?"

Mark shook his head no. "It's him though," he repeated. "I'm sure of it. Tony Milasi is your twin."

Roger wanted to believe this, yet why should he? Mark Frattalone was obviously excitable, and he was young. As Roger had guessed, he was only eighteen and he was a student at Miami University. Then too, Roger had never believed the discovery would happen this way, the result of a coincidence, or an accident, in a crowded highway coffee shop. His dreams of finding his brother always were romantic. He and his twin would be brought together on the Ed Sullivan television show with millions looking on, or they might face each other for the first time as opposing World Series pitchers. Once, he saw them meeting on the stage of the Metropolitan Opera, where he had been starring as a lead tenor.

"Mark, could you find out when Tony was born?" he asked. "Could you call that Great Books Company? They might know."

Using Roger's change, Mark Frattalone telephoned long distance to the Great Books office in Buffalo, New York. Although it was Saturday, a secretary answered. She remembered Mark and agreed to check Tony Milasi's file for him.

"Anthony Joseph Milasi," Mark said loudly, beginning to relay the information, "was born . . . in Binghamton . . . on May the twenty-eighth, 1938 . . ."

"That's the same day," Roger said softly, as though to himself, "that I was born."

"I told you! See, I told you!" Mark said. "Tony *is* your twin. He really is your brother."

Roger could feel himself giving in under the increasing weight of this circumstantial evidence. Still, he kept thinking: it's a coincidence. That's all. A lot of people were born May 28, 1938, and maybe the Binghamton part in Milasi's file was a mistake.

Having allowed himself to give expression to his doubt, Roger suddenly was afraid. He feared being wrong, of again being disappointed and of appearing the fool to those in his adoptive family who had maintained, over and over, that he had no hope of ever finding his brother. His adoptive mother had urged him to forget his brother; she hadn't even wanted him to know he was a twin.

"If only I could see a picture of Tony Milasi," he said to Mark.

"Sure, that's what you need," added the busboy, "and that's easy. Tony is in the Great Books newsletter. It's called *The Phoenix.* I've got a copy."

Their next stop was Mark Frattalone's dormitory room on the Miami University campus. Mark had indeed saved a back issue of the newsletter, which listed Anthony Milasi as one of the company sales leaders—only the space above the name was blank, and the caption explained, "Picture unavailable."

Mark then decided they should drive into Miami to the local Great Books Company office, which they found closed. But an hour later the door was unlocked and inside was Peter Koister, division manager. He produced a current *Phoenix,* and on page six Mark saw five rows of sales stars, with handsome, dark-haired Anthony Milasi among them. He pressed his index finger under the photograph.

"Now," Mark asked Roger, triumph in his voice, "do you believe me?"

Roger stared at the picture, but before he could answer Mark turned to Peter Koister to ask: "What do you think? Does this picture look like my friend here?"

"If they wanted to," Koister said, "they could pass for twins."

"Well, I don't know," Roger said, but it wasn't the truth. Much later, he was to say, "In that moment I knew this was my brother. I was proud, yet I was also terribly afraid that something might go wrong to keep us from ever meeting. I was badly confused as to what to do next."

He took the Great Books magazine home but said nothing of it to his mother or grandmother, for until he was certain that Anthony Milasi was his twin, he didn't want anyone in his adoptive household to know. He hid the little orange and black magazine in his dresser, burying it under his socks and underwear. Next morning, after he had made his bed, he transferred it to a safer place, slipping it under his pillow.

There was only one person to whom Roger was willing to trust his news, Aunt Millie Brooks. Since he was ten years old, his Aunt Millie had been his confidante. It was she who suggested now that he take his incredible story to the local

Family Service agency where, as a boy, he had, for a time, been counseled. As Mildred Brooks explained to her husband, "If this proves to be only a coincidence or, God forbid, it doesn't work out at all, the Family Service people will know how to shield Roger."

It was nearly 4:30 P.M. Monday, October 8 when Roger reached the Family Service office on Northwest First Street. He outlined his story to the casework supervisor, Miss Catherine M. Bittermann, and when he came to the discovery of Tony's picture, he pushed the crumpled magazine across her desk.

"Well," Miss Bittermann said, "there is a certain resemblance, isn't there?"

Nevertheless, Miss Bittermann explained this was a matter that called for a deliberate and circumspect inquiry. She suggested he leave the initial details to her. She would write first to the Binghamton, New York, Family Service, and someone there would contact the Milasi family.

"You understand," said the social worker, "that we must have the consent of the adoptive parents before any contact can be made. The family, of course, has the right to prevent what they might consider an invasion of their private life.

"I don't mean to discourage you," Miss Bittermann continued, "but you should guard against romanticizing this relationship. Remember, you and this other boy, who may be your brother, possibly have little in common. As yet, there are no shared experiences to bind you together, to give you a true sense of his being a brother. You don't know his religion, whether he has other brothers and sisters or even how he lives."

Roger left the Family Service office then and was only dimly conscious of the traffic, the noise and the warm evening sun that forced him to walk in the long shadows of the building line, taking the shade wherever possible. He was wondering what Tony Milasi was doing. He had already begun to think of him, this dark stranger, as his brother. He knew that no matter what this Family Service learned, he was going to find the courage to telephone the Milasi home in Binghamton, New York. He was prepared to risk any disappointment, for this was not simply a brother: this was his identical twin!

He knew that he should have impressed this upon Miss

Catherine Bittermann. He should have explained how for ten years, ever since he learned he was a twin, he had wanted to find his brother. He should have told her of the nights he lay in bed waiting for sleep and how his mind oftentimes drifted to thoughts of his brother. She had said they had no shared experiences. Well, he believed they didn't need any. They were twins, and that was enough. They were the same blood and had the same genes; they had begun life together, in the same womb. Roger knew and understood all this.

"What more," he asked himself, "do we need to be close?"

More than fifteen hundred road miles to the north, in the city of Binghamton, New York, Tony Milasi was absorbed by thoughts of his own. He was home for the weekend from Buffalo, where he was working as a book salesman, and on this October morning was having a cup of coffee in a restaurant a block from his parents' apartment. Surrounded by a number of friends, several of whom had been in the service with him, he was reminded of his worry-free years in the navy. For some reason, unfathomable to Tony at the time, his thoughts focused upon a spring day in 1958 when he had met a sailor named Glenn Logan. They were both members of Fleet Air Squadron 102 at the Norfolk Naval Base in Virginia.

"You look familiar to me," Glenn Logan had said to him as they stood at the sandwich counter in the post exchange. "You ever been in Miami?"

"Nope."

Logan, whose home was in Hollywood, Florida, persisted: "I could have sworn I saw you around Miami in civvies."

"Not me," said Tony, "must have been someone who looks like me. Some other handsome guy."

"Matter of fact," Glenn Logan said, "this fellow was better looking than you. You have any brothers who call you 'Ugly'?"

"I don't have any brothers," Tony said.

He had said it without conviction, though, for Tony Milasi knew that he had been born a twin and that he and his brother had been separated as infants. To spare him from worrying, his adoptive mother told him that his brother most likely had died. But Tony never had been convinced this was the truth. When he was much younger, he had dreamed of his twin and continued even now, when he was twenty-four years old, to hope that he and his twin someday would meet.

2

Roger and Tony

It was Saturday, May 28, of the busy 1938 Memorial Day weekend in the old factory town of Binghamton, New York. The Elks were holding their spring dance in the clubhouse on Washington Street; thirteen Girl Scout leaders left excitedly for a three-day canoe trip and at 93 Riverside Drive the James H. Crowleys, owners of the local dairy, and prominent socially, held an open house. Meanwhile, across the Susquehanna River at City Hospital, a strikingly pretty young woman in her early twenties signed herself into the emergency room, complaining of labor pains. She said she was Maria Brooks, Italian Catholic, married six months to Jules Brooks, a fifteen-dollar-a-week salesman of Jewish faith. On her admitting form she explained that she had received no prenatal care and asked then to have an Italian doctor deliver her.

Just after dark, Vincent M. Maddi, doctor of general medicine and city councilman from the Seventh Ward, backed his new Chrysler into Carroll Street and easily covered the familiar one mile from his home to the red-brick City Hospital maternity building.

The doctor normally delivered Mrs. Brooks's full-term baby, a six pound and four-ounce boy, strong and sound. It was, the thirty-five-year-old doctor told himself, a routine delivery. Still, he was nonplussed, for this slender woman's abdomen remained obviously distended. Was this to be a multiple birth?

"Doctor Maddi," he heard the nurse's voice saying. "I think . . . my God, yes! There is another!"

The nurse was correct. There was *another;* a boy and an identical twin. Within five minutes he too was delivered, sending the lone nurse rushing away for help and to order a second bassinet in the nursery. In all the excitement, the twin was given his brother's figure of six pounds, four ounces, and if he was in fact weighed, there is no record of it. Doctor Maddi, however, remembers that he was the smaller and paler of the pair. The hospital recorded only these few details:

Baby boy A, born 8:31 P.M. Color good.

Baby boy B, born 8:36 P.M. Color white.

No names were given the uncommonly healthy twins because their mother had no forewarning she was carrying two children and, more to the point, Maria Brooks had no thought of keeping her baby—now babies. Upon learning that she had given life to twins, she loudly insisted she meant to give them away. Shrilly, she protested that neither she nor Jules Brooks wanted the infants.

"O, God no!" she cried. "I don't want them. I can't care for them," and to Doctor Maddi she said, "You've got to help me. Find a family that wants them and will look after them."

This was not a new request to Vince Maddi, because 1938 was neither a stable nor a confident time for a great number of Americans. The nation was not yet out of the Great Depression and in Binghamton, as indeed all across the country, times were hard. This was the time of the sit-down strike, the four-day week, President Roosevelt's CCC army and the New Deal "rehabilitation communities."

Dr. Maddi listened to Maria Brooks, and he sympathized with this stranger to Binghamton who told him her family home was ninety miles away in Utica, New York. He felt certain, though, that she was going to want to keep her twins and, at first, he did nothing. Two days later, however, he spoke with her a second time and became convinced she was not to be dissuaded. He decided then that this was the very opportunity for which his friend, Mrs. Pauline Milasi, had been waiting for so long.

On most nights, Pauline Amadeo Milasi lit a devotional candle and slipped to her knees to pray. In the close familiarity of her bedroom, comforted by the soft darkness and friendly shadows, she began by fixing her small, dark eyes on a painting of a young Saint Anthony of Padua that hung protectively above her bed.

"Great, glorious Saint Anthony," she prayed in Italian, "lighten the burden of my miseries. Grant me this one grace."

As a young girl in her home town of Reggio Calabria, Italy, Pauline Amadeo had taken a vow to Anthony, the miracle worker. She promised a life of devotion in return for the saint's intercession and favor. She prayed now for his favor, but as she knelt long and faithfully, Pauline Milasi had in mind a miracle. She was forty-six and believed herself cheated. The one thing she most wanted from life was being denied her.

Seven times she had felt life and seven times Pauline Milasi had suffered despair. Three of her pregnancies ended in miscarriage; two others produced stillbirths and two children, born healthy, died of sickness in infancy. So, childless and discontented, Pauline Milasi looked upon every healthy baby as beautiful. She stared lovingly after children whom she passed on the street and pampered those who came into her husband's grocery and meat market to press up against the penny candy case. She even kissed photographs of infants, murmuring again and again, *Quanda bella, quanda bella . . .* such a beautiful baby!"

This bitter-tender story of Pauline Milasi was told and retold in the Seventh Ward, where the Italians had settled in two- and three-story graceless frame houses, each with its vegetable garden in the narrow backyard. They had come at the turn of the century, drawn by the work available in the Endicott-Johnson shoe factories spread throughout the Triple Cities of Binghamton, Endicott and Johnson City. Here now, stout, kerchiefed wives sat in painted wood rockers on their front porches and thoughtlessly accused their neighbor.

"Too much Pauline wants a baby. She's going to kill herself trying for a baby."

They were gossiping, but a thread of truth ran through their prattle, for Pauline Milasi was on warning that at her age, and with her history, another pregnancy was a risk. To gain a life, she must be prepared, possibly, to sacrifice her own. She understood this, and therefore, in addition to daily communing with her saint, she carried on a second and wholly secular campaign. The focus of this effort was the same Dr. Vincent M. Maddi, aggressive defender of Italian-American causes and, importantly, a regular customer in Milasi's Market ("Free Saturday Deliveries," read the awning), where invariably he was consulted across the meat counter.

"Ah, Doc-tor Mad-di," Pauline Milasi would first greet him, rolling her words inside a tone that signaled immense respect. "You are a good man. You help me catch a baby?"

"Pauline," said the doctor, mildly irritated. "Please, I'm a customer now."

"Doc-tor Mad-di, I'm sorry. Only you my *lasta* chance."

Vince Maddi knew this was the truth. Pauline was too old to adopt a child through normal channels. And yet, even as these two tilted with each other, they both understood how their common concern was to be resolved. The doctor would deliver—and Pauline and Joseph Milasi would adopt—a child whose natural parents would be anxious to place it, most likely because they couldn't provide for it.

When he left the hospital after seeing Mrs. Brooks that day, Dr. Maddi telephoned Pauline Milasi with what he considered his incredibly good news. But this woman who had begged him to help her find a child disappointed Vince Maddi. She sounded thrilled at first, then her mood darkened: the thought of twins overwhelmed her. She argued that she was too old, too sickly and tired, no longer sufficiently strong to care for two infants and manage her responsibilities in the family store. Vince Maddi recognized that, in the main, this was true. Joe Milasi depended on his wife to help out in the market. The doctor knew that Pauline often worked an eight-hour day, even taking her turn at the butcher's block while her husband was busy elsewhere or on his meal hour.

Pauline Milasi ended her speech to Dr. Maddi by imploring him to allow her to adopt only one of the infants. The doctor, understandably, was reluctant, but when he relayed the unusual request the mother herself had no objection to separating her twins. In retrospect, it was all too quickly and expediently agreed upon by all parties. The Milasis were to have one child, and it remained for them to make their choice.

Pauline Milasi first saw the twins in Dr. Maddi's office when they were just two weeks old. She hefted and she hugged each baby, kissing first one, then the other, and then the first again. Predictably, she whispered, "*Quanda bella. Quanda bella.*"

The twins no longer were simply "Baby Boy A" and "B." Their father had named the first-born Russell; his brother was Roger. Pauline Milasi loved them both, yet her brown eyes were brighter when she held Russell, the redder, fuller-faced infant. His puffed cheeks were as tiny red balloons, and to her mind's eye, fat was blessed. But Dr. Maddi counseled her to take his slighter, paler brother, explaining that in his experience thin babies were consistently healthy. This advice confused her. She turned instinctively to her husband.

"Do you still want," she whispered, "to be a father to one of these boys?"

Joe Milasi is five feet, five inches tall. Yet, people who know him rarely mention his size. The talk instead of how hard he's worked all his life and they say he is a solid man, in all his ways.

"You want with one heart," he said, beginning to answer his wife of twenty-two years. "Well, I want more than you even. I want like I had two hearts!"

His wife understood that, having seen them, he was pre-pared to make a home for both babies and that he wanted no part of picking only the one son. She knew, as well, that her respect for Dr. Maddi was too great to refuse his counsel, and so she denied her own heart. As the doctor had pro-posed, she chose Roger, the second-born.

Early on the morning of July 6, 1938, after a blood test of the child and a routine examination of the Milasi home, the transfer of the Brooks twin became a legal adoption. In the imposing sandstone and marble courthouse downtown, County Judge Thomas A. MacClary put his signature to the blue-backed court papers, and the clerk fixed the State of New York seal. A nervous Joseph Milasi, who for this memorable day had closed the store and dressed in a business suit, white shirt and broad satin tie, reached up to the bench to accept the papers. Only then did Pauline eagerly, joyously lift the baby from the arms of its mother, whose angular face strangely showed no recognizable emotion. In this moment, the boy became a Milasi. He became *Tony Milasi*.

A long time before this, the couple decided not to give their son the father's name, as was Italian custom. Pauline knew that she must honor Saint Anthony, who had kept his promise, one made to her on a soft, spring night some six years ago. The humble and boyish-faced saint, who during the thirteenth century literally worked a spell over great, worshipful crowds in France and Italy, had appeared in a dream. The Anthony who healed the deaf and blind, who straightened hunchbacks and whose preaching zeal earned him the title Hammer of the Heretics stood in Pauline Milasi's narrow, darkened bedroom framed with a white light.

"Have faith, be humble," he told her. "Ask whatever you believe good for your own soul."

In awe, in full humility, in conversational Italian, the butcher's wife had spoken with her saint, explaining how her heart longed for a child. Her patron then said, "You shall have a son, and you may call him after me."

To someone other than Pauline Amadeo Milasi this incredible experience might have been suspect. But her faith is a passion, rooted deep in her native Calabria and in her family.

From the county courthouse, the Milasis went quickly home to their apartment on Susquehanna Street, insisting that Maria and Jules Brooks join them. Pauline had promised to cook Maria a dinner, gently telling this woman, at least twenty years her junior, that she was "too skinny." Around the long dining room table then were relatives, neighbors and even the court clerk, who had been paid five dollars for his troubles. There were fresh-cut steaks, large bowls of spaghetti and Joe Milasi poured a heavy, aromatic red wine that he made in wooden barrels in the cellar beneath his store.

"It's just for salads," he would explain to the suspicious state liquor inspectors. "You know, flavoring."

The dinner party soon became a happy, noisy celebration with the baby, Anthony Joseph Milasi, propped up for all to see in a blue bassinet beside his mother's place at the foot of the Milasi table.

"You would have thought," said James J. Barber, a friend

as well as the family lawyer, "that Pauline had delivered the baby herself. She was that proud and, well, just too happy to ever describe."

Italians from Reggio Calabria did what they called their part. Much of doing your part was in paying respect, to your elders, the Church, every good and decent person and the dead. By doing your part, you kept your own respect in the community. In entertaining the woman who called herself Maria Brooks, Pauline Milasi believed she was doing her part. And although she knew very little about her, Pauline liked the young woman. Perhaps it was because she felt sorry for her. She looked so sad; it was clear that she had suffered. Still, Pauline Milasi asked herself, "How does any woman, especially an Italian woman, give up her baby?"

Now here she was saying goodbye, shaking hands weakly, walking hurriedly down the stairs with Jules Brooks behind her and out into Susquehanna Street, without so much as a kiss for her boy or a wave over her shoulder. Mother of God, some people in this world are strange.

Pauline stood by her front window then, thinking how all winter she had been fighting the aches in her body and a mood of defeat and despair. She too had been sad, and for the first time in her life, she felt very old. But things were different now: there were diapers to wash and hang, formula to make, bottles to scrub, and she knew there was plenty of good life ahead. God bless the gift of life. God bless her Tony and Saint Anthony for sending him.

She was left with only the one regret, that she had been forced to turn away the other twin. On this excitingly happy and exhilarating day, he was a forgotten child. Over the days and months to come, whenever Pauline Milasi returned in her mind to the picture of the mother, leaving her home without a kiss for her son, she wondered: "What kind of life is ahead for that other boy? What is to be with my little Tony's brother?"

3

Tony

Anthony Milasi was taught to believe that he was special, as truly he was to Pauline and Joseph Milasi. But beyond this, he was to understand even in his earliest years that he was a *Milasi*, and in Binghamton's Seventh Ward it was a name that stood for something. It told of a hard-working, stubbornly proud and decent family. Though working-class people who lived by a narrow budget, the Joseph Milasis were first on Susquehanna Street to have a radio, a big standup piece of furniture that cost five hundred dollars in 1921 and was bought with cash. Two years later, they were also first with their washing machine, and when television sets came on the market, they were the first family to watch Milton Berle in their own parlor.

Joe Milasi was just eighteen in 1911 when he came to the United States from Reggio Calabria and joined the march of immigrants into the Endicott-Johnson Company shoe factories. It was the regular E-J paycheck and the benefits, including a free pair of shoes for every baby, that lured thousands of eastern Europeans to the Appalachian Valley.

Over the next twelve years Joe Milasi worked at a stitching machine, sewing soles onto shoes and boots, and when he gave up the shoe factory, it was for good reason! He was going to open his own grocery and meat market. Before long he had won new respect as the owner of a growing small business. He even built a following, people who said: "Joe Milasi knows his meats." This respect and the status in the ward of being a storekeeper's son automatically belonged to young Tony and helped contribute to what is remembered as an uncommonly happy childhood.

"I never worried, and I was almost never sad," Tony has said. "I had everything. I even had seven bikes—because they were always getting stolen or lost—and when there was nothing for me to do, I could always stay around my dad's store."

He alternated then between the store with its atmosphere of loud, talkative grownups ("Hey, Tony, when you take over this business?") and the security of his home. It was in the home that he often heard his mother declare her devotion. Still vivid in his memory is the night, he might have been eight years old, that he lay close to sleep, listening to his mother and a friend. They were arguing softly in the kitchen.

"If you had taken a girl," the other woman said, "she could have helped with the housework. Why didn't you make it easy for yourself?"

"I got a good boy," Pauline Milasi said, immediately defensive.

"Yes, but you should have a daughter."

Tony raised himself up on one elbow to listen closely, and he heard his mother's voice become firm as she answered, "My Tony not a son of my blood, but he is my son from the heart. *Per lui daro il mio cuòre;* him I would tear out my heart."

In Tony's mind, the incident is worth recalling only because it tells of his mother's loyalty, which was so strong and pervasive that he was able to make a simple adjustment to the knowledge that he was an adopted child. "I don't remember the exact day when she told me; I just remember that I took it very well. I didn't have any grudge, nor did I wonder about any other mother and father. I had my parents. And I loved them. That was all I needed to know."

As soon as he had turned seven, Pauline told him of his adoption and his natural mother, whom she described as a good woman. She coupled this with the fact that he was a twin, adding as gently as she knew how that his brother had died. Dr. Maddi first heard this report, carried it back to the Milasis and thereafter it was whispered about the ward. The doctor had also learned that Maria and Jules Brooks left Binghamton, a circumstance that displeased him. He had never been paid for the delivery.

Tony accepted these disclosures on faith, with one exception. He wasn't satisfied that his twin was dead. Strangely, he kept going back to this point, asking his mother if she believed it was true.

"I think so," she would answer him. "Dr. Maddi thinks so."

Pauline Milasi felt that it was better Tony accept this version. He wouldn't then grow up wondering, perhaps even searching for his lost twin. She generally smoothed over this early history by recounting her vision of St. Anthony. This story had the effect of endowing Tony's adoption with a divinelike interpretation; it was as though his mother were explaining, "You were sent to us; it was preordained by Anthony of Padua."

"I loved that story," he said. "I guess I heard it a hundred times and I loved it each time. I suppose that's why I always loved my name, too."

Still another measure of the security that was a part of his everyday environment came from his being among relatives who were important in Seventh Ward community life: his Uncle John Milasi, owner of the best Italian restaurant in Binghamton; Uncle Bruno, operator of a billiards and card parlor; and his godfather, Dr. Maddi. But the most notable tile in the mosaic of young Tony Milasi's security was The Block, a four-story, yellow-brick building at 47 Carroll Street, which housed two ground-level stores and six family units. In February 1946, Joe Milasi bought The Block for $15,000 in cash and notes, and moved his family into a comfortable five-room apartment directly above his store. The second storefront was rented to Uncle Brono, and his Carroll Street Billiards.

This south end of the ward was in decline, yet there was a country character that offset its drabness. Although within sight of the green-domed courthouse at the center of the city, the Milasis' new home was also just two blocks from the Susquehanna, which the Iroquois had accurately called "the long and crooked river." The Appalachian foothills formed a distant backdrop at both ends of the block while giant Dutch elms built a leafy canopy above, shielding Joe Milasi's building from the oppressive summer heat. Still, the attraction for those who lived here was in the pattern of the human relationships. The Italians, and the Negro families who melded into the neighborhood, all trafficked in first names, and it was an expected thing to borrow, whether it was a spice, a cup of sugar or an hour of companionship. No family along Carroll Street was ever lonely, except by its own choosing.

Each of the Milassi family members had a personal reason for enjoying The Block. Joe Milasi liked being a landlord. Rents were payable the first of every month. Pauline was pleased that from her second-floor porch she could see the Gothic tower of St. Mary of the Assumption Church on Hawley Street. Called simply St. Mary's Italian to distinguish it from St. Mary's Irish, this was her church, and now she had its physical as well as spiritual shadow over her.

Tony was eight when he moved onto Carroll Street and had typically boyish reasons for liking his new home. Directly across the street was Christopher Columbus Park, with a Little League field, basketball courts and a small swimming pool, while around the corner was St. Mary's grammar school. All his world was now familiar and at hand, and as a symbol of this familiarity, his days all began with a signal from his father—a rattling of the steam pipe in the store below. In this way, Joe Milasi was telling him that it was 7:30 A.M., time to get up and dressed and hurry downstairs with a milk bottle filled with Italian coffee. Then father and son breakfasted together.

As Tony grew older, he was routinely expected to work in the store, waiting on customers and stacking shelves. Saturdays he delivered orders for his father, who assured him, "Work is good, never kill no one." Most of Joe Milasi's views were similarly uncomplicated and, to a ten-, eleven-, and twelve-year-old boy, difficult to accept. Tony often found his father's example too tall a challenge, and sometimes with good reason. In his helper's role, he was expected to assist in the killing and cleaning of chickens, and together father and son annually slaughtered goats.

"Someplace in the Bible," Tony remembered, "it says that at Easter you sacrifice a goat. We had regular customers who always wanted goat meat around Easter. So we kept two or three kid goats down our cellar, all ready. I didn't want to kill the poor goats, only my father said, 'It's okay. It's in the Bible.'

"Then I had to hold the back legs, and the minute my father took up his butcher's knife that darn goat knew exactly what we meant to do. He started naaing; my dad would plunge the knife into his throat, and boy, swoosh! Mr. Goat crapped all over me!

"It happened every time, and my father always would say, 'Okay. Okay. It's in the Bible.'

" 'Well, never mind the Bible,' I told him. 'I got goat shit all over me.' Boy, how I hated that job."

While Tony earlier had enjoyed the advantages of the store, namely the candy, ice cream and soda for himself and his friends, he came to feel differently. In his young adolescent years, his work at the store continually cut into his play hours. Now, in fact, there was little about the market that he liked. Whenever he saw the chance, he bolted, easily disappearing into Columbus Park. Occasionally, he slipped some change, or even two single bills ("a loose deuce") out of his father's register before he fled. Joe Milasi pretended he hadn't seen, and said nothing. If the father was hurt, Tony never heard of it, for Joe Milasi couldn't bring himself to discipline his only son.

In almost every other way, though, Joe Milasi was a hard man, and there are stories about him to prove it. When he first worked in the E-J factory there was one stitcher faster than he was. No matter how long a day Joe Milasi worked, this other pieceworker outproduced him. One night after everyone had gone home, a completely frustrated Joe Milasi took up a ballpeen hammer and smashed his rival's machine. Two days later, the man, intimidated by this, was allowed to transfer, leaving Joe Milasi thereafter unchallenged as the fastest stitcher in his 35-man section.

Whenever Tony tried to manifest a like toughness, it was uncharacteristic and most often misfired, as it did the time he thoughtlessly aimed his BB gun at one of the stray cats that patrolled the dark corners of their store. Guilt-ridden and unsatisfied that he had proved anything to himself, he spent the next week nursing the wounded animal with warm milk.

In most ways then, Tony was not Joe Milasi's son. Unlike his adoptive father, he was neither persevering nor single-purposed and not at all tough-fibered. Rather, he was impressionable, imitative and perhaps because he was a handsome only son, vain. The descriptive words outsiders most often applied to him were "spoiled" and "lazy."

So a pattern of permissive indulgence had begun to shape the boy, some eighteen years before a psychologist would comment that the man Tony Milasi was less interested in struggle and achievement than he was in "recourse to unearned essentially magical, extravagantly happy endings."

4

Tony

As she would dust around the store, or stand at the stove in the kitchen humming her favorite *Calabrezella,* Pauline Milasi would cast out bits of her philosophy. Tony called them her parables.

"Play with those who are your betters," she would say, and when she had disciplined him with a reprimand, "He who makes you cry loves you; but he who makes you laugh hurts you."

Behind her gentle nature was an iron will, and the boy grew up almost entirely at her direction. Joe Milasi was busy in the store. He had neither the time nor the understanding to have a catch in the park or to take his son to a Boy Scout jamboree. Pauline filled the void, making most of the decisions affecting Tony. She decided that although many of their neighbors could not afford the $12-a-year tuition for Catholic schooling, the Milasis could, and she fought with the Irish Mother Superior to enter Tony in the first grade before he turned six.

She saw to it he had a football helmet and shoulder pads, a complete Scout uniform costing $30 and a new $150 trumpet. Of course, he needed private lessons, too. She dressed him in the best that Fowler's department store carried, and by the time he was twelve Tony had become so clothes-conscious he refused one morning to go off to school wearing a brown shirt and brown pants with *blue* socks.

His mother instilled in him that Milasis were good people, deserving of full respect. She explained they had as friends two doctors and a lawyer and that all four families played as equals in the same poker club. Then, she greatly impressed him with the fear of the Lord. She led him to the devotional candles flickering on her dresser close by the large painting of Saint Anthony, and here she taught him his prayers and the rosary, first in Italian and later in English.

"I was taught to pray hard," he remembers. "Some nights I'd be kneeling there and I actually felt that God, or the Blessed Mother, was in the room with me. I'd be so scared then that I'd promise in my prayers not to swear or talk fresh and that I wasn't going to put my hands on this neighbor girl's breasts anymore."

This was his earliest understanding, that God was just, but wrongdoers must be punished, even twelve-year-old boys sneaking a feel. Eager to stay right with his Lord and to make his mother proud, Tony enthusiastically became an altar boy. When Father John J. Conway, the pastor of St. Mary's Italian, learned that young Milasi lived only around the corner at 47 Caroll, he told Pauline that "God was well pleased" with her boy. On snowy mornings when another acolyte would call in sick, the pastor could almost reach out and pluck little Saint Anthony Milasi out of bed and rush him onto the altar as the substitute server of the Mass.

Tony immediately fell in love with the job, for up on the altar he was at the center of attention. He sensed that people were watching *him*, Tony Milasi, as he carried the holy water, moved the Book, rang the bells at the Consecration and sang his part of the Latin Mass.

"*Dominus vobiscum . . .*" sang the priest. Tony would answer in his high, toneless soprano, "*Et cum spiritu tuo . . .*"

He was tall for a twelve-year-old, standing five feet, six inches, and when he wore the long black cassock with its white lace surplice, he felt handsome, holy and, best of all, important. He liked all the sensations that went with being an altar boy: that deep stillness that fell over the congregation just before the Mass began; kneeling at the altar rail, smelling the sweet, smoky incense and the burning candle wax. And he felt good and clean inside as he sometimes stared up at the multicolored ceiling panels, the seven physical and spiritual acts of mercy. Yet, he never deluded himself. He wasn't as truly religious, or righteous either, as his mother. His only goal, one that had no spiritual value, was to win Altar Boy of the Year and a week's vacation free at a Catholic Youth Organization camp. Tony never felt that the Holy Ghost had slipped inside his body to guide him through his altar boy chores, nor did he ever enjoy what was known in the Seventh Ward as a religious experience. Rose Finelli was one who did though—and Tony was jealous.

Rosie was a deeply religious twelve-year-old classmate of Tony's who went to Mass every morning and the year before had been selected by the nuns to be Mary in the Coronation of the Blessed Mother Festival. At noontime on Jauary 19, 1951, a Wednesday, Rosie was kneeling in Assumption Church praying to the Blessed Mother that she would do well on her math test in Christopher Columbus School when it happened! The four-foot-high statue of Mary moved. Rosie saw the Virgin Mother's eyelids flutter, and her hands, clasped in prayer, also parted.

Rosie Finelli raced from the church with her girl friends Lorraine Bennett and Carmela Capozzi trailing her, all three excited, crying and calling out their news.

"It moved. We saw it move!"

"The hands, the eyes—they moved!"

It being the noon hour, word of the vision quickly spread. Father Conway and the principal of Columbus School took the three back into the church to investigate. Again, all three girls, with Rosie being the first and the most vocal, saw the Virgin Mother part her hands and raise and lower her eyelids. However, the priest and principal saw nothing unusual, a circumstance that frustrated the girls.

"I don't even belong to this church," Lorraine Bennett said, "and *I* saw it."

Father Conway again studied the statue, touched it as though to reassure himself and measured it to establish that it hadn't grown, shrunk or moved on its pedestal. While he had reservations, he was chary of ridiculing the young girls' faith and so simply announced to all, "It is one of those things."

If the pastor had his doubts, they weren't shared by his congregation. Until 8:30 P.M., when the big oak doors were finally locked for the night, hundreds trooped up the cement steps and slipped into the pews, many of them bent on receiving a "sign."

One of those who came in the later afternoon was Tony Milasi. He sat in a front pew before the statue. He bowed his head, folded his hands and then held his breath, beginning his concentration.

"If Rosie saw it," he told himself, "I can see it." Silently he prayed: "Move . . . please, move! Blessed Mother, move! . . ."

His reasons for wanting to see the statue move had nothing to do with faith. Tony saw the receiving of a sign as a sure way to become, in the language of the street, *somebody*. He knew, as well, that his mother would be proud, but foremost was what it would mean for him. He would be important, a boy with a story to tell: people would ask him questions about his experience. Maybe they would even ask his blessing. He automatically would become Altar Boy of the Year and be excused from religion class.

In the flickering candlelight of St. Mary's Assumption, he continued his vigil, praying. "Move, just a little. Please move, one time. Please, Mother." It was to no avail, though, and in the end, only Rosie and her friends received the sign. Tony went home as before, second tallest of the altar boys and only son of Pauline and Joseph Milasi.

By his thirteenth birthday, Tony was almost a head taller than his parents and resembled neither very closely. His father's face was broad and square, with a strong chin, but Tony's baby-face was oval. It was closer to Pauline's, although both she and her husband had brown eyes. Tony's were blue, and he had dark brown hair, which he kept neatly parted. Joe Milasi's brown hair had a reddish cast to it and was combed straight back. Considering these obvious differences, and the active Seventh Ward gossips, it was remarkable that Tony reached teen age before he heard in the street just how he was *different,* that he was born of an Italian mother but was only half-Italian because he had a Jewish father.

It happened then on a hot and tedium-filled night in the summer of 1951. He was sitting with a group of neighborhood boys and had been bragging about his mother's cooking, when suddenly one of the number turned on him, "Yeah, well you're not Italian like the rest of us. You're half Jewboy, Milasi. A Jew like your real father."

Tony was hurt and confused. He had sensed there were gray areas of his life about which he knew nothing. Was this one of them? His mother had told him about Maria, yet she had said little of his father. Could he be part Jew? Tony didn't want to be. He believed all Jews had money, lived in big homes in that other world on the West Side and their sons voted to keep Italians out of the high school fraternities. Tony said nothing in denial, however, and from the silence of his friends he judged the accusation must be true. Rocco, Dino, Fortune, Ernesto: none of them had rushed to his defense. He wanted to run away from this scene, but to flee now would have been to admit his guilt, so he stayed out until the street lights went on. He raced home then to sit beside his mother at their porcelain-topped table in the kitchen. He quickly told her everything and waited, his heart setting up a quick pounding in his chest.

"Am I *different*?" he asked. "Am I Jewish?"

Pauline Milasi had believed this time would come, and she wasn't unprepared. She kept the inviolate adoption papers hidden in her cedar chest in the dining room, safe yet accessible for emergencies. She took them out now, and with Tony looking over her shoulder she read aloud, " . . . This child, hereafter known as Anthony Joseph Milasi, is the legally adopted son of Pauline and Joseph Milasi."

She pointed to the language that established under subdivision 4, section 112 of the Domestic Relations Law that this was a valid adoption proceedings, and she repeated what Jimmy Barber, the lawyer, had told her that day thirteen years ago: "Everything that matters is in that one paragraph."

"So," she said, "it says you belong to Pauline and Joe Milasi! Nobody else your mother and father."

Slowly and hesitantly at first, Pauline moved to the explanation of why his natural mother had given him up, again putting only the kindest interpretation on the facts. His mother was poor; she had been sickly; times were hard. Not everyone had a store like Joe Milasi. Few families ate as well as the Milasis, through bad times and good. Tony knew this was the truth.

Laying her rough, worn hand on his arm, Pauline said, "Your first mother tell me: 'I give you this boy with a whole heart because I know you will make him a good home!' She was good Italian Catholic woman."

Tony listened, thought for a time and then asked quietly, "But what about my other father? Was he a Jew?"

Pauline Milasi didn't want to answer. Neither did she want to lie. "I saw your father one, maybe two times," she said and paused. "Nice-looking man. Tall, like you. He was no Italian. People talk he was a Jew. Maybe, I say: 'Who cares?' "

She paused again, this time longer than before, and becoming emotional, said: "You speak Italian. You eat Italian. Your family is all Italian. Whoever says you are no Italian is crazy."

She had a way of putting things right. It had always been this way, starting with those nights when he would call her into his room and they would say his prayers together. He looked forward to those times; he enjoyed listening to her, the way she spoke with her face turned up to him with that brightness, like a fire, in her dark eyes. Her hands were always in motion and her shoulders rose and fell, adding to the passion and meaning of her words. Tony felt good when his mother had finished her explanations. He went to bed reassured that because his natural mother had been Italian he was, truly, Italian. He was no different from any of his friends.

He dreamed that night that he was living in New York City, in the Bronx. He was a member of a fighting street gang that wore black jackets and was getting ready to rumble with a rival gang. For Tony, it was an ugly and unwanted dream, a nightmare. He always had difficulty remembering dreams, but this one stayed with him. When he recounted it for his mother he told her its object lesson was that he was lucky to have such a good home and fine parents, that really, he had everything—everything, that is, except his brother.

There was one other dream that Tony remembers from his boyhood. It was a recurrent dream and one that was pleasant, far kinder to him. In this dream he was playing in the backyard of the old house of Pine Street, where the family had lived before moving to Carroll Street. He was with his twin; sometimes they were together on the swings. Generally, after this dream, Tony would again ask his mother if she thought his brother was dead.

"I think so," Pauline Milasi answered and usually added, "Dr. Maddi think so too."

Although the answer was always the same, and left small room for hope, Tony never gave up asking. Secretly he wished that someday he might hear a different answer.

Until then, however, he would continue to ask, to wonder, and to fantasize.

5

Roger

It was ironic, and pitiful. Ten days after Tony Milasi had begun his new life as an adopted only child, his twin was rushed back to City Hospital with second- and third-degree burns covering the left side of his seven-week-old body and threatening his life.

The hospital on July 16, 1938, listed his condition as critical, and the following day a Binghamton newspaper story told how the baby's mattress had caught fire mysteriously. The news account mistakenly identified the infant as Gene Newman. A series of bizarre events had occurred in this other twin's life in the brief space of ten days. There was no question, though, that he was Tony Milasi's brother, the first-born twin and that same puffed-cheek baby Pauline Milasi initially had chosen to be her son. Police and court investigators established this, just as they also fitted together the assorted pieces to the larger story.

This full story begins with the revelation that the natural or biological parents—Jules Brooks and the young woman we have called Maria—never were married. They actually had met a year before in Utica, another of upstate New York's small and largely isolated cities, when Jules came calling in his salesman's role, hoping she would buy his silverware, kitchenware or bed linens. He was thirty-five, divorced and darkly handsome; he was also glib with an almost compulsive eagerness to impress.

"I suppose you've noticed," he often told listeners, "that I'm some kind of an intellectual."

Maria was twenty-three, lonely and miserable. Five years before, she had married a laborer, who during their marriage had been arrested and jailed four times and was away now, serving a federal sentence as a counterfeiter. Maria and her two children by this man, known here as Renato, were living on welfare.

So Jules Brooks and Maria, both hungry for companionship, became friends. Before too long, Jules was an overnight visitor to her second-floor apartment, tiptoeing up the back stairs with his little suitcase and inexpensive toys for her children. During these nights and days he heard the pathetic story of her life: how her father, while still in his early forties, was struck and killed by an automobile. One of six children, she had to quit school then, at fourteen, to help her mother. At eighteen, eager for a life of her own, she fell in love and was married. But in her first year with Renato, her dreams of a good life were crushed. He seldom had a job, was almost constantly in trouble and from the outset they were a welfare case.

Her husband's large family, who lived all around Maria, closely watched her comings and goings from behind partially drawn shades. When they saw her now with Jules Brooks and counted his shirts on her washline, they were convinced she was a wicked woman. Unwilling to endure this neighborhood vigil, Maria took her two small children and in January 1938, fled with Jules. They lived then in a third-class hotel in Binghamton, sharing a six-dollar-a-week room that had light housekeeping—a small stove, an icebox and the one double-sized bed.

Mostly, they had moved to escape the prying neighbors, but adding to their concern was the fact that Maria was five months pregnant by Jules. In early March Renato's family discovered the runaway couple and swore out a complaint against their daughter-in-law, accusing her of being a neglectful and unfit mother. Maria was forced to return to Utica and ignominiously stand trial in the local children's court. For two days, she sat and listened as witness after witness, nearly all of them her husband's people, testified against her. Much of it was gossip; of Mr. Brooks kissing her; of a time she hid him in a closet because there was a knock at the door; of a night he wanted his back washed.

The judge asked the witness, "How do you know he wanted his back washed?"

"I heard it through the wall," the woman answered. "My kitchen is near her bathroom."

Maria's own testimony was ineffectual. She told the court, a little naively, there was nothing incorrect in her friendship with Jules Brooks, that she loved him and had no intention of going back to her husband. She denied she was ever a neglectful mother. "My children were never in need and what's more, Mr. Brooks likes them, too."

This seemed to be the truth for, surprisingly, none of the witnesses offered any story about Maria being a poor mother. In fact, her welfare worker, though protesting he was neutral, helped her case.

"For the court's information," he said, "this woman has tried to be a good mother, but there has always been this antagonism between the family and her. If she hadn't done anything wrong, they surely would have driven her to it.

However, there was no arguing away the affair with Jules Brooks. This was the main thrust of the prosecution's case, and after reserving decision for a week, the Italian judge found the children were without proper and sufficient guardianship and directed they be placed with the Welfare Bureau. A police detective called at Maria's mother's home that night, pulling up in front in a black, unmarked car. He said the children were being taken to a Sisters of Charity Institution, and softly, reassuringly told Maria, "The Sisters will look after your kids just fine."

Denied her children and convicted of being an unfit mother, Maria went back to Jules Brooks, back to the little room in the Binghamton hotel, with its dim hallways and mingled cooking smells. This is where she chose to wait the nine weeks until she would give birth to her bastard child. As bad as her life seemed then, it suddenly turned worse, for she had twins! Now she and Jules Brooks, this footloose man she loved, had *two* children that neither wanted.

Jules is unsure of the sequence of events that followed the births of the twins but does remember that he abdicated all responsibility to Maria and candidly admits, "I only considered what was expedient. I suppose my reasoning was I just didn't want to be saddled with two children."

He recalls the adoption by Pauline and Joseph Milasi as "a half-hour in court, a signature, everything cut and dried, with their mother handling the whole business.

"I'm not trying to hide anything," he protested. "It's just that I don't remember. It was a long time ago."

Jules has good cause to forget, for what occurred next seems almost beyond belief. It was as though this couple was clearing out of the hotel room, which was the case since they had decided to live with Maria's mother back in Utica, and among the items for which they no longer had any use was their child, the leftover twin. Jules then had what he considered a stroke of luck. He had met this Jewish couple in the hotel some weeks back. Hearing of his problem and being childless themselves, they came forward to suggest they take the baby. Jules sent them to Maria, who after listening to their offer, promptly agreed to surrender her infant son. With absolutely no legal force to this impulsive and heedless act she handed over her child to almost total strangers, two nondescript people she knew only as "Mr. and Mrs. Newman."

Hers truly was behavior born of desperation and calculated, perhaps, to help her hold onto Jules Brooks.

"I didn't know what I was doing," she was to say years afterward. "I was all confused. I'd only just lost my children and I wasn't myself. Can you blame me?"

Jules Brooks knew at the time and was to admit a long while afterward that "the Newmans weren't married, and their reputation wasn't the best." He meant that they both drank heavily, and although neither partner worked, they always had a little money. The man had told Jules he was "somewhat of a ne'er-do-well."

In the hands of this pair, the child was literally in danger, a fact that becomes patently clear from a reading of the Binghamton police investigation into the fire. The account begins with the statement that Mrs. Newman had a police record and continues:

"On the evening of Saturday, July 16, 1938, she apparently was under the influence of dope, or liquor, and fell asleep on the bed with a lighted cigarette. The baby was next to her. The bedclothes caught fire, and before the woman was aroused by neighbors, who smelled smoke, the child was badly burned."

The police promptly referred the case to the Binghamton Children's Court, which, after having made its own inquiry, found the Newmans unfit parents.

Six weeks after the fire, on August 29, the city hospital discharged the baby as completely well but with raw scars on his left arm, along his left side and on the left knee. It was feared these scars would considerably lessen his chances for a permanent adoption and, quite possibly, impair his use of the arm. At least this speculation became a paragraph in his record as he was transferred to St. Joseph's Infant Home for orphaned and neglected children in Utica.

He was sent here because legally he was a ward of his mother's home county and, like his mother, a nominal Catholic. Oddly, Maria volunteered almost no information to the home about her son's natural father or his Jewish faith. Therefore, the boy was admitted and baptized a Catholic. Across the top of his admitting form was written, "Father still unknown."

Only three months old, this pathetic infant, now called Gene, had already suffered a series of incalculable emotional shocks. Consider: he was illegitimately born, rejected by his mother, deserted by his father, almost burned to death and consigned by a state court to live in an orphanage. Finally, he was separated from his twin, seemingly with no hope of ever again finding him.

It was unfortunate, but none of those involved with either twin had a deep enough understanding of monozygotic children. In their ignorance, they had no appreciation of what it means to an identical twin to lose his life partner. They were unaware of the unhappiness and loneliness implicit for both twins because of the forced separation.

The loss of his twin was to be a recurring theme in the

lives of both boys but would be particularly traumatic to this first-born child, because his was the difficult beginning and his was to be the emotionally deprived adolescence. The contrast between them then was to be extreme. It was as though some unseen force were predestining their environments—establishing an experiment with separated monozygotics.

6

Roger

St. Joseph's Infant Home in the late summer of 1938 was a cold, formidable-looking Gothic structure standing two and a half stories high. It had been built 106 years before of imported Scottish brick as the finest private home in Utica, but its occupants now numbered 115, all county wards under six years old. Despite this overlarge census, each child's progress was meticulously charted, and the records show that for his first-year physical examination Tony Milasi's twin measured thirty-one inches and weighed twenty-two pounds. He seemed normal in every respect. The examining pediatrician noted: "Drinks from cup with help, sits on table, is pleasant and affectionate."

At two years, however, the effects of his rejection began to flaw his development. On his twenty-four-month tests he had difficulty combining words and was unable to fit sticks into a toy punchboard. Overall, he was judged to have a mental age of nineteen months. After making note of his obvious burn scars, the doctor reported: "Five months retarded. Probable cause, born out of wedlock and rejected by mother."

There were other, more poignant examples of how rejection affected the child. "He will watch people and then if caught noticing, will smile and walk away," a remarkably sensitive nursery report began. "But Gene is a very attractive blond boy, tall for his age. He has blue eyes and hair of light sand shade. He shuffles his feet a little and his knees are inclined to knock. . . . Eats a goodly amount of food but is not neat and plays at table, passing his own food or taking someone else's. . . . Gene seems nervous, impatient and hard to interest. . . . Special attention to advance his speech, yet only slow progress can be seen."

At night he was even more insecure: "Lies awake rolling in bed and calling to other children. Other times Gene likes and looks for affection in a shy manner."

Clearly, he showed a need for his mother, but so too did the boy seem to exhibit a longing for his twin. The image of him tossing in bed, unable to sleep, calling to the children around him is reminiscent of analyst Dorothy Burlingham's stories of the twins Bessie and Jessie. In her research, Miss Burlingham saw a parallel between separation from the mother and separation from the twin, writing that both "have the same emotional value and produce the same reactions."

Moreover, it is also likely that Gene's growth progress suffered because he lacked the companionship and assurance of his brother. For it is not uncommon that when arbitrarily separated, identical twins suddenly do poorly. The pediatrician Benjamin Spock once declared that "to separate twins when there is no need is foolish and cruel."

Unaware that he was an identical twin, the superiors of the infant home believed the panacea to most of Gene's problems was placement in a family situation. So in May of 1941, a week before his third birthday, he was sent to a foster home in a rural community an hour's drive west of Utica. Over the next fifteen months, he lived here on a small farm, and although he had the companionship of brothers and sisters, his life was neither easy nor pleasant. Gene was one of six county children in the home, and his one clear memory is that of being whipped with a strap because he had wet his bed. The foster mother was an authoritarian with a grammar school education and said to be "highly nervous." She was also the third woman to act as a mother to the boy and Children's courts of two cities had judged his others to be unfit.

In August of 1942, Gene was unexpectedly rescued from

this environment. He was just four, yet recalls patches and flashes of this long ago summer day when he knew that he must be ready and waiting outside because he was going to his permanent home. His foster parents told him he had been chosen for *adoption;* a magical word to the abandoned child.

He remembers standing in the backyard on the cinder drive, clutching a paper sack with his extra clothes. He had on freshly laundered clothes and was wearing his first new shoes, Buster Browns.

His foster brothers and sisters were waiting with him, too. A long, dark-colored Packard automobile came up the drive then, and when it had stopped, a woman got out. She walked toward him, smiling as she drew closer, and then she was bending over him, taking his one free hand in both of hers.

"Hello, Gene. I'm going to be your mother," she said. "I want to give you a home of your own. I want you to be my son. Do you think you're going to like that?"

She paused, waiting for his answer. Gene said nothing; he couldn't find any words. Instead, he began to cry, not because he didn't like this lady or her wonderful ideas, but through his sad little noises he protested he didn't want to leave his playmates, the ragtag group that stood about him, mute and wide-eyed at the presence of the huge, new Packard.

However, this well-intentioned and persevering woman was not about to be deterred now by a few tears, for she had reached this moment only after expending considerable time, patience and both physical and emotional energy. Moreover, she desperately wanted this boy, actually seeing his adoption as her duty, for she was Mildred Elman Brooks, wife of Jules Brooks. Just recently she had learned of her husband's illegitimate sons, and her compassion went out to this lost twin. Determinedly, she had set out then to locate him and convince her husband that he must be a father to his son. Her assignments seemed equally difficult.

There had been two courtships and marriages between Mildred Elman and Jules Brooks. They first met in the winter of 1930 aboard a New York-to-Boston steamer, a romantic beginning followed by a series of original love poems from Jules and an impressive, catered June wedding. Mildred's father, Sam Elman, a successful clothing manufacturer, hosted the party and gave the newlyweds a cash gift large enough for them to buy a bookshop on upper Broadway, close by Columbia University.

Mildred ran the bookstore while Jules sat in the back figuring out pinochle hands, reading Swinburne and waiting for the late results from the California horse tracks. Not surprisingly, the business failed after a year, and the marriage, which had produced a son, Rodney, ended in divorce four years later. Jules became a door-to-door salesman then, and one winter morning in 1937 he was in Utica, flattering a blond young housewife named Maria.

He has explained that he stayed with Maria through the birth of the twins—although he was nowhere to be found when she stood trial as a neglectful mother—because he was not the kind "who just runs out." In the fall of 1938, however, caution dictated that he leave Utica. He was warned that her husband, Renato, was getting out of jail.

Over the next two years he continued to sell silverware, blankets and dishes throughout northern New York State. He liked his traveling life, eating in new restaurants, meeting new people and, best of all, trying new horse tracks. Gambling, admittedly, was the one true and constant excitement in his life during these years.

"The world of the track is a different world," he has said, "and I love that get-away feeling, the feeling that you are away from everything. They say gambling is part of a self-destructive urge. Maybe it is; I just know that I gamble, and losing horses have plagued me all my life."

In the spring of 1940, though, Jules grew nostalgic. He was thirty-eight now and wanted to see his son Rodney, a bright child nearly eight years old. The boy and his mother were living in a Boston suburb, and it was arranged that father and son have an outing on Father's Day.

They met in Boston Common, and this day unlocked a storehouse of memories, for Boston had been Jules's home until he was ten. His mother died of tuberculosis that year, and he remembers that he never again had the feeling of family. He was placed in a Jewish orphans' home and later lived with relatives in New York.

After their Boston reunion, Jules saw Rodney several times more, and in July he and Mildred remarried. They began this second life together more modestly, renting a drafty old house in Syracuse and vowing to fill it with children and laughter. For two years they tried to have a second child, but without success. Neither of them thought about adopting until the day Mildred inadvertently discovered Jules's secret.

She answered the door one morning to find a swarthy little man. He said his name was Renato and that he wanted to see Jules Brooks on personal business. The name meant nothing to Mildred; she was hearing it for the first time, yet the meeting is still a clear memory, because the man's eyes terrified her: "They were dark, little eyes and there was violence in them."

Her husband's reaction that night did nothing to diminish Mildred's fears. Jules paled on hearing the story and instructed her to say that he wasn't home if the swarthy man returned. It was up to Mildred's brother, Lee Elman, a boarder in her home and in whom Jules had confided, to clear up the mystery. He convinced Jules to tell his wife the entire story; so, as best he could, Jules explained about his affair and the twins. But when Mildred heard how the boys were separated and that the first-born, whom Jules had given his mother's maiden name of Russell, had been left with the questionable Newman couple, she was enraged. A sentimentalist who all her life has befriended wandering cats and dogs and keeps pet birds, she couldn't abide the thought of an abandoned twin.

"What kind of people," she screamed, "separate twins? In God's name, will you tell me?"

"It was all *her* fault," Jules tried to protest.

"You gave them away? Both of them? What possessed you?"

"She shouldn't have gotten pregnant in the first place," Jules answered, obviously floundering. "Besides, I never wanted you to find out."

"Well I did find out," Mildred shouted, growing more angry with each exchange. "And don't try and tell me it isn't my concern. I want that child!"

"Why? For God's sake, what for?"

"Because I deserve him," Mildred Brooks said, "and because God is punishing us. He's not letting us have another child of our own because of *this*. To bring children into the world and . . . and then to abandon them, to turn them over as though they were hand-me-down mackinaws is cruel."

"Well, how are you going to find him? I don't know where he is anymore."

"Don't worry. I'll find him."

Jules hurriedly left the house then, and as far as he was concerned the argument was ended. Furthermore, his wife should forget these twins. Mildred had other ideas.

"That child became my obsession," she remembered. "I simply had to have him. Things were going poorly in the marriage, and I really came to believe that we needed him, poor soul, as much as he needed us. My arms were hungry to hold him and I just made up my mind that I was going to find the boy."

When she was fifteen, Mildred's father had divorced her mother. There were angry scenes in the home and accusations that to an impressionable teenage daughter were unforgettable. For Mildred, a world filled with comfort and security was torn apart. As the youngest of five children, she had been a favored daughter to her overprotective mother and prosperous merchant-father. Following the divorce, she lived with her mother, Bessie Elman, and money was an almost constant worry, because their only income was a small alimony.

The idea of divorce was understandably repugnant to her, and when this second marriage to Jules Brooks began to fail she became a regular visitor to the marriage clinic at the Syracuse Psychopathic Hospital. Here, she found enthusiastic support for her idea of adopting the displaced twin. A social worker eventually located him through the county Welfare records under his mother's name. He traced the child from Binghamton City Hospital to St. Joseph's and then to the rural foster home, reporting to Mrs. Brooks that while the boy had survived his first years in fair physical condition, he obviously was now suffering emotionally and quite possibly was retarded. Mildred didn't care. She told the worker what she had said to Jules: "I want that child."

But because she and Jules had no intention of raising the boy in his Catholic faith, St. Joseph's Home could not release him to their care. However, the home was willing to return him to his natural mother and she, in turn, could surrender him to the Brookses.

So Mildred Brooks went alone, and in trepidation, to see the natural mother, quite prepared to beg for the boy. She found, however, that Maria had almost no reason to frustrate her. She and Renato were reconciled, had reclaimed their two children from the Sisters of Charity and had added a third and fourth child to their family.

The couple agreed the Brookses should give the boy a home and no mention was made either of Renato's mysterious visit to Syracuse or of raising the child as a Catholic. Curiously, though, Maria would surrender custody for only six months at a time. This meant that final adoption would have to wait. Still, Mildred Brooks made no objection. She had possession, and this was all that mattered; and when finally she helped the frail little four-year-old into her automobile that summer day in 1942, she was positive hers was the right decision. It was right for her—and surely it was right for him.

As soon as they reached home, Mildred promptly fed and then bathed the boy and had only to study his frame to see the neglect.

"Oh, he was a funny-looking thing then," Mildred Brooks remembers. "He looked like those magazine pictures you see of starved orphans. He was a regular waif."

A pediatrician confirmed that the boy was, in fact, malnourished. Vitamins were prescribed, along with exercises for his eyes, which were weak and tended to cross, and on her own Mildred fed him carrots at three meals and meat twice a day. He seemed totally unfamiliar with most meats and, allowed all the milk he wanted, drank nearly a quart at some sittings.

On their first shopping trip, Mildred bought him new shoes because his other pair, though new to him, were county hand-me-downs and much too tight. Apparently, all his shoes had been small because both his big toes were black and blue.

Within six weeks, the boy put on weight, his eyes grew stronger and, after giving him an intelligence test, a psychologist at the hospital clinic assured Mildred that his IQ was average. He most definitely was not retarded. Equally pleasing to Mildred was that his personality, repressed for so long, began to manifest itself. Almost from the first day, he was an unusually loving child, much more so than her own Rodney. Mildred recalls that he was a "cuddler," who would climb into bed between her and Jules every morning. This was hard on Jules. He had promised to ignore the boy.

"Let him believe," he instructed, "that he's our foster child. Don't tell him, or anyone else either, that I'm his father."

Mildred found her husband's attitudes laughable. Of course, no reasonable adult can ignore an energetic, affectionate four-year-old. As for Jules pretending he wasn't a blood relative, Mildred said: "They looked so much alike that anyone with two eyes could tell they were father and son."

And after she had made new sailor suits for both Rodney, who was ten, and his stepbrother, Jules went walking in the neighborhood with his well-dressed and handsome sons.

"Oh, how he was proud of them that day," said Mildred Brooks. "They were like three peas out of the same pod. He took pictures of the boys and sneaked them into his wallet, hoping to keep it a secret from me."

Mildred and Jules decided their new son was to be called "Roger." Both liked the sound of the name and agreed that it went well with Rodney. So, this twin whom Jules had first named Russell, and who later became Gene Newman, now and finally had his permanent identity. He was *Roger Brooks,* the name originally given his identical partner.

One afternoon during this summer of 1942, and less than one hundred miles southeast of Syracuse, Tony Milasi was riding his three-wheeler on the sidewalk in front of his father's store. In one hand he clutched a soda bottle. No one knows exactly what happened next, but he fell over the handlebars, the head of the bottle shattered and the jagged glass tore a gash into the soft underside of his left arm. Dr. Maddi closed the wound with eighteen stitches, and thereafter, Tony had a four-inch ribbed scar running down his forearm.

Now, strangely, both twins carried scars on their left arms!

This unusual coincidence, however, was only one of a very few ways in which the first five years of the two lives showed parallel events. For while Roger Brooks had just become a member of a true family, with its attendant routines and natural securities, Tony Milasi had been at the center of his family since he was six weeks old. When he took his first step two weeks before his first birthday, he was applauded by

Pauline and Joseph Milasi and several visiting relatives, among them his Saraceno cousins.

When at eighteen months Roger began to walk, only the nurse on duty in St. Joseph's Home was there to record the information on his nursery chart.

By the time Roger Brooks had his first pair of new shoes, Tony Milasi already had had fourteen new pairs. Roger Brooks had never been to a birthday party until he was five years old. Tony Milasi had one every year. Roger Brooks in the first four years of his life never had his picture taken, except by welfare people anxious to see him adopted and no longer a public burden; Tony Milasi was regularly posed in a studio by his cousin, Frank Saraceno, a professional photographer.

In his pictures, Tony is smiling, and his is the boyish face of innocence. Roger's welfare poses show him unsmiling, and his look is that of a boy who is unsure and wary. His eyes are not innocent, and in these pictures he is not a twin to Anthony Milasi.

7

Roger

Despite the new love that Roger brought into the Brooks home, he was too late to save an already troubled marriage. The strains upon it were too numerous and constant. Jules spent too much time and money at racetracks, and in March 1943 when he slipped behind in his rent, the landlord threatened to lock the family out. Mildred had warned him that his next trespass would be his last against her, and they had a bad scene.

The couple had used up their reserve of positive memories. Time had dulled them first, and then their anger destroyed whatever fragments were left. All that remained were two fallible people, once in love, but suddenly, irrationally committed to hurting each other.

Mildred vowed she was returning to her mother. Jules wrote a poem:

> What matters all the beauty in the universe
> while suffering and agony are still here?
> You'll show me laughter and happiness everywhere
> and I'll drown them all with one tear.

and turned to the horses to forget.

"If I have a little money, it will soon be gone," he said, trying to explain what happened in Syracuse a long while ago. "I don't know, maybe if I were a different person and led a conventional life, which I haven't, it could have worked. Still, if she were a different woman? I'm trying to be candid and remember it just as it was."

Mildred has no such problem remembering. "I told him that I'd had it! I was tired of always ducking people at the door because we owed them money. I didn't want to live that way, humiliated all the time. I told him to get out!"

A few days after their blowup, Jules obligingly packed and left quietly. Although Jules remembers he was angered and hurt by this breakup of his second marriage, he took no legal action, and it was Mildred who finally sued for a separation. He, meanwhile, went back to his traveling life, and his family hardly ever heard from him. Mildred and the two boys, and her mother, Bessie Elman, lived together then in an old, ramshackle fourteen-room house on Cherry Street in Syracuse. To support her family, Mildred opened a neighborhood beauty parlor in the late fall of 1943. But the house was so drafty and cold and the furnace so small and impotent, that with the coming of winter she had to close her beauty shop.

Through the long winter months, the two women and two young boys kept warm nights and early mornings around a potbelly stove in the kitchen. The boys—Rodney was eleven, and Roger five—hated to leave the room to go to bed. "I fall asleep counting my shivers," Rodney told his mother.

It was apparent to Mildred that her family couldn't safely

spend another winter in northern New York State, at least not on their paltry budget. Jules' support for Roger and Rodney was twenty dollars every two weeks but was sent infrequently, and so Bessie Elman's alimony, amounting to thirty-five dollars a week, was their financial mainstay.

Bessie had come to the United States as a young girl, fleeing an oppressive Poland, and she clung to the immigrant's dream that the American land held the answers to most of life's problems. She had once visited Florida and believed this was where they should be living.

The sun is warm, the streets are clean and the sands are white as snow," she told Mildred and the boys. "And flowers and fruit trees grow everywhere. Even in your backyard, they grow."

This little speech, repeated from time to time, soon convinced Mildred, and the family began to save for Florida, hoarding their loose change in one cracked coffee cup and their rationed gas stamps in another. Then, from an unexpected source, an offer of help reached them. Mildred's wealthy and eccentric father, a determined enemy of tobacco, wrote proposing a deal. If his daughter quit smoking and gave up her "headache child," sending Roger back to the county, Sam Elman would send her a twenty-dollar check each week. Sam obviously wanted his daughter close by him in Florida, where he was living in semiretirement. However, he had chosen the wrong way to influence her. The proposition infuriated Mildred, and she replied, "We're fighting a World War to rid the earth of dictators like you. Give up Roger? Over my dead body. Now that he doesn't have his father, he needs me more than ever."

Mildred Elman Brooks was steadfast in her belief that no matter how difficult things were, Roger was a far healthier, happier boy than he would be as a ward in a foster home. She delighted in his enthusiasm over each new experience, such as his recent trip to Missouri with Rodney. They had traveled alone, by train, so Roger could be circumcised. Her brother Robert was a surgeon in St. Louis, and despite the prevailing family opinion that Roger was a burden she didn't need, he had offered to do the operation as a favor to Mildred.

Roger returned home with several long, glowing accounts of the trip and life in "Uncle Robert's hospital." He was met with the happy news that after ten months of self-denial and enforced savings, the family was ready to move to Florida. In the first week of October 1944, Mildred shipped her refrigerator ahead and sold the other furniture, with the profits going to buy a four-year-old Chrysler. Rodney's bike was strapped to the front of it, and then they were off, leaving behind a grim Cherry Street and Syracuse winters with bitter winds blowing off nearby Lake Ontario.

Three days later they wearily crossed the state line into Florida. Within the hour the skies grew leaden, the big palms blew and tipped and the rains seemed to explode above them. Then the roads ran with torrents, and driving, in fact all traveling, became impossible. A hurricane was blowing up the peninsula out of the Caribbean.

For two days and nights they waited out the storm in a roadside cabin, bundled in warm sweaters and huddled under blankets. Grapefruits thumped down on their roof at night, waking and, at first, frightening the women. Rodney, a sophisticated twelve, and six-year-old Roger, were thrilled. To them, this was adventure.

Although she said very little about it, Bessie Elman was quietly determined to frustrate her daughter's plan to eventually adopt Roger. She knew that before too many years Rodney, uncommonly self-sufficient, would be on his own, setting her daughter free—free to travel, to remarry, to have her own life. With Roger clinging to her, she was already more restricted, and this is how it was going to be for a long time.

At dusk during the hurricane, Bessie stood in front of the small cabin window and recited her Hebrew prayers, staring up at the forbidding sky as she asked for health and peace of mind. Afterward her thoughts naturally turned to their predicament. She and Mildred had only a little money left. They had no place to live in Miami, and the boys needed new clothes and shoes for school. Her ex-husband had been right, calling Roger a "headache child." If only Mildred could accept Sam Elman's offer. Send Roger back to the Catholics and collect twenty dollars a week. Who would turn down this kind of proposition? Only her Mildred!

Across the room, Mildred Brooks sat on the edge of the bed, studying her strong-willed mother. She knew what was on Bessie's mind. They had argued it out before, and she was sure they would argue it further. Mildred disliked living contrary to her mother's wishes, and on most subjects she bowed to her father's counsel. This was partly out of fear: "As kids we never disobeyed him, because when he roared at us, the whole house shook." Yet, if she did as they both wanted and gave Roger up, he truly would be *lost*. She was convinced of this, and so would hold on to him as long as she was able to withstand the pressures from her family.

"Roger needs my love," she told herself, "and whatever little security I provide him. If only we can turn a corner here in Florida. . . ."

There was an almost classic disparity in the way each of the twins was received into his home. Tony Milasi was a miracle child and assumed, if only in his mother's eyes, the incarnation of saintly, angelic-looking Anthony. From his earliest, few demands were made upon the young Tony. He had only to be himself and return a measure of the love that each day was his.

Roger Brooks' world would be far different. Quite by accident Mildred had learned of him, and he was to become much less than a son to the Elman family, where he was a reminder of Jules Brooks, the rogue who twice wronged—by marrying, never adequately supporting, then divorcing—their youngest member. Simply by his presence, Roger was an unwitting yet inevitable source of friction, and the antipathy for the father oftentimes was unfairly directed toward the son.

Bessie Elman was ordinarily gentle and charitable. Yet, during their first day together, she had mistreated Roger. She was seated at the piano. Drawn by her music, he climbed up on the bench beside her. Impulsively she swung her arm, catching him across the face. He tumbled over onto the hard wood floor, breaking a bone in his right foot. Since he was only four at the time, it was a simple matter to explain that the boy had suffered an accident.

Roger has no memory of his *accident*. This is not entirely because he was too young to remember or that his recall is poor. Rather, it is because he has completely walled out whole segments of his boyhood. It is as though he were looking through an old photo album of his earliest years and dismissing as inconsequential those snapshots that are unpleasant reminders. This, of course, is his defense against rejection, the severest of all the cruelties to threaten a child's emotional security.

So, he chooses to remember Bambi, the family terrier; Rodney as his constant pal; his mother as a Cub Scout den mother; and the long trip to Florida, the hurricane and the nights they were marooned in the roadside cabin become an excitement.

"I remember that Rodney and I put all the grapefruits in piles, like cannonballs, which made Grandma Elman laugh."

He has no memory of his grandmother being harsh with him, just as he has forgotten that Jules and Mildred argued and that his father left during the night while he slept. He has lost the image of the afternoon, some years later, when he sat across from his social work counselor and asked: "Why is it that everyone I love always leaves me?"

8

Roger

Florida was to be different. Mildred and Bessie Elman promised the boys they were heading straightway to better times, but it just didn't happen. When Roger thinks back to his early Miami years, from the time he was six until nine, he remembers: "We were always moving, so I never had many friends."

This was a particular hardship for him, because friends were important to Roger Brooks. They were the surest proof that he was well liked. He courted the few he had and was willing to make considerable sacrifice to gain others. One morning shortly after moving into a new neighborhood, he found four boys aiming stones at an empty can. They agreed to let him into their game, only first he had to hold the can on his head.

"Don't laugh," he said a long time afterward. "I wanted friends so badly I was willing to do most anything to make them like me."

Each boy then fired a stone and, inevitably, Roger was struck. Blood spurted from a forehead wound. He ran home and, bloody and crying, burst into the house, only to be shouted at to be still. His mother and grandmother were sitting before a table radio, themselves in tears. An announcer was saying in a hushed and dramatic voice that the thirty-second President of the United States, Franklin Delano Roosevelt, was dead at Warm Springs, Georgia.

Early in 1948, when Roger was still only nine but already had lived with four different sets of parents or guardians, in nine different homes, he was finally able to set down roots. Lee Elman's compassion for his aging mother and troubled sister ended the family's wandering; he had a small brick duplex built on an inexpensive lot in southwest Miami. The women rented out one side and moved into the other, a two-bedroom unit painted bright yellow. It had a narrow screened porch in front and was on a typical Florida block: quiet, two-lane blacktop with white crushed-coral shoulders; one-story homes in pastel colors and sheltered by palms; runabout boats parked under carports; Bermuda-grass lawns and swimsuits drying on clotheslines out back. It easily was the most attractive and comfortable of their homes but remained an unusual household, in part because of Florence Dwyer. She had been the Elman family housekeeper when Mildred was a girl, and over the years the two women had grown close.

"Without Florence," Mildred liked to say, "I feel lost."

Since Mildred Brooks disliked housework and at times was out of the house, working as a practical nurse, Florence assumed charge. Being indefatigable and compulsive, she got the meals, cleaned, did the laundry and saw to it that Roger and Rodney were washed and well-mannered. Her own manner was brusque, and perhaps because she was English-born, Florence held rigid ideas about child behavior. So this was an entirely female-oriented home, managed by women of differing temperaments and disparate ages: Mildred, early forties; Florence, past fifty; Bessie Elman, late sixties. They had in common that they were all divorcées and shared much the same mental scenery: recurring loneliness, frustration, and an outspoken antipathy toward the men who allegedly had wronged them. The boys, and Roger in particular, were often the outlets for abuse.

"If Roger so much as dropped his socks," said a regular visitor to the home, "one or the other of them was on top of him."

One result of this tripartite arrangement was confusion. Roger complained at the time of "too many bosses. One says do this; the other do that!" Further, he was constantly being reminded not to upset Florence: "She'll leave and then where will we be?" Consequently, he tried avoiding her, with mixed success. Sometimes when through a boyish failing, such as tracking grass into the house, he provoked her, she sent him to bed without supper.

Not only older by six years, but a gifted student, Rodney retreated into his books, and while largely uncommunicative and withdrawn, he stayed busy. To earn enough money for a clarinet he had built up a paper route and once he had the instrument was a religious practicer. "Toot, toot, toot," Florence complained. "That's all I hear. Toot, toot, toot. Doesn't he ever stop that thing?"

The clarinet was to be Rodney's escape, literally. In the fall of 1948, when only sixteen, he left for the University of Florida at Gainesville as a music scholarship student and thereafter was only an infrequent visitor in his mother's home. His unquestioned scholastic brilliance eventually earned him a fellowship to study physics at Harvard University.

Roger wasn't nearly Rodney's equal in intelligence, but he had a greater capacity for enjoyment. He would play outdoors until the last patch of daylight was gone and then race home to endure, with a sheepish grin, the reproach that almost certainly awaited. His mother and grandmother wished he didn't eat so sloppily and was better than a C student. "Rodney never had any trouble," was the censure he often heard, and in her crackling, high-pitched voice, barbed with the English accent, Florence regularly dismissed Roger as "a little snot."

No one bothered to consider why his teachers described him as an "underachiever" in *every* marking period, nor did they trouble to discipline his study habits. Instead, they lamented, "He doesn't have the Elman brains." They of course had no way of knowing, but in the same grade school years his identical twin was an honor roll pupil at St. Mary's in Binghamton, and Roger Brooks was capable of at least equaling his twin's achievements.

By contrast, Tony Milasi's home life was permissive, as well as indulgent. He largely made his own routines, and the family happily fitted its life around them. Then, because his happiness was paramount, Pauline Milasi was always ready to set another plate for one of Tony's friends. Her zest to please through her meals was also an Old World quality and peasantlike in its effusiveness.

Finally, Tony's mother believed that her responsibility required she be her son's constant champion, and if there had been trouble at school, she would have speedily attended to it. Pauline Milasi wouldn't have wanted the Irish nuns calling her Tony an *underachiever*.

Although Roger is reluctant to admit it even to himself, Bessie Elman had a stronger influence on him than Mildred Brooks, his adoptive mother. For it was Bessie's verve and intellectual curiosity which stimulated their home, and it was her true versatility and forceful personality that predominated. Despite her sixty-plus years, Bessie Elman was an activist, a liberal humanitarian with a love of music, gardening, Jewish literature, card games and, when she wasn't sulking over something Mildred had said or done, an engaging sense of humor. It was Bessie whom neighbors came to visit; it was Bessie who saw that the radio was tuned to classical music, and it was Bessie who insisted the Negro be accorded full respect in their home, forbidding use of the word *nigger*. And although she knew little about baseball, she celebrated Jack Roosevelt Robinson as a great American. Together, she and Roger saw the movie *The Jackie Robinson Story;* together, they went to temple Friday nights, and together, they planted shrubs, flowering bushes and fruit trees in the backyard, Bessie Elman instructing her stepgrandson that fish heads made the best fertilizer.

Without any conscious design, they drew close, and Bessie imparted to Roger her sensitivity and appreciation for beauty. Many nights when Mildred was out, off to a square dancing class or on assignment as a practical nurse, Roger sat home on the couch between Bessie and Snoopy, the cat. They listened on the radio to "The Shadow" or "The Fat Man," and when she became bored, Bessie Elman took out her lapboard and played solitaire. Moving close beside her then, Roger watched and spoke up when he saw a move. He had only a dim understanding of it at the time, but with hindsight he can appreciate that this diminutive old woman he so loved, and called "Grandma," was genuinely getting to like him.

Mildred Brooks had done enough reading in psychology texts to know the home she was providing Roger was lacking, and when he was nine, she asked the Miami Family Service Bureau for help. Actually, her hand was forced, because Roger, ordinarily good-natured and shy with new friendships, began brawling with other boys at a Young Men's Hebrew Association summer camp, seemingly for no good reason. Over the next three years, Roger spent two or more hours a week with his Family Service counselor. Invariably, this came on a Saturday and, as Roger remembers it, was the happiest day in his week.

The days began alike, with the morning spent in the YMHA where he played Ping-Pong, shot baskets, took a long swim in the steamy green-tile pool and weighed himself on the free scale. After two hot dogs and a grape soda he caught a second bus downtown and then ran the last long block to the Family Service office on First Street.

"They had these real slow elevators," Roger said, "and after what seemed a long ride, I'd jump out and just about explode through the frosted glass door. Inside, my worker—either Mr. Harris, Mr. Nappan or Miss Naomi Grossman—would be waiting for me."

Miss Grossman was young and pretty and Roger's favorite. She drove her own car and pretended she liked to fish, even to baiting her own hook, a fact that impressed a nine-year-old boy.

The workers saved Roger for their last appointment, which enabled them to spend more time with him. "They tried to plan something different every week," Roger explained. "We went fishing, played carpet golf, built a model airplane or maybe we just rode out to the airport. The most important thing was the way I was treated. They gave me a feeling that they wanted to see *me,* and I thought of them as my friends. I remember looking forward all week to Saturday and wondering where I was going this week."

At first, though, Roger had resisted the social workers. He denied there were problems with his home situation and wouldn't talk about himself. His initial interview ended with the case worker noting, "Clearly repressed the negative." It was Miss Grossman who eventually broke through his defensive shield.

"Do you like me?" Roger asked one Saturday.

"Yes, I do," she answered. "I don't like some of the things you do, but I like you, as a person and no matter how poorly you behave sometimes I shall continue to like you."

"Always?"

"Yes, always!"

"Forever and ever?"

"Yes, forever and ever."

Through her actions, as well as her carefully thought-out little speeches, Naomi Grossman convinced Roger of her genuineness, and then he confided in her. The result is a file 3 inches thick and totaling 126 pages. It is laced with social worker phrases describing a small boy choked up with confusion, anguish and repression: ". . . initially demanding . . . underlying hostility . . . identity crisis . . . not aggressive by nature . . . fears doing harm to others . . . doesn't enter in easily . . . is an underachiever . . . represses anger . . . wonders about biological mother and father."

Roger had cause to wonder about many things. He wondered why Mildred and Bessie argued so often, confessing to Miss Grossman he was afraid they might someday strike and hurt each other. He wondered, too, why they favored Rodney and why Jules and Mildred hadn't been married when he was born. And why—wasn't there anyone to tell him?—had his natural mother given him up?

These were extraordinary burdens for a nine-year-old, and until he began with Family Service he had no one to whom he regularly could turn for help. From his first days with Mildred Brooks she had explained he was her adopted son and Jules his natural or *real* father. Thereafter, she tried to answer him when he came with a question, but her poor regard for Jules, which was reinforced by both Florence and

Bessie Elman, soon conditioned Roger to avoid mention of his father.

He also learned he wasn't to speak of his real mother: "I just knew I wasn't supposed to ask Mildred about her, which I accepted. I mean, what could she tell me? She hadn't known her."

So it was Miss Grossman and her coworkers who helped Roger sort out his confusion as he moved searchingly through the adolescent years from nine through twelve. They explained there were many thousands of boys and girls like himself who never knew their natural mothers and lived apart from their fathers. They helped him understand that he was as good as any other child, and that he was fortunate to be in a foster home with a loving and well-meaning mother *and* grandmother. They consistently encouraged him to talk and with intelligence and compassion, they responded.

His Family Service counselors all saw an unusual sensitivity in Roger, exhibited in part by his desire to share. He would insist that whenever he was having fun they join him, and frequently he made them little gifts. He responded to their every kindness and long after he had forgotten the details of his sessions with them, he would remember all their names and recall their treatment of him.

In addition to these social workers, there were several others who were important to Roger's development in this period. Rabbi Morris A. Skop was particularly helpful. Roger and the rabbi's dark-eyed, handsome son, Ray, met memorably on a sandlot baseball field. As the two sides were being chosen, Ray Skop announced, a bit imperiously, that he was a pitcher.

"Who wants to catch me?" he asked.

Everyone knew that Ray Skop threw hard and wildly, an intimidating combination, and there were no volunteers. There was only indifference and silence until Roger Brooks, never in his life a catcher, stepped forward.

"Give me the mitt," he said, striving for nonchalance. "I'll catch the kid."

Even at nine, Ray Skop knew a good thing. He had found a steady catcher, and Roger, just ten, had his first best friend. The Skops' fine home in Coral Gables now became as familiar to him as his own. He slept over, had icebox privileges and invariably shared their Shabbas table, putting on his yarmulka and joining in the prayers and songs. This close-knit family drew Roger with an almost hypnotic pull.

"For a young boy he had a deep sense of religiosity," Rabbi Skop remembers. "He was fascinated by the Zmirot, our table songs that we chant after the meal. In fact, he was fascinated by the entire service. He liked the idea the mother was Queen of the Sabbath and lit the candles; that the father blessed the wine and the family blessed the bread."

Long afterward, Roger explained that religiosity, neither his nor Rabbi Skop's, had anything to do with the enjoyment of his friend's home. "I liked things with people," he said, "and there was always good talk and excitement at the rabbi's. Ray had a brother and two sisters, and the family was together and happy. After our Shabbas meal we all walked to temple. I got to sit in the front row and I felt important. I would sing out loudly, which made Ray giggle. The rabbi would wink at us—all of this was fun. Then, nine times out of ten Mrs. Skop asked me to stay the night. To my grandmother, overnight at the rabbi's was better than if I got invited to the White House."

There was only one other home in which Roger was as comfortable; that was the apartment-home of his Aunt Mildred and Uncle Lou Brooks, who came into his life when he was ten. In the summer of 1948, when Lou Brooks was forty-three, married, the father of a seven-year-old daughter and a veteran of twenty-two years in the navy, he received a disturbing letter telling him of his brother's illegitimate twin sons. Written by a gossiping cousin, this letter suggested he open his home to "the boy without a father."

Lou Brooks was shaken by this news. He felt a responsibility to his nephew and so sent his wife from Richmond, Virginia, where they were then living, to Miami to meet him.

Roger's Aunt Millie was thirty-four, brunette, with long, well-groomed hair, clear skin, eyes so dark they seemed black and, because she was North Carolina-born, a beguiling drawl. Roger believed her the most beautiful woman he had ever met and surely the most beautiful who had ever kissed him.

"He tried hard to act grown-up," Lou Brooks' wife remembered, "but there was this thrilled little boy's look in his eyes. It said: 'Is this really happening?' "

Roger and his new aunt felt a deep affection for each

other, and Mildred Jordan Brooks carried this report home to her husband. Several months later, Lou Brooks sold his restaurant business in Virginia and moved to Miami. Almost immediately Roger became a "weekend child," and Aunt Millie, an omnivorous reader as well as an occasional short story writer, became his tutor. She hounded him on grammar and pronunciation and corrected neglected table manners. Roger loved every bit of this extra attention and still remembers many a late afternoon when he all but held his breath, waiting to be invited to stay for supper and overnight. Although the Lou Brookses never did adopt Roger they were, importantly, a loving aunt and uncle.

"There was no one," he says, "like my Aunt Mildred. She was special. I even confided in her more than my own mother, and I always knew that whenever I needed her, she was there."

It is an odd fact that Mildred Elman Brooks never legally adopted Roger either. She had only the temporary custody order signed by his mother. But none of this mattered to Roger, because during the three years he lived in the little duplex in southwest Miami he was remarkably happy.

"I believe that Roger made himself happy," his friend Ray Skop has said. "He had a great natural ability to adjust."

In the late summer of 1950, when Roger was twelve, a new domestic crisis in his home tested this ability. Mildred Elman Brooks announced she was remarrying. Once more, her family suggested Roger be sent back to his natural mother, but again she opposed them.

"The woman doesn't want him," she remonstrated. "She hasn't once tried to find out how he is, or even where he is!"

With Rabbi Skop's help, it was arranged then that Roger should go to a Protestant boarding school at Montverde, Florida, north of Orlando near the center of the state. Mildred was heartsick over leaving Roger, yet felt she had no choice. Seeing her own life slipping away, lonely to the point of desperation, she had married an alcoholic. She knew her home was no place for Roger now. Perhaps it would be in time, when she had rehabilitated her man.

"Please trust me," she wrote Roger at Montverde. "The school is the best place for you. It's healthy."

"No, it isn't," he wrote back, and because he was miserable and homesick he lied. "They beat me here. They have a

big paddle and my house father makes me hold my ankles
and swats me hard on the behind."

Despite his initial unhappiness, Roger became reconciled
and by his fifth week had grown to like the school. He enjoyed the sports and fraternities and took pride in being able
to keep up in his classes. For the first time he was a C-plus
student. Of all the new routines, though, Sunday was his favorite, because it meant no classes, no work in the fields—
where they grew all their own vegetables—and a chicken dinner followed by a movie.

He remembers, with unusual clarity, the cold Sunday in
January 1951 when the movie was *The Prince and the
Pauper*, the Mark Twain story in which the two lead players,
who closely resemble each other, exchange clothes and life
roles. Later that night Roger woke out of a dream about the
film. He was actually shivering. Yet his hair and forehead
were moist from perspiration. He had dreamt that he was a
twin, and this had excited him. Could it be true?

Mildred had told him Jules Brooks was his father and explained that his natural mother had placed him in a foster
home, where he had been burned when his crib accidentally
caught fire. There was nothing here to say that he didn't have
other brothers and sisters: one of them could be his twin!

"What's the matter with you?" asked his roommate, who
had heard him stirring. "You wet the bed?"

"No," Roger answered. "I dreamed I was a twin."

"Go to sleep," his roommate said. "You'll feel better tomorrow."

"I feel fine," said Roger. "It feels good to have a twin.
Who wouldn't want to be a twin?"

There was no answer this time. His roommate was already
asleep again. This disappointed Roger. He wanted to talk
about his dream. "Shoot," he thought, "If I did have a twin I
bet he would stay awake and talk with me."

Lying there in the dark then, Roger contemplated what it
must be like to have a twin. He knew it was better than having a plain brother. Brothers were always younger or older
and never wanted to do what you wanted. He remembered he
had this problem with fussy Rodney. A twin, though, that
was different. It would be like having a partner, another *self*.
Roger could think of many times he had wished he were

twins. For one thing, he'd like to have a twin to help him in the vegetable fields. The twin could do half his hoeing down those long rows of beans.

Roger walked around for the next two days believing he was a twin but saying nothing to anyone at the school. Then he wrote his mother, explaining his dream and asking her to please tell him that he was a twin. "It's true, isn't it?"

Mildred Brooks believed she was justified in lying. She answered he certainly was not a twin, that he should put such foolish notions out of his head and concentrate on his studies. She sincerely believed her untruth was sparing him from still more anxiety, but Roger uncharacteristically decided to ignore his mother's letter. He wanted to believe he was a twin; he liked the feeling "there was someone exactly like me."

He told his roommate and his friends in the fraternity how he luckily had discovered that he was a twin. Most of them remained skeptical.

"Well," he challenged, "just how do you think I got these scars on my arm and my side and my knee? Huh? How do you think they got there? I'll tell you! We were Siamese twins and got separated at birth!"

His roommate hung a crayoned sign on their door:

> Peak at The FREAK
> 25¢ to Look
> 50¢ to Touch.

Literally overnight, Roger Brooks was an attraction. From all over the campus, the curious came to view his allegedly celebrated scars. Roger didn't take their money, though; he was satisfied just being the object of all this attention. The caper was short-lived, however, for word of the phenomenon soon reached the dormitory proctor, and under his gentle interrogation, Roger confessed. As punishment he was required to take up the French horn in the school band. He couldn't then appreciate the humor of this discipline, but as the dean explained in his report to Mildred Brooks, "French horn players are as scarce here as separated Siamese twins."

In his second year at Montverde, Roger was completely happy. He was an eighth-grader, a veteran French horn player and no longer needed to resort to fantasy to overcome his loneliness. But at the close of the spring term the school abruptly, and permanently, shut its doors.

"I don't know which was worse," Roger said, recalling his feelings at the time, "hating the school and having to stay or liking the school and being forced to leave it."

Roger's dream, like that of his identical twin earlier, seems to support the hypothesis of researcher Dorothy Burlingham, who wrote the fantasy of having a twin is a common daydream, particularly where the child feels thwarted or unloved. Believing himself rejected by his parents, he conjures up this image of a constant companion; he creates a twin, and together they escape from loneliness.

Surely, Roger Brooks was troubled by these feelings. After his final session at the Family Service, during which he asked: "Can children ever divorce parents?" his counselor reported: "Roger has a constant problem. He believes that whenever people grow to like him, they leave him. His natural mother and father left him; his brother left him to go to school and now his mother, Mildred Brooks, is leaving him to marry."

So there is no mystery behind Roger's dream, but what of Tony Milasi? He was at the very center of a loving, close-knit family and growing up in an Italian environment where children, sons especially, are the protagonists of life. Everything in his daily routines spoke of security and attention to his smallest wants. Yet, he too dreamed of a twin and remembers how he often felt prompted to ask whether his twin wasn't alive.

In Tony's dream, he and his twin were playing behind a house where the family had formerly lived. Curiously, Tony saw himself as the big brother: "I felt that I was the older, that I was born first." Otherwise the dream, much as Tony's early life to date, was without conflict. It was simple, prosaic and happy.

A further element in the twin fantasies, as reported by Miss Burlingham, is that of narcissism. A child who feels himself thwarted cannot imagine anyone more satisfying than himself. He creates an image of himself, and this object-love of the twin acts as a cover for self-love.

Quite possibly narcissism was a factor in Tony's creation of a fantasy twin, for Pauline Milasi has described her son as vain. She remembers how even as a nine-year-old he used to comb his hair while standing on the toilet seat and admiring himself in a wall mirror.

It becomes significant that *both* Roger Brooks and Tony Milasi dreamed they had a twin—and that Roger's dream even predated knowledge that he was a twin. Going beyond the Burlingham analysis for an explanation to cover the two cases, it is tempting to advance the possibility that as identical twins Roger and Tony weren't creating fantasy at all. Rather, they dreamed and speculated not about a fantasy twin but of their lost twin.

9

Tony

By the time Tony Milasi was fourteen, he no longer dreamed of his twin. It wasn't that he had forgotten; it was only that life was too busy. There was no room for other preoccupations, not when he had The Seventh Ward Saints.

Becoming a Saint was the biggest thing in Tony's life since he took first communion, and when he wore his black and white jacket with the scripted *Saints* across the back, he carried himself with unmistakable self-confidence. He had no doubts as to his identity then, or his acceptance in this peer group.

The Saints, of course, were rascals, athletes and characters with names their mothers never gave them. Among them were Il Duce, Benny the Blood, The Horse, The Head, and Punchy; and although most of them regularly attended Mass and confessed their sins, they didn't otherwise qualify for sainthood. Still, they were unlike their big-city counterparts.

Rarely were they all antisocial on the same night, and so mercifully most of their conflicts were quickly put down or hushed up, whichever seemed more expedient. The school strike, though, had a nasty look when it began. Dino Pirozzi was the instigator.

With his pale blue eyes, virile Roman face and an incongruously dimpled chin, Dino was every Saint's ego ideal. In addition to good looks, he had the well-developed body of a halfback and a questioning mind that would ultimately lead him to the works of Aldous Huxley and a rejection of most recognized authoritarian orders, including his own Catholic Church. But at the moment he was celebrated as a gifted athlete, a churchgoer, a swain and to the Saints he was *Il Duce*.

On this particular noonday, Dino stood in the Christopher Columbus Junior High School playground and glaring up at the principal's office, announced in a scream: "We strike!"

As the ace softball pitcher, he wanted four Saints to walk beside him in the halls carrying his golden throwing arm extended restfully on a little pillow. The pinch-faced Irish principal balked. So, after the last bell, eleven Saints clapped, stomped and noisily yah-hooed around the school yard until the nervous educator summoned *Il Duce* to his office, where they agreed to a compromise. Dino Pirozzi was allowed *two* bearers as he and his golden arm moved from class to class.

There were no other Saints with Dino's natural leadership qualities, and the remainder of the gang were mainly followers. The most faithful of these was Tony Milasi, for he saw the gang as the source of all the drama and tension in his life. The Saints were his surrogate family, and as such, all-important to him in the years from fourteen to seventeen, when he was freeing himself from the hold of his protective and determinedly possessive mother.

The truth, though, is that Tony didn't belong in the Saints. He was never a street fighter and had neither the ability nor desire to be a high school athlete. In puberty his hulking body turned soft and fleshy. He was known then as "Bottle Ass" or "Moon," for his round face, and "Awk," which was short for awkward. (At about this time, Roger's starchy diet also began to mark him. Because he too was bottom-heavy, at Montverde School he was called "Light Bulb" or "Duck Ass.")

"Tony was so clumsy," remembers George Tomaras, a

Saint who went on to earn a master's degree in social work, "that watching him as an altar boy you had this terrible feeling he was going to trip or drop something."

Moreover, Tony was too naturally cautious to run with the Saints. He didn't challenge life physically, as so many of them did. Every summer they all risked breaking a leg jumping into the Susquehanna River from the Rock Bottom Bridge, a drop of thirty feet. Tony could never bring himself to jump with them.

"I always wanted to," he has said. "I don't know why I didn't. I suppose I was afraid."

Nor did he relish their brand of trouble. The night they were all smoking and the barn caught fire, he wasn't around. He was busy, too, the night the gang decided to "sneak" into the movies by threatening the ticket-taker. Actually, the threat didn't work so, instead, the War Lord of the Saints, a prizefighter, flattened the youth with a left hook. The Saints then filed quietly into the darkened theater. But Tony wasn't this kind. He was a laugher and fun-seeker.

Pauline Milasi never forbade her son to be with the Saints. Rather, she encouraged him to make friends with those who were his superiors. She had in mind, for one, Ernie D'Aristotle. A tall, gangling, intense boy, with deep-set brown eyes, he was too fine a student and too serious a saxophone player to make cause with the Saints. Ernie was Tony's good friend through high school, helping him with homework and his trumpet lessons and doing his utmost to dissuade his impressionable pal from squandering his potential. For Ernie was aware, as he was growing up on Carroll Street before going on to St. Bonaventure College to be an honor student and class president in each of his four years, of the direction the Saints were traveling. Yet, he understood the attraction they held for his friend as well as why the gang welcomed Tony.

"Tony was accepted because unlike other Italian kids he was never openly jealous or even suspicious," he explained. "He wasn't a threat to anyone. That was important to some of the gang. Instead, Tony was easy to be with and always quick to laugh. He was principally looking to have fun, and since the Saints made the most noise in the ward they seemed to have the best fun. They were the big operators, and by being one of them, you automatically were *somebody*—that goal to which every Italian-American boy aspires. Putting it all together, you can appreciate that Tony was naturally drawn to the group. Their ends became his ends; their values became his values."

All activity for the gang began at Michael-Angelo's, whose sobriquet had nothing whatever to do with sixteenth-century art but derived from the first names of its owner-brothers. A lunch counter, a dozen formica-topped tables, orange-plastic-covered booths and a jukebox is all there is to "Mike's," but it is friendly and noisy and was the Saints' turf. Every mother in the ward knew it, and so the "nice" Italian girls were forbidden even to walk the sidewalk past the address.

At Mike's the gang squeezed into the booths six to a table and sat while the hours slipped away on the Genesee beer clock overhead. They drank coke or coffee, bummed cigarettes and flattered some co-ed, whose family believed she was in the public library, into playing the Frank Sinatra or Joni James ballads on the jukebox.

Boredom was the enemy, and at each session someone invariably lamented, "There's nothing to do in this town. Nothing! You know what I mean?" This was a cue, opening the meeting to propositions. One of the zaniest adventures began one spring evening in 1952, when Tony was fourteen. Four of the gang, Tony included, abruptly decided to drive to New York City, about two hundred miles south. The purpose of the trip was a well-kept secret.

After more than four hours of steady driving the Saints double-parked in front of the Waldorf-Astoria under a Park Avenue moon and strode up the carpeted hotel steps into the cavernous lobby, past the potted palms and two out-of-town ladies discussing the United Nations tour. They circled the great Waldorf clock, which they read was built for the Chicago World's Fair of 1893, and then single-filed into the men's room with the sign on the door reading: "Gentlemen/Hommes/Caballeros."

"I'm a caballeros," Tony said. "Which are you?"

"You look more like a hommes to me," Dino said.

Afterward, they retraced their route, drove back out of the city and over the George Washington Bridge. They ate breakfast in a diner on Route 17 in New Jersey. Stopping only the two times, they completed the four-hundred-mile round trip and once more took their places in Michael-Angelo's. It was now Saturday morning, and they didn't have to wait long until some dum-dum fell into their elaborate trap.

"Hey, where did you guys really go last night?"

"New York," said Dino offhandedly.

"Yeah, what for?"

"Take a leak in the Waldorf," said Tony.

"Come on, don't give me that."

"Honest to God," Dino insisted. "Something wrong with that?"

"Sure," Tony said, building on the gag, "they got a real clean men's room in the Waldorf."

"They even have a guy who holds your towel while you wash," said George Tomaras.

"It's nothing like Mike's," Tony added, working to get in the last line. "They never run out of paper at the Waldorf."

It was a gas, a big laugh and for Tony the fun of being a Saint. This was an experience to share boastfully in conversation: "Hey, did you hear what Dino and us pulled?" Being in with the Saints was important to Tony; his membership and his jacket were his credentials, proof that he was popular. Unlike his identical twin, Tony never questioned his place in the home, but outside on the street he was less sure of himself, and acceptance in the peer group was necessary to his sense of well-being.

Tony always took a particular pride in being well liked. He remembers that he was "friendly to everyone, and I could get along with everyone. I probably got this way from helping my father in the business, waiting on so many customers. Anyway, I like activity with people."

Just as Roger Brooks believed that he was drawn to Rabbi Skop's home because of the excitement of people—"I liked things with people"—so does Tony describe his fascination with Uncle Bruno's pool parlor to a liking of "activity with people." True, Carroll Street Billiards was unusually active for a small, storefront operation. One of the reasons for this success was that with the fall of darkness the pool cues were racked in favor of serious card games and, on certain designated nights, dice rolled across the smooth green of the backroom tables. The old red-brick police station was only four blocks east of Uncle Bruno's, and when the games went on year after year, reasonable men concluded the detectives didn't care.

As a boy, Tony had run hero sandwiches and cold beer from the store to the card players next door. Later, these men knew him as the pest who lived upstairs, the one who practiced "Joy to the World" and "Santa Lucia" on the trumpet while they tried to concentrate on their cards.

Tony enjoyed standing around Uncle Bruno's, sucking a toothpick and studying the players, each with his own style. They had the unworried look of strong men who seldom worked terribly hard, which very nearly was the case. In the summer, they took jobs in construction and worked outdoors, getting tan to their waists. During the long upstate New York winter, when there was little construction work, they were free to spend time in the Carroll Street storefront. The regulars at the parlor all shared the belief that if you were clever, you didn't have to "break your hump." Their aim was shrewdness, and with them idleness was a badge of status. Tony was intrigued by their trafficking in whispered deals, horse tips, word of bargains in used Cadillacs or a quick profit from turnover in watermelons. Yet, with all their inside knowledge, these men who proclaimed they lived by their wits were unprepared when police apathy toward their crap games ended. Two carloads of detectives burst in this night, scooping up the money and dice, and that was the beginning of Binghamton's "Protected Gambling Case." A grand jury returned twelve indictments and there was a trial then. One of the first witnesses was Tony's father. Although Joe Milasi paid little attention to what went on at his brother-in-law's billiards parlor, he was the landlord and, under the law, responsible for what took place there. So, he was made to sit up on the witness chair, his red butcher's hands in his lap. To Joe Milasi, this was stupid. He wasn't going to tell the court anything to hurt his wife's people, his *compare* from Reggio Calabria.

The prosecutor ignored his opening profession of ignorance. "Mr. Milasi," he asked, "don't you know that gambling is against the law in New York State?"

"I don't think so," Joe Milasi answered. "Not all gamble."

The prosecutor was taken back: "Can you explain your answer to this court, Mr. Milasi?"

Tony's father began by saying that every year he bought a five-dollar ticket to the Police Department picnic. "I have clams, sausage, corn on the cob and beer. When it gets dark they hang down a light bulb on a cord and everybody shoots the craps. I see policemans there and sometimes a mister judgeman. Okay for *you* to gamble, I think okay *everybody* gamble."

The answer was struck as immaterial, irrelevant and unresponsive and after three or four more questions, Joe Milasi was dismissed as a hostile witness. But the trial dragged on, and with appeals, the case was in the courts a year until nine of the twelve accused were acquitted. Tony's favorite cousin, Uncle Bruno's son, was among the three who were convicted, which brought a sadness to Carroll Street. On an overcast winter's morning a group of crestfallen family members gathered in front of The Block to wave goodbye as a stoical, unsmiling Cousin Memo surrendered to serve a year in prison. Up at the windows stood the women, crying soundlessly into their handkerchiefs. They knew that Memo, in his early thirties, was taking his father's place, for the family had agreed Uncle Bruno was too old to go away. In the argot of the street, his boy was *taking the rap*.

Tony was proud of his cousin, just as he had been proud that day in court when his father stood up to the asinine DA. In years to come he would tell both stories again and again. To him the two incidents spoke broadly of the same thing—of a proud minority group that in some quarters of Protestant Binghamton was still regarded suspiciously as "foreign-born" and Catholic; of an underdog people opposed to certain demands of the bureaucracy.

Tony was told then that, at least in the Seventh Ward, law was a contest, the outcome of which sometimes depended on "who you know" downtown and how much you are able to spend for a lawyer. The larger concept of American justice had nothing whatever to do with the practice and observance of law in the ward.

Through adolescence, Tony lacked the example and tutoring of a figure strongly committed to tolerance, integrity, social justice. He had no Bessie Elman to espouse the rights of the Negro or to explain the horror and sting of prejudice. Roger remembers well a night when he was fired from a busboy's job because he was found to be Jewish; he recalls how Bessie immediately began a one-woman crusade whose lesson was an editorial in religious tolerance.

The Milasi family code accented hard work, patriotism,

charity, yet Tony tended to look past his positive models, many of them embodied in Pauline, to be more impressed and thus imitative of the negatives in his environment. Of the twin partners, his was the lesser social conscience.

By the time the Saints were fifteen, girls and drive-ins had taken the lead in their value system. A number of Binghamton career girls, some of them off farms back in Oswego, Chenango Forks and Speedville, lived at the YWCA and ate their meals in Michael-Angelo's. They were soon being courted by the Saints.

"Want to go for a walk down by the river? We can sit in the grass and listen to the falls?"

Again, Tony was more a follower than pacesetter, and feeling a pressure to catch up to the veterans of sex, he was ready to pursue any opportunity. One cold spring night he and Mitch Pirozzi, Dino's younger brother, were at Tony's when there was an odd phone call.

"Are you that Tony Milasi?" a girl's voice asked.

"Who wants to know?"

Tony could hear giggling in the background. The caller explained she had seen him around and thought him cute. Didn't he and a friend want to come over? She and her friend were alone.

"Oh, oh, there's got to be a hooker here someplace," Mitch Pirozzi said.

"They're probably two dogs," said Tony.

Still, they decided to chance it. The address was a farmhouse eight miles south of Binghamton and off the main route. When he saw the house, set far back from the road and dark except for a single light in a front room, Mitch was sure it was a trick. But just then the girls came out and stood on the porch, waving and giggling.

"They must be hard up," Tony said.

"Who says *we're* not?" Mitch added.

Following self-conscious introductions and a can of beer each, they paired off, and someone turned out the single light. Tony's date took his hand and led him into one of the sleeping-rooms, where they fell onto the bed and began to pet. Suddenly, the bed heaved and a dog skidded out from beneath. He stood barking loudly at the intruder, who had lost both his composure and all desire for love-making. Tony yelled for Mitch, and they left hurriedly but not before making loose arrangements for a second rendezvous. That very next night, Tony borrowed a car and drove back out to pick up his new girl. He waited until his mother had gone to play bingo and then slipped the girl into his house, promising her they would be safe from barking dogs.

With this conquest, Tony proved to the Saints that he was a bold innovator, capable of maneuvering a girl into his own bed. He followed up with other such nights, even finding a ready partner in a girl who lived on his block. But as he continued his teenage philandering, he was careful to maintain his good standing as an altar boy. He told himself this was to keep his mother from being hurt. Along with others in the Saints, he was willing to risk an occasional mortal sin, only he couldn't stand to see his mother suffer because: "There isn't a bad bone in her body. She is nothing but good."

Still, as Tony moved through his sixteenth and into his seventeenth year, areas of open dissent grew between the boy and his parents, and it was clear that Tony was unyielding. For one, he rejected the store as any way to make a living. Little was said, yet he made it plain he had no patience for a job that chained a man from early morning until late at night seven days a week and returned him only a modest living.

In June 1955, Tony was graduated from Central High. A lazy student in high school, he finished in the last quarter of his class with no mark higher than C. But Pauline and Joe Milasi hoped that he was ready now to settle down, take a job with IBM or Ansco, the film company, and marry a good Italian homemaker. They had saved $1,500 toward this day. Tony, though, had other ideas. He didn't want to back up his father at the butcher's block and had no thought of settling down—not if that meant driving over the Susquehanna every morning with a lunch sack beside him in his little used car with thirty-nine payments to go. No thanks! Movies, television, magazines and the Saints had whipped up his hungers beyond that. At the moment, it was his thought to buy a new, paid-up automobile. If his father would just give him that cash gift, he'd be on his way. He could start to live a little.

Joe Milasi thought his son too young for a new car and said as much: "Poof, and the money is gone!" So there was a test of wills, an impasse. The differences continued unresolved, for father and son were unable, or unwilling, to talk things out. There was a remoteness that precluded meaningful discussion. When both were younger and there seemed more time, there was some dialogue. Generally, it came after the store was closed, for only then could Joe Milasi relax. Many days he worked in a controlled fury—patient with his customers—gruff and short-tempered with the help, and this included his son and his wife. Joe Milasi's code demanded that a storekeeper never sit, and no customer was ever kept waiting unnecessarily. Pauline Milasi has always said her volatile husband saw four customers when he had two and eight when he had four.

But at night, after closing, it was different. He locked the front door and slowly climbed the eighteen dusty, linoleum-covered stairs to his apartment, with everyone in the house recognizing Joe Milasi's end-of-the-day tread. Oftentimes he carried a fresh-cut sirloin. Over the sharp protests of his wife he would cook the steak and then wake his son. Together, the father and the boy would eat the steak, meat enough for four. Now Joe Milasi was being a father, and although he was incapable of articulating it, Tony understood the old-country attitude: "You're my boy. I'm your father. No more talk is needed.

It hadn't been that simple of late because Joe Milasi couldn't understand his son's new rebellion, this desire to break from the traditional mold. Tony, meanwhile, was impatient with his father's old-fashioned ideas. Neither could communicate it verbally, yet both knew they were becoming strangers to each other.

"There are people in this town," explained Ernie D'Aristotle, "who say Tony Milasi was spoiled so rotten he never did anything for his father. I know that isn't true. He collected overdue bills and rents for his dad and he was good at it. Tony was smart with money; in fact, he wasn't dumb about anything. He just wouldn't apply himself, wasn't willing to pay the price to be outstanding at any one thing. Like all the other Saints, he believed it was dumb to take a book home and studying was for jerks, the suckers.

"Maybe he did have it too easy, I don't know. I know that it hurt his mother and father when they had to make him do things he didn't want to, like work all day Saturdays. That's when Tony started having trouble with himself. He rebelled, although I doubt that he saw it as such. Still, he always did what he wanted—no matter what anyone else told him. In that way, he was terribly spoiled."

Tony remembers with some shame that he sometimes took advantage of his parents, particularly his father, and with a small boy's cruelty tried to punish him. He recalls that when he was around ten, his bicycle was stolen, and this time his father refused him a new one. They were in the store alone. Tony sat down on a pile of cardboard cartons by the beer cooler and refused to speak to or even look at his father. One, two, two and a half hours passed. Finally, Joe Milasi stood above his son, pulled up his bib apron to get at his money and silently counted out twenty-five dollars.

"Careful riding home," he said.

When in the summer of 1955 his father refused him the money for a new car, it was the same thing all over again. Tony delivered his ultimatum: "If I can't have a car, I'm joining the navy." This time, Joe Milasi stood firm. He thought the navy would be good for his son. So, on the sunny humid Monday morning that was August 23, 1955, seventeen-year-old Anthony J. Milasi left Carroll Street for Bainbridge, Maryland, and a four-year enlistment. Pauline Milasi stood on the corner in front of the store and watched until he was out of sight. She had her apron up to wipe her tears, which she could no longer hold back. The last thing Tony saw of the old neighborhood was his mother's tiny figure shaking with sobs. He walked faster, afraid that he too would cry.

"Ma, I'm sorry," he began his letter home that night after less than a day of navy discipline. "I wish I was home. Believe me, the way they cook is awful. Tell Dad I wish I was back home—without the car. Could you send me $10 until payday? . . ."

10

Roger

Roger Brooks' adolescent years were marked by a succession of disorganizing twists and turns. It was as though he were caught in a maze, yet each time he chose the logical opening or was led toward it, it proved to be a wrong one.

In the spring of 1952, after the Montverde School shut down, Roger went home to his mother in Miami. Mildred Brooks' third marriage had ended, predictably, in a separation, and she was back living with Bessie Elman and Florence in the duplex. All three women welcomed Roger after his two-year absence. He was taller, a little heavy for fourteen, but a handsome boy, and to Mildred Brooks, his irrepressible spirit and laughter were a tonic.

"People always said I shouldn't worry about Roger," she told a friend once. "They said that with his smile he'd always make out, and he had the personality to sell ice to the Eskimos. Even when he was a little fellow, his teachers told me this."

It was the side of Roger that everyone saw: his readiness to laugh; his sense of wonderment; his trust in those who showed him any kindness. Not as easily discernible were his restlessness, his insecurity and a disappointment in his home life, characteristics that manifested themselves in his being incorrigibly sloppy. Moreover, when he could get away with it, he was lazy around the house and hard of hearing when the speaker was Florence. Of course, these were muted expressions of hostility, which the Family Service workers had detected when he was nine.

Shortly after his return home, these traits worked him into trouble with his old antagonist, Florence. It started because Bessie Elman mistakenly had the idea you could drown chinch bugs through a daily watering of the lawn. Roger thought it stupid, "Standing there for an hour or more with a little hose." On this particular evening, he forgot, and Florence regarded his failure as a serious breach of discipline.

"You bastard," she screamed, leaning on the word, her face set and hard. "Don't give me that dumb look either. You know what I mean. You are your father's *bastard!*"

Florence had consistently portrayed Jules Brooks to Roger as insensitive and irresponsible. "Oh, it's easy for the man," she had said. "He gets his pleasure and then the woman has to support the children. Look at your mother!"

But this was only half of her thrust. Her other attack centered on Roger, who she predicted was growing into another Jules Brooks. Whenever he displeased her, it was because he was acting "just like your father." Roger wasn't entirely sure what his father was—he had almost no memory of him—but with Florence hectoring him, he reasoned he didn't want to be like Jules Brooks.

Now this new accusation. "My God," Roger thought, "am I illegitimate? A bastard son?" Fighting back the tears that he didn't want Florence to see, he fled on his bicycle. Even at fourteen, his bike, a second-hand model, was still the one sure escape. He rode around for what seemed hours, not knowing where he wanted to go. Aunt Mildred's was his first choice, but talk of Jules Brooks made Uncle Lou nervous. Invariably, his uncle went for a walk when the conversation was about his brother. Roger's second choice was the home of his Uncle Lee and Aunt Frances Elman.

When she saw him pedaling into the drive, Frances Elman knew something was wrong. Roger was unsmiling and had a funny, hurt look. After only the slightest coaxing, he told her what was troubling him. He asked his aunt why Mildred

Brooks had kept this from him, and who was his real mother? Was this the reason she gave him away?

Since her husband, Lee, was the first of the family to hear of Jules Brooks' twins, Frances Elman knew the whole story and was profoundly glad now that she did. She was also knowledgeable in child psychology. She believed this situation called for an immediate remedy.

"Roger, all of us in the family," she began, "have been saving a secret about you. We've been waiting until you were old enough. Well, I happen to think you're ready to hear it. The secret is that you are a unique young man. Roger, you are a twin!"

Roger let out a whoop. "Ya-hoo," he cried. "I knew it. I knew it all along, Aunt Fran. I even dreamed it at school. Hey, I'm a twin!"

That night Roger stayed with the Lee Elman family, sleeping in the backyard in a tent with his cousin Raymond. The two stayed awake talking excitedly of Roger's discovery and of ways he might find his twin.

"I know," Roger said, "I'll go on television, on 'This Is Your Life.' My brother will see me, and that's how we'll meet."

Frances Elman was gratified, seeing that she had, if only temporarily, directed Roger's thinking away from the cruel discovery of his illegitimacy. But she had angered her sister-in-law. Mildred Brooks complained, "The boy already has two strikes on him. God knows, it's ridiculous to hold out hope he'll ever find his twin. He'll spend the rest of his life wondering about him."

In one sense, Mildred Brooks was right. Roger was going to spend a share of his life wondering about his twin, for that twin no longer was either a dream or a fantasy. His twin was now a reality, and Roger's life search for a sense of family became narrowed in focus, centering entirely on his brother. It was perhaps immature of him, but he strongly believed he was going to find him, and here Mildred Brooks was wrong. It was not anxiety that Roger felt, at least not initially. The subject of his twin and the idea of finding him gave his life continuity, purpose and a vague feeling of hope.

"I remember," Rabbi Skop says, "that Roger did a lot of talking about his twin, mostly about how he wanted to find him. Of course, I didn't put too much stock in this, but nobody could discourage him. When I saw this, I realized it wasn't fair to even try. He needed to hang on to this."

Three weeks later, a fresh excitement occupied Roger. He was going to Cincinnati, to join his father for a ten-day vacation. The trip and the reasons behind it were typical of Jules Brooks. Still a drummer, selling door to door, he had scored a nonpareil week, clearing better than one thousand dollars selling house siding. So he decided to treat Rodney, the family's first college graduate, to a holiday. At twenty, Rodney Brooks only recently was graduated with honors from Florida University and was now a trainee for the General Electric Company in Cincinnati, where Jules, fortuitously, had a brother living. According to his plan, he would meet his two sons there and they would all stay at his brother's home.

Aunt Mildred and Uncle Lou drove Roger to the Miami airport, lecturing him not to give his father any trouble. Those who loved Roger were united in their desire that Jules and his fourteen-year-old son get on well. They saw how much Roger needed his father.

It had been almost ten years since Roger and Jules last saw each other. Yet, when Roger came down from the plane, holding onto his borrowed brown leather valise with straps, Jules acted as though they weren't strangers after all. He clapped Roger on the back, joked over how big he had grown and laughed a deep, hearty laugh. Next, he took out his wallet to show Roger a tiny, square photo of himself.

"See," he seemed to be saying, "I haven't forgotten you. I carry your picture."

Then he promised they were going to have a great time. Their first stop was across the Ohio River in Covington, Kentucky, where Jules easily found a horse room, and so Roger spent that first afternoon watching his father bet the horses. He didn't understand most of it, yet found it exciting, for the room was noisy and smoky and crowded with grownups, all of them men.

After the first afternoon, Jules put a little effort into the vacation. He took Roger sightseeing, to movies, shopping for shoes, and every night they met Rodney after work and ate in a different restaurant. It was a wonderful reunion, and Roger believed he was getting to know his father, whom he regarded as brilliant, smarter even than Rodney. There seemingly wasn't any subject that Jules couldn't discuss; and it was plain he was a reader, for he was always talking about books. Roger saw how wrong Florence had been to belittle Jules Brooks. Further, he understood how foolish he was, not wanting to be like his father.

When it came time for Roger to leave, Jules said they should talk, man to man. He came right out then and asked Roger if he would like to live with him and his wife, Jennie, back in Schenectady, New York. Eagerly and unashamedly, Roger answered yes, yes, yes! He checked his emotions, trying to behave as an adult with Jules, but that night in a letter to Ray Skop he unloosed his true feelings: "Hey, I'm going to live with my father. He wants me to be his son. Tell your dad he can't adopt me anymore. I've got my own father. . . ."

Having watched him spend money in Cincinnati, Roger concluded his father was well off. The moment he saw their Schenectady home, he knew this couldn't be true. They lived in a third-floor walkup apartment, a block from the traffic, noise and dirt of the downtown city and Roger slept on a couch, a soiled relic in the living room. Later, they moved into another old frame house, occupying four rooms on the second floor. This time Roger was assigned his own room. Actually, it was closer to an alcove with a sliding drapery giving him a small measure of privacy. In this setting, Jules Brooks was a greatly changed man. He showed little resemblance to the happy spender Roger had known back in Cincinnati. He was away much of the time now, selling or with Jennie at the track. Some evenings Roger would get home from his after-school job as a stock boy at Stella's Dress Shop to find an empty apartment and a melancholy note, "Dinner in icebox. Warm it on stove. We'll be home late, Dad."

Roger hated being alone. Still, it wasn't much better when Jules was there, faulting him for talking too much, not reading, not doing well in school and for not being more Jewish! Jules insisted that he join the YMHA, enrolling him in a Jewish history course. Roger daydreamed during the lectures. He found Jewish studies difficult and of no help in his everyday problems. Not even Rabbi Skop's patient cantor in Florida had been able to pull him through Bar Mitzvah studies. Roger had skipped so many classes that his grandmother eventually surrendered, allowing him to drop out.

"He doesn't have a Yiddische kopf," Bessie Elman had lamented, "and a rabbi he isn't."

To please his father, Roger now let his regular school work suffer, giving first priority to the Jewish history course. But Jules refused to understand why his son couldn't hold a part-time job, have several close friends from the better Jewish families and also keep up with *all* his studies. As Jules analyzed it, Roger was spending too much time "loafing around his room" and so forbade him to be in the house until he arrived home and dinner was ready. Roger waited for his father then, hiding in a car that had been junked and was sitting on blocks in a lot alongside their house.

"I spent hours in that old car," Roger remembers. "It was a Nash, and I used to pretend that I was driving it. At the same time, I was watching a girl sunbathing next door. She would lie there in tight shorts or her little bathing suit, teasing me. I was too shy to do anything, though. I never spoke to her, didn't even know her name; I just made up daydreams about her. I dreamed she was in love with me and we were taking off somewhere, racing the Nash sixty miles an hour. I know that she liked me because she was there practically every afternoon. Still, it was all so silly. The old car, the girl, me waiting for Jules to get home. The hours used to drag."

While Roger Brooks endured his unremittingly bleak life in Schenectady, less than 150 miles west, Tony Milasi's life in Binghamton was a sequence of agreeable events. There were trumpet lessons, Saturday football games with the Central High marching band, long rides home in the noisy, darkened bus after an out-of-town game and then Saturday nights in Michael-Angelo's with the other Saints, and the career girls from the YWCA.

"I know now that a lot of it was silly," Tony has said, "but I just had to be out of the house every night. I would go down to Mike's or one of the diners."

"We sat for hours over one cup of coffee," Dino Pirozzi explained. "Someone told stories, George Tomaras did crossword puzzles and we argued: football, religion, sex, money and Sinatra."

"I don't think I did homework once in four years," Tony said, "and if it wasn't for Ernie D'Aristotle I never would have studied for tests."

The pattern left little or no time to be alone, and to be contemplative or analytical was to risk ostracism from the

Saints. So Tony Milasi glided easily along the surface of life with neither the disposition nor any reason to go deeper, to ask himself:

"What is happening?"

Roger spent most of his nights in his bedroom, lonely but glad for the moment Jules wasn't around. Yet, even here he felt trapped, with no one to whom he could look for help. Jennie was kind. She got his meals, kept his clothes clean and got him off to school each morning. Still, she wasn't his mother; he didn't even know her well.

As the months passed and he began a second year in Schenectady, one subject occupied most of his thoughts. He wished there was someone to share his loneliness and that this someone was his twin. The more Roger thought of his brother, the greater was his desire to learn about him; he realized that Jules was the only one who could give him any information.

One evening he stretched out on his bed, and stared up at the faded, sterile wallpaper. He let his eyes follow a seam up to the ceiling and then along a plaster crack that somehow led him to the realization that this was the first room he had ever had. For all of his fifteen years, he had slept either on a couch or daybed in a living room or porch. The thought slid him deeper into the ditch of his depression. He traced the seam back down, circling each of the stains in the paper. Next, he began to study the pattern of the cheap drapery when suddenly it was flung back and the heavy-set figure of his father stood in the passageway.

"Don't think you're fooling me," Jules said. "I know what you're thinking. It's about your brother. Well, someday when you're older, maybe I'll tell you the whole story. But for now, forget it. You're too young."

Jules was determined Roger must never know anything of his biological mother. He knew that Maria and her husband had become reconciled and even had other children. He felt no one had a right now to disrupt these lives. As for the other boy, Roger's twin, he knew very little. The respected Italian couple in Binghamton had him, but this was also a part of the dead past. What could he possibly tell Roger that would help him? He was better off as he was, knowing nothing.

Jules tried to explain all this and turned away then, letting the drapery fall back across the opening. Behind it, he could hear Roger beginning to cry.

"Oh, I was hurt and let down," Roger recalls. "I cried because I had learned nothing of my twin and because now I was sure Jules didn't want me around anymore. If he did, he wouldn't have hurt me that way, not telling me *something* about my twin.

"He didn't even leave me any hope I would find my brother."

There were other, even clearer evidences of Jules' dissatisfaction with the relationship, and Roger no longer could rationalize them away or continue to wait for some improvement. Mostly, it was in the way his father behaved toward him in front of others.

"He would say something about me and then get right off the subject," Roger explained a long time afterward. "It was as though he were afraid someone would ask him where I came from. He spoke of 'my son Rodney.' I was always just plain Roger. He was ashamed of me. I could sense it. I got so bad that I was ashamed of myself. I began thinking of myself only as a *bastard*. When I first told Rabbi Skop and Ray the story, I was able to laugh. I even made up a little song, like Gilbert and Sullivan: 'A bastard am I; oh, a very, very bastard am I.'

"After two years with Jules I couldn't laugh about it anymore, and there was one other thing. Never—not once—did he put his arms around me. I know, because I remember, that we never kissed. I got no physical love from my father. It just never happened, if you can imagine such a thing!"

Roger was prepared for Jules when he came to him at the close of the school year in 1954 to propose that he go back with his mother in Miami. Jules apologized, saying it had nothing to do with how he felt toward Roger, it was only because Jennie was too nervous with him in the house. The following weekend, he borrowed fifty dollars out of Roger's savings from his after-school job and suggested they have a farewell outing. They drove into Albany on a Saturday afternoon in June, and while Roger and Jennie waited in the car Jules went off to bet the first three races. In an hour he was back: all smiles, obviously a winner. Over a Chinese dinner they celebrated, and then continued on to the Albany airport where Jules paid for Roger's ticket out of his winnings. He said nothing of the fifty-dollar loan.

When the moment came for goodbyes, Roger gave Jennie a kiss on the cheek and shook hands with his father. They both promised to write, knowing that neither of them would. Jules told Roger it had been good living with him, that the two years had gone by all too fast. Roger nodded and walked quickly away, not wanting to cry.

Once he was on the plane, though, there was no holding back the tears. As a boy he had often cried, sometimes for foolish reasons. But if he was quick to become emotional, Roger was unnaturally slow to anger. Perhaps this is because anger is a luxury that belongs to the secure, and there was little about the first sixteen years of Roger Brooks' life that gave him cause to feel secure. Even now, as the plane carried him away from Schenectady, he felt no rancor toward Jules. He didn't blame him for what happened.

Years afterward, Roger would be asked what was the single greatest difference in the disparate environments that he and his identical twin had known. He replied: "A father . . . Tony had a father."

11

Roger and Tony

It was a poor time for Roger to come home to Miami, and he quickly understood this. His mother finally was getting a divorce, and the court delays and expense frustrated her. Grandma Elman suffered with ulcers now, and Uncle Lee Elman, whom Roger remembered as broad-shouldered and powerful, was being wasted by cancer. The whole family was depressed by this sadness, and understandably, the prevalent mood in Mildred Brooks' home was melancholia.

Fearing he might be an added burden, Roger, a husky sixteen-year-old, took a night clerk's job in a drugstore, and Saturdays he worked in a supermarket. He insisted on paying board and continued to carry this demanding schedule over the next fifteen months until his grades at Coral Gables High School skidded to the failing level in every subject except history and dramatics.

In twelve years, Roger had been a student at eight different schools, in four cities, and this unnatural shifting with the accompanying disruption had flawed him as a scholar. The time in Schenectady was particularly harmful: three schools in two years, coupled with a bleak home life. Roger knew that he was paying for his nomadic school career and that if he continued to work nights and Saturdays, forfeiting time he ordinarily might have used for study, he was going to have to repeat this junior year.

At almost the same time that he became aware of his predicament, Lee Elman's condition worsened. The family decided to move him into Mildred's duplex, where she would be better able to nurse her brother. This of course meant there was less room in the house and less time in Mildred's life for Roger.

Realizing this was a time to make a decision, Roger did what he believed would prove most helpful to his family. He joined the air force for four years, giving up his space in the home. Since he was only seventeen, Mildred Brooks had to sign his enlistment papers giving parental consent. She then suggested that he call his father and give him the news. In the week before he left, Roger telephoned Schenectady collect. The deep and unmistakable voice of Jules Brooks demanded, "Who calls?"

Roger recognized his father's Chinese accent and heard the operator say, "Mr. Roger Brooks in Miami."

"So solly," his father said. "Mister Brooks no live here anymore. Gone away."

Roger next heard the metallic click. His father had hung up on him.

It took Roger several minutes to put it all together. He had heard Jules use this Chinese routine before, mostly when he was ducking customers with complaints. But why tonight? With him? Then, he remembered the fifty dollars.

"Oh, my God," Roger thought. "I was calling to tell him that I had enlisted, only he figured I was calling about the money he owed me."

On August 15, 1955, seventeen-year-old Roger Brooks reported to Lackland Air Base in San Antonio, Texas, to begin basic training. He told himself there was no turning back from this decision, that he must like the service, and he did. Almost from his first day he adjusted to the life, finding the regimentation and discipline difficult yet satisfying. He quickly made friends, took up weight lifting to harden his body, and for the first time had a true sense of well-being, a confidence that he was capable of governing his own life without interference from his mother or grandmother or tedious Florence. At year's end, he was a radio operator in Japan, proud of his first stripe and the title Airman Third Class.

On his first overnight pass at Johnson Air Force Base, near Tokyo, he walked out the main gate and into the Orient, with its exciting world of new sounds and smells and, for teenaged Roger Brooks, adventures. Close by was a narrow café, dark inside, with wooden bar stools on a damp cement floor. It was filled on most nights with the omnipresent odor of fish and rice but was nonetheless a romantic spot to the American airmen because of its uninhibited bar hostesses. Here, Roger met a laughing little girl who introduced herself as "American name Ginny, Japan name Sachiko."

Thereafter, when she wasn't giggling or drinking orange soda from a bottle, without benefit of a straw, Ginny was staring at Roger with eyes as dark and round as plums. She would squeeze his biceps and exclaim: "Oh, *takesan* big. You good *Sumo* boy. You number one boy!"

This was commercial affection, but a pliant Roger was a willing victim, on the verge of his first sexual experience. For 800 yen, less than $2.50, Miss Sachiko had agreed to spend a segment of her night with a now thoroughly aroused *Rogersan*.

At times during his early teens, Roger had felt a stirring toward Shirah Skop, the rabbi's shapely daughter, and cousin Diana Brooks, a willowy brunette who would mature into a beauty and a photographer's model. But he had believed that sex, primarily, was for the marriage bed. In high school he had only a few dates and hadn't learned to dance until he was assigned to the air force radio operator's school in Mississippi. At a commercial studio in Biloxi, he naively paid $95 for ten one-hour lessons and then was too shy to ask his hostess for a date. Back in Miami one night, a girl he was dating had encouraged him to feel her breasts, only he became so excited that he caught his hand in her bra, spoiling it for both of them.

Miss Sachiko made it all simple and guiltless. She led Roger up a flight of back stairs, through sliding doors with rice paper panes and into a perfectly square little room that startled him. There wasn't a single piece of furniture in sight. Sachiko quietly slid other doors, producing two Japanese-style bed rolls called *futons*. She performed with not the slightest embarrassment and, facing him, she undressed. Only then did she turn out the light and lay down to wait.

Roger now undressed hurriedly, hesitating only to bunk his wallet in his left shoe. But as he started to crawl in beside Sachiko, he felt suddenly weak, even light-headed. He had lost his ardor. Guilt, inexperience or inferiority had drained him of his strength.

"That's okay," said Sachiko, reassuringly. "You come back. Tomorrow night okay."

Roger did return the next night and, as Sachiko promised, it was okay. He decided then to stay the night with his gentle, childlike whore who giggled when he flexed his muscles and had taught him to make love. Holding to a pleasurable body fatigue, a sensation entirely new to him, Roger Brooks smoked a last cigarette before giving in to sleep and told himself that this man's air force wasn't bad.

By a coincidence both remarkable and unaccountable, the separated monozygotic partners had entered the military just eight days apart: Roger Brooks on August 15, 1955, and Tony Milasi on August 23 of the same year. And just as the personality of each was reflected in his personal reason for enlisting while still underage, so too was it a determinant in the choice of service.

Roger had chosen the air force largely for negative reasons. The army was out because he had flat feet, a condition that resulted from his spending too many childhood years in ill-fitting, cheap shoes; marching would have been torture for him. He rejected the marines after having heard stories about drill instructors who punched recruits; Roger wanted no part of any violence. In this regard, he was much like his twin. He undoubtedly would have been drawn by the excitement of a gang such as the Seventh Ward Saints but was no fighter or athlete either and no more suited for membership than Tony Milasi.

The navy didn't even merit Roger's consideration, for despite Uncle Lou Brooks' fine repertoire of old sea stories, he had a definite prejudice against sea duty.

"I didn't exactly have claustrophobia," Roger explained, "but I was afraid of being cramped up on some little ship. I didn't want to be way out in the middle of the ocean with nothing to look at but water."

But for Tony Milasi, there was only one service. "Go Navy," read the sidewalk posters. "Travel, adventure, career." He accepted this injunction on faith and believed the recruiter's every blandishment; indeed, in his seventeenth year Tony saw all of life as an exciting scenario. He sat through movies convinced the images on the screen were genuine, that real people were giving truthful portrayals of life. He stared at them and recognized people from his own experiences. Secretly, he saw something of himself in each cinema hero and not surprisingly, his view to the future was similarly unrealistic.

Asked what he hoped to do with his life, he had answered seriously: "I want to be a disc jockey, become discovered after a few years and go to Hollywood."

Actually, both monozygotic partners showed naivete, yet this shared characteristic was expressed differently by each. Roger tended to undervalue; Tony had no such inhibitions. When something good happened in his life, Roger reacted in wonderment and with appreciation; Tony *expected* only good things to happen.

On completing his ten-week boot camp in Maryland, lighter by twenty-six pounds and in the best physical shape he had ever known, Seaman Apprentice Milasi set out for Norfolk, Virginia, and his first ship. He was confident this was the beginning of his biggest adventure.

It was past 10:30 of a soft November night in 1955 when

he stood before the U.S.S. *Fremont,* a long, rectangular metal tub whose mission was to ferry marines about the Caribbean.

"In the dark, and with only a few lights on her," Tony remembers, "the *Fremont* looked like a sleek tanker. I thought, 'Wow, here I am, in the great big United States Navy.' I walked up that gangplank to request permission to board and I felt I was Davy Jones."

Two weeks later the *Fremont* put out to sea, bound for Caribbean ports of call. Seaman Apprentice Milasi's assignment was the ship's records office where he was a yeoman, or clerk, who had access to all the personnel jackets. He often took out his own and read the paragraph that described him as an adopted son whose name at birth had been "Roger Brooks."

"Naturally," he said, "this set me thinking about my twin. I wondered if he was alive: I just couldn't accept that he had died. I wondered too where he was, whether he looked like me and what his name was . . . it's funny, but I never thought to look for another jacket under Brooks. I don't know why; I suppose I never thought I had any chance of running into my brother. Certainly not in the middle of the Caribbean.

"Even after that, when I was back in the States and on leave I didn't really look for him. Once or twice I met guys who asked me, 'Hey, don't I know you? Haven't I seen you before?' I never gave it too much thought. Toward the end of my time in the navy, though, I decided that when I got home to Binghamton I was going down to the county hall of records and ask them to tell me, once and for all, if my brother was alive, and if he was, how I could find him. I knew they had my adoption papers on file and they would probably have that information.

"What more could I do? I couldn't go around in the navy looking for my brother. With all the people in the world, what are the chances of bumping into your twin?"

Since the day over three years before when Roger Brooks had learned from his Aunt Frances Elman he was a twin, he had built haunting daydreams in which he was a passenger on a plane or a train that passed his brother, yet neither was aware of his partner going by. Roger quickly would shake off this image, returning to wish-fulfillment. In this latter mood, he was confident. He became, uncharacteristically, a braggart who had absolutely no doubt that he was going to find his brother.

It was a paradox then that Tony Milasi, who believed his life was running to schedule and plan, lacked assurance he would find his brother, while Roger, who had repeatedly experienced disappointment and rejection, made a show of his conviction that he was going to discover his lost twin.

On the day that he left for the air force, Roger had walked across the street to a neighbor's and told the woman, Mrs. Eleanor Bak: "Before I'm twenty-five years old, I'm going to find my brother. You'll see."

12

Roger and Tony

"Hey, I know you!" the strange voice said. "I've seen you someplace. . . ."

Airman Third Class Roger Brooks had been staring out of the air force bus at the Japanese countryside, fascinated by the economy of the local farmers who had planted the slopes and hillsides, even to the shoulder of this narrow blacktop road. He hadn't noticed the airman in front of him until he turned to face Roger.

"Sure, I know you," he said again. "We played basketball against you. You were St. Mary's CYO, right?"

He was a three-striper—an Airman First Class, red-faced and loud. He was also drunk. Roger's answer was apologetic, "Not me, airman. I think you have me confused with someone else."

The airman persisted, "Hell, no. I don't have you confused." His tone now was superior: "I never forget a face. Your name ends in *s-k-i,* or *s-t-i.* You're Catholic, right?"

Roger wanted to laugh. He wanted to say, "No, I'm Jewish and I'm on my way to services at Yokota Air Force Base. My friend Rabbi Schwartz is expecting me. I'm his Yiddische altar boy." Instead, he again answered tactfully: "Sorry, my name is Roger Brooks. I'm from Miami."

As he spoke, Roger held his wallet open to his air force identification card, letting the other man read his name and home address.

"Where did you say you think you saw me?" Roger then asked. "What city was that?"

"Binghamton, New York," the airman answered. "That's where I know I saw you, Brooks. Let me tell you something —I never forget a face!"

The airman turned back around in his seat and pitched his garrison hat forward until it shielded his eyes. It was a contemptuous gesture signaling the end of the conversation. Roger immediately began to sort the loose pieces. He knew that he was born in the Binghamton City Hospital. His birth certificate had told him this much. He had always believed, however, that his twin had moved away from Binghamton at a young age, just as he had. But now he wondered: if his brother had grown up in Binghamton he could have played basketball in a church league like the Catholic Youth Organization. Roger liked the game himself and during his Schenectady years had played on the Shield of David team in the Young Men's Hebrew Association league.

Roger was presuming that his brother was a Catholic, but this was a logical presumption. His biological mother was Italian Catholic; Mildred had told him this long ago. So why couldn't his twin, as a Catholic, have played CYO basketball against this loud-mouthed airman?

Roger leaned forward and excitedly tapped the airman's shoulder. "Excuse me, do you remember the address of that St. Mary's Church in Binghamton?"

"Hell, no," the three-striper answered. "You expect me to remember everything. I was there only one time. The night we played you St. Mary's guys. Like I already told you."

When the bus reached Yokota the tippled airman walked toward the enlisted men's club, and Roger went to Shabbas services with Rabbi Schwartz. But as brief and unsatisfying as this chance meeting in late November 1957 had proved, Roger couldn't put it out of his mind. In the week that followed he had new pictures of himself made and then sat down before a writing table in the service club. He began a letter to "Saint Mary's Church, Binghamton, New York, USA."

After explaining, in considerable detail, that he was a twin separated from his brother, he asked, "Do you have anyone in your records born at City Hospital on May 28, 1938? He would be an adopted or foster son and possibly played on your CYO basketball team during the mid-1950s. To show what he looks like today, I've enclosed several pictures of myself. I'm sure my brother resembles me. Please, do you have any information that will help me? . . ."

On the back of the photographs (he sent both profile and front-view poses. Roger had written his height, weight, hair and eye color and included a description of his burn scars.

"I figured," he explained, "that when they're young, twins sleep together, and if I was burned in a crib fire, my brother must also have been burned."

Roger believed that at last he was doing something to find his brother; he was also sure good would result from this letter. This was his new confidence speaking.

"I always felt in the air force, that someone was watching out for me. I had faith that things could work out for me, and I had faith in myself."

This new feeling had started with his very first assignment. Out of a thirty-eight-man training class, thirty-seven radio operators were sent to what everyone called "HARDSHIP STATIONS"—Iceland and Alaska. Only Roger Brooks drew the Japan duty, which led to more good things. He had then met the scholarly, understanding Chaplain Schwartz, and once they became close, Roger volunteered to teach Sunday school to the officers' children. It wasn't entirely religious zeal that motivated him, although he enjoyed the teaching. He calculated that his charity was almost certain to redound to his benefit, and he was right. He naturally became friendly with a number of officers, and they protected him from all the unpleasant enlisted men's assignments, including night guard duty. Later, he was selected to be master of ceremonies for the USO shows, and after just two such appearances, he was a well-known and popular camp figure. Roger enjoyed this notoriety; it was a new experience.

He began then by answering mail call completely confident. But when three weeks passed with no news from Binghamton, he felt his old depression beginning to build, and on the morning the mail clerk handed him an envelope with a pen-and-ink sketch of St. Mary's Church in the upper left-hand corner, his hands shook from anxiety. He tore it open, telling himself—as though it were fact and not entreaty: "They found my brother."

The letter was short and its message disappointing. A nun, whose name Roger has long since forgotten, said she was sorry. They could be of no help at St. Mary's. She counseled him to pray and had enclosed a string of rosary beads "to speed your prayerful efforts to relocate your dear brother."

Roger was badly let down. He fingered the beads and then flung them into a trash barrel. "As if these could help! As though prayer were going to find my brother!" He knew almost nothing of Catholicism, but what he did know seemed absurd. Ray Skop had told him Catholics believed Christ was born of a Virgin, had walked on water and raised up the dead, and Catholics confessed their sins to a priest who forgave them if they did penance by saying prayers called "Hail Marys." All this sounded so silly, and now this! A set of little wooden beads to lead him to his brother!

Roger couldn't wait for Friday, when he would tell Chaplain Schwartz. Usually, after services the rabbi invited him for chopped liver, bagels and lox and hot tea. The rabbi's lovely Israeli-born wife served and also joined in their talks. This night the chaplain listened patiently to Roger's long story, and after he had finished, he laughed.

"What's so funny, rabbi?" Roger asked, disappointed with his friend's reaction.

"You!" the rabbi said good-naturedly. "My Hebrew school teacher with rosary beads."

"I don't think it's funny," Roger answered. "I say they're stupid people. That nun never really answered my questions. She didn't tell me whether she had looked for my brother. I don't know what to think now. I have no idea what her silly note means—"

"Well, all right," the chaplain said, becoming serious. "The point is you're seven thousand miles from the problem, and there isn't terribly much you can do. Besides, you've got a job right here and it takes precedence. For the time being, put your brother out of your thoughts. Mind you, I'm not counseling you to give up the search. To the contrary, I think you're on to something, and with some hard work, plus a little luck, and a *Jewish prayer* or two, it's possible you can find your twin."

"How, rabbi?" Roger asked . "Where do I start?"

"I think you must begin by going to Binghamton. Stay a week or more. Move around; get to know people. Go to that church and try to find an old priest who has baptized every child born into the parish for thirty years. Convince people of your sincerity. You're a very appealing young man, my friend. Someone will remember something, and by being on the scene you'll find ways of advancing your search. Only the time for this maximum effort is after you are discharged. Now, you must concentrate on keeping up a good service record."

Roger disciplined himself then to give full attention to his radioman's job, and shortly after this night was one of twenty-two operators chosen for special assignment. For the next half year, he served on two tiny Pacific islands and was a part of an historic experiment, the atomic test of 1958. On Eniwetok Island he witnessed the literally unforgettable A-bomb explosion. A week after the test Roger's unit was transferred to Tarawa in the central Pacific, where the loudest noise was the soft sound of the waves washing over the coral reef that surrounded the eight-square-mile island. Roger at once fell in love with Tarawa. To him the isolation, the natural beauty, the tropic stillness gave him a deep and unique feeling of peace, and he was to describe the island in years ahead "as a paradise, exactly like you read about in books."

"We were one degree above the equator," he remembers, "yet there always was a breeze, and it never rained, at least not for more than ten minutes. I loved the stillness, and it was a perfect opportunity for me to think. Sometimes, sitting alone in our mobile radio van I got really carried away. I would start to sing and let my mind just drift. I used to think about my life, what I wanted to be like someday. I told myself that I wanted someone to know that Roger was around."

*   *   *

Anthony Milasi would have been unhappy, if not miserable, on faraway Tarawa. He was too restless, too much the fortune seeker to have been content among palms, sea gulls and wild flowers on a slender strip of coral in the middle of the world's largest ocean. He saw his time in the navy not for thinking and self-evaluation, but rather as time for *living*. Moreover, he admits candidly that as a serviceman he was easily misled and spent at least several of his shore leaves unwisely. One weekend he and two shipmates checked into a Washington hotel, made frequent use of room service and left unpaid a bill of more than one hundred dollars when they fled down the fire escape. Another time he and his shore-leave buddies exhausted their money and when they grew hungry broke open a gum machine. None of these off-duty peccadillos found their way into his navy file, however. The record showed only that he served well and honorably. It also reflected he was a good yeoman who had risen in grade to Petty Officer Third Class. But during the spring of 1959 he had his biggest navy misadventure. It very nearly was his undoing.

With only six months to serve, he was given duty in the records office at the Norfolk, Virginia, Naval Base. One of his responsibilities was to issue ID cards, an item indispensable to every sailor intent on a night of drinking in town. Because a great many of the sailors at Norfolk were younger than the state's legal drinking age of twenty-one, there was a lively traffic in bogus cards. A nineteen-year-old Seaman Second Class, who said his name was Fred, was one of those who, for ten dollars, bought a phony—a card that exaggerated his age by twenty-four months. Petty Officer Milasi had sold it to him, and when the Shore Police discovered this fact, they brought Tony up on charges before a special court-martial.

At the trial, Fred changed his story. He insisted that he had bought the card in a darkened tavern from a Marine, whom he couldn't describe. The court-martial lasted twelve minutes and closed with a Tony Milasi finish: swift, theatrical, unearned.

All that Tony wanted then was to get home to Binghamton, and the navy obliged by granting him an early discharge. He had only to say goodbye to his navy girl, a WAVE with whom he worked in the records section. On their last night, he and the girl lay side-by-side on a deserted Virginia beach.

Staring up at the stars, he told himself that for the first time he was truly in love. At the same time, he was afraid. The girl was an anomaly: a Kentuckian off a farm and a Protestant! He was an Italian Catholic from a northern city. Each had grown up believing the other wasn't to be entirely trusted. So as their time ran out, they left their deepest thoughts unspoken. They turned to inconsequentials and Tony became a braggadocio.

"I'm going to make a lot of money. I'm going to build a big house, with a white fence around it. Everybody in Binghamton will look at the house and say, 'That's Milasi's place. He made it *big!* '"

"Why do you want all that?" the girl asked.

"Because I'm a materialistic person and a big house will show I'm a success."

"And how do you figure you're going to make your money?"

"I don't know," Tony said. "I'm still working on that part."

They both laughed, but Tony continued, serious once more, "Maybe as a disc jockey. You know, I'll start small, get discovered and next stop, Hollywood."

"You're cute, Tony."

"You don't believe me? Well, I'll make you a promise. Someday you're going to read about me in the newspapers. And I'm going to make a lot of money. . . ."

Then, not knowing why he was saying it, yet powerless to brake himself, Tony declared: "I'm a twin, you know. Did I ever tell you?"

"No, I don't remember *that* lie, sugar."

"It's the honest-to-God truth. Come to Binghamton and ask my mother."

"I'd sooner ask your twin. Where is he at?"

Tony hesitated: "I don't know. He may be dead. I don't think he is, only I'm not sure yet."

Airman Third Class Roger Brooks was honorably discharged on August 24, 1959, and this time his homecoming to Miami was a completely happy one. As he came up the slate-and-cement walk in his starched suntans he walked tall and straight, affecting his best military posture. His grandmother waited at the screen door. When he drew close, she threw it open and Bessie Elman reached out with both her arms. She grabbed for him, pulled him close, and then Roger saw the tears sliding down her lined face.

"My grandson," she said, and, "Oh, I missed you so. I didn't know until you were gone how much I loved you, my grandson."

All his life, Roger had been more loving than loved, a fact that was to create myriad guilt feelings in most of those who had been close to him. Even while overseas, he had been constant, sending his mother a twenty-five-dollar allotment every month. He also shipped home souvenir gifts, birthday and mother's day cards, choosing fancy, frosted ones with sentimental messages. Oftentimes, there would be a five-dollar check inside the card. And whatever he sent his mother, he tried to match for Bessie Elman.

Years afterward, Mildred Brooks admitted, "Rodney was a source of pride, but Roger always gave me the more love. I only wish I could have enjoyed him more, and done more for him."

She was speaking of a time passed. Now, in late summer of Roger's twenty-first year, it was another beginning for them. Roger slept late, went swimming at Miami Beach afternoons and spent his nights with Ray Skop, then a pre-med student at Miami University and intent on becoming a psychiatrist. The family was glad to have Roger home, to see him matured, and these next few weeks were for him, to do as he wished. No one really worried about his getting a job because he was obviously eager to "prove myself on the outside." He wanted to save money, to buy his first new car and be independent.

"All I ever heard when I was growing up was money," he once said. "Money, money, money. I promised myself I was going to have money someday and spend it whatever way I wanted."

There was another reason behind his eagerness to get going. He hadn't forgotten that strange meeting on the air force bus in Japan. He was still troubled by the memory of it and the belief that the airman had mistaken him for his twin. Nor had he rejected Chaplain Schwartz's suggestion that he take up his search in Binghamton. Still, this was no time to wander off, looking for someone of whom he had no first-hand knowledge. As Mildred Brooks was always quick to point out, he and his brother might be fraternal twins and not even resemble each other.

"So you tell me," she cautioned. "how in God's name you're going to find him? You don't even know his name. You can't walk the streets looking for someone born May 28, 1938! The whole thing is preposterous."

It wasn't the difficulty of this task that worried Roger. He was more concerned with being ready to meet his brother. "Before I start looking I want to be completely settled. I want to have a respectable job, to have money saved, to be independent and be, well, a little successful. I certainly don't want to find my brother and then not have him proud of me."

The concept of being "settled" and "responsible" was one that now weighed heavily on Roger. He understandably equated responsibility with the successful personality, because he had grown up hearing of his father's irresponsibility; he was even lectured about this being the underlying cause of the failure of his mother's and father's marriages, the reason that he was denied a father. Moreover, he saw that in his home to be responsible was to win love and approval. The thought of reuniting with his brother before he had become fully responsible was an intolerable one.

In his rush to be employed, though, Roger took the first job offered him and went to work as a clerk in an aircraft factory employing four thousand persons. He sensed he was starting down a dim corridor toward a dead end, but the restrictive Miami job market plus his own limited background left him, he felt, small choice. Further, no one counseled him differently, and he therefore began his campaign for security and independence, which was to occupy him for three years, at $60 a week. Inside of ten months, however, he had worked himself up to expediter on the assembly floor and was earning $120.50 a week. Now he was able to give his mother $20 every Friday and to buy a new automobile, a two-door white Ford with blue interior. It was an $1,800 purchase, and although it had the conventional shift and no extras, not even a heater or radio, Roger was as proud as though he owned an Alfa-Romeo.

"I never knew Roger when he wasn't saving," Ray Skop said years afterward. "Some weeks when he didn't have spending money left, he went without, because he never dipped into his savings, not even the loose change that he saved in an old jar on his bureau."

"And he never missed a day at that old factory," said Ray's wife, Alva. "I remember once he went to work with a cold that sounded like it was pneumonia. He just drove off with a box of tissues and his little sandwich bag. I used to tease him about taking lunch and eating when the whistle blew."

It was the truth, though. The factory workday began with the 7:30 A.M. whistle and ended with the 3:45 P.M. whistle. There were two ten-minute breaks during the day and half an hour for lunch. Roger hated the factory; he realized that, ironically, his civilian life was narrower and more regimented than his life in the military had been. Because of the unrelenting sameness of all his days and the tedium that marked them, he built a second life away from the factory. Together with Ray Skop, he joined a theater group and quickly established himself as a talented amateur. He was a good mimic and conscientiously followed stage direction, for beneath his passivity was an arrested need for self-expression, as well as a great desire to do well among those whom he judged superior to himself. In time, he became a good enough actor to carry a lead part. His comic's portrayal in one play earned him this praise from a local newspaper critic: "Roger Brooks' was the best-played role in the delightful performance."

"To me it was just a hobby," Roger explains. "My mother pushed it, though. She always thought something might come of it. I knew better, but I'll admit that I liked the applause. I knew then that people had accepted me and this made me feel good."

Roger also liked the theater because of the people with whom he worked. They were filled with ideas and ambition, interested in self-improvement, in becoming involved with issues and causes. Alone, Roger Brooks was satisfied to be a spectator, willing to wait until Ray Skop was free or even to stay home. He was, in many ways, a manchild, still the boy of whom the psychologist at St. Joseph's Home wrote, ". . . looks for affection in a rather shy manner. He will watch people and if caught noticing will smile and walk away."

With his theater friends, though, he was more confident,

competitive and purposeful. He went to operas and ballets and he started voice lessons. For two years, from 1960-1962, he studied opera and here again, did passably well. Feeling himself grow, he even dreamed that someday, possibly, he might be a professional. Once or twice he let his imagination run, until he saw himself as Rodolfo in *La Boheme*, singing on a broad and well-lighted stage in some magnificent old opera house.

"If I were a star," he thought, "My brother might come hear me. Then, we would meet. . . ."

13

Tony

By the time he turned down Carroll Street in his beige-colored Chevrolet convertible, dusk had begun to settle over the block. This was the dinner hour in the Seventh Ward and no one was around to see civilian Tony Milasi come home in his new chariot, with the top down, showing off the gold upholstery.

Weeks before, Joe Milasi had telegraphed his son the news: "Your money is waiting." Tony knew this meant the entire $1,500, saved all during his boyhood, was finally his, and because he wanted this car in which to drive home, he had bought it in Virginia the same day.

The navy had released him two months early, so on May 27, 1959, the day before his twenty-first birthday, Tony had set out early and traveled hard all day, stopping only for gas and to eat. He had hoped to reach Binghamton while it was still light, but now as he made the turn off Court Street into Carroll it was quiet all down his block.

"Holy cow," Tony thought. "Nothing around here ever changes."

But in the next moment he saw the "For Rent" sign in the storefront at 47 Carroll and he realized that the neighborhood was older and had indeed changed. Milasi's Market was gone now. A year ago a modern supermarket had opened only four blocks away. Joe Milasi understood that his Tony never wanted to be tied to the store's long hours and uncertain profits, and at sixty-five he was too old to fight alone; so he sold the stock and locked his door for the last time.

Tony had written his parents they were wise to sell, and when he saw them waiting together at the head of the stairs, he was even more certain they had made the right choice. They seemed old, not as he had remembered them. His mother, who was sixty-seven, was much thinner, and to go with her complaints of a weak heart she had new ones describing arthritis and an ulcer.

Joe Milasi, also sixty-seven, remained stoical and uncomplaining, yet he too was markedly changed. There were new lines in his face, he was a little more round-shouldered and Tony was used to seeing his father in his butcher's bib-apron. Without it, he seemed out of character.

Unchanged, however, was the Milasi spirit, the wellspring of the family strength. Pauline and Joseph were unashamedly emotional over having their son home and stood ready to support him in any undertaking. The first, launched within six weeks of his return, was his own business: "Tony's Snack Bar." It was located in his father's vacant store, and the specialty was a submarine sandwich stuffed with Pauline Milasi's home-cooked meatballs. There were also pizzas cooked to order, and a teenage chef handled cold sandwiches.

"Right away I began to dream," Tony remembers. "After a year, I would add maybe a second and a third place. A couple more years and I'd have two more. I was even scouting locations. The guys used to kid, calling me Tony, the Submarine King.

"But why not dream big? The place wasn't three months old and I was pulling down a hundred dollars a week. Then, I don't know what happened—it all came apart."

Misled by the early success, Tony paid too little attention to business. Even Pauline Milasi laughs when she thinks back: "He puts the young boy in charge, and goes out, riding around. No good for business, this way." Bankruptcy papers were filed just 117 days after the red, white and blue grand opening bunting was tacked over 47 Carroll Street, and Tony began to skip from job to job.

He worked for a car rental agency, he sold real estate, and he drove across the country to Porterville, California, where he and four others from Binghamton intended to get a free junior college education. Sitting in Michael-Angelo's one morning, they had taken the idea from a newspaper story. Tony attended classes for two weeks and even tried out for the football team. He showed up for three practices and was described in a news photograph as "one of the four biggest men on the squad and a promising lineman."

The same day his picture appeared in the newspapers back in Binghamton, Tony left the school. He held and quit two more California jobs, made side trips to Las Vegas and Hollywood and then returned home tired, jaded, unfulfilled. Bowing to the persuasions of his family, he tried working for International Business Machines, Binghamton's premier employer. He was hired for a night job; he lasted just eight months. Finally, after two and a half years of frustration, of drifting from misadventure to disappointment, he decided upon a sales career. He drove 196 miles northwest to Buffalo on Lake Erie and in January 1962 became a door-to-door salesman of Great Books of the Western World.

While the one monozygotic partner was groping, failing, aimlessly moving with the ebb and flow of Seventh Ward indolence, living off unemployment insurance as he watchfully waited for the one big deal that would change the course of his life in a swift stroke, the other *human carbon* was almost the epitome of constancy.

Roger Brooks' life was measured in shifts at the aircraft factory, by the number of biweekly voice lessons he took and the small yet regular deposits he made in a growing savings account. Self-discipline, responsibility, punctuality: these were the markers along the highway he traveled.

If twenty-three-year-old Tony Milasi seemed determined to prove that he was a product of his heredity and nothing more, totally ignoring the example of Joe Milasi's life, then Roger Brooks at twenty-three was at the other end of the pole; he seemed equally determined to prove that environment was the only motivator to which he responded.

Tony and six other sales beginners were given a five-day training course and on an overcast Saturday morning were grouped on a Buffalo street corner with their instructor. He shook their hands and followed with the challenge, "Now go out and sell!"

An apprehensive Tony Milasi walked down the street and turned into a housing project. He stared up at the buildings, wondering where to begin. Then it started to rain, and Tony ran into the nearest vestibule, hesitantly pressing the first apartment bell. A man, about forty, opened the door to ask, "What do you want?"

Everything Tony had been taught and had faithfully committed to memory went right out of his head. It was as though he were seized with amnesia *and* speech paralysis. He blurted, "Want to buy some great books?"

"Absolutely not. I'm too busy to bother with your books. I'm an engineer."

"Wait," pleaded Tony. "Give me a break. I get a dollar if I make my presentation. Besides, I need practice. You're my first customer."

He unquestionably needed practice, but he wasn't paid for a presentation. Still, this business lie was the wedge that put him into his first apartment. When the engineer agreed to give him ten minutes and called his wife to join them, Tony quickly took off his coat and squatted down on the floor. He spread out his life-size picture of the set of fifty-four Great Books costing $398 but payable over thirty months, his index book called the Syntopicon and his mimeographed sales speech. He began by declaring he was going to try something different. He was going to make his pitch exactly as he had been taught.

"Now, I'm supposed to say, 'Hi, I'm Tony Milasi: M-I-L-A-S-I, of the Great Ideas Program and I'm here to talk about education!' Then I get you to fill out these forms, which tell me your occupation and how many children you have. This is to help me sell you. If you have children, naturally I slant my pitch in that direction. Get it?

"I explain the Great Books are a complete indexing of all the great minds of the world by ideas. Napoleon, Shakespeare, Dostoevski—did I pronounce that right? Well, you name him and we've got him right here," he said, slapping the Syntopicon.

"That's a gesture," he said. "I've got a repertoire of gestures. They're to keep you alert. If I catch someone dozing, I'm supposed to accidentally drop the Syntopicon; Bang! Wake 'em up."

The engineer's wife laughed; her husband's face softened; Tony was encouraged. He continued: "Now, I have to tell you that to accomplish this program took ten years—think of THAT—and cost one million dollars. Right here I say, 'Isn't that fantastic! Ten years and one million dollars.' "

He could feel the sale beginning to tip his way and this made him confident. Pointing at his speech, he said, "Say, I have three more *fantastics* coming up and twice I have to say, 'Isn't that amazing?' The *fantastics* win over the *amazings*, four to two."

This time, both the wife and her husband laughed. "Please, please, no applause," Tony said, and knew this was the time to begin the serious talk. "What do you think of capital punishment? Undecided? All right, let's find out what the great minds have to say. It's all here in this handy-dandy Syntopicon, which gives volume number, page number and even the section of the page. We look up Shakespeare on capital punishment, then maybe Napoleon and finally another great *Frenchman*, Dostoevski.

"Now, completely well informed, you are prepared to make up your own mind. We at Great Books, I modestly claim, have led you into thinking for yourself. Isn't that a *fantastic*—that's Number Two, two to go—way to get your children to read, to learn and to think!

"Heck, I've got a lot more spiel to go through, but you've heard enough. You've both been good listeners. I want to thank you, too."

"Well, good going," the engineer said. "I changed my mind and you've just made your first sale."

"It was refreshing," his wife said. "So honest."

When their sales trainer met them back on the same corner for review at four o'clock in the afternoon, Tony was the hero. While the others all had drawn blanks, he had made two sales and had the engineer's check for the full amount. The commission on each sale was one hundred dollars and over the next three months Tony averaged two hundred dollars a week. One week he sold seven sets by Thursday and took off the rest of that week.

"I found myself in this job," he explained. "I always was a good talker, able to convince people, and this is what I was doing with Great Books."

Getting them to take the pen and commit themselves to the thirty payments was the toughest part of each sale. This was *the closing* and Tony saw a number of otherwise good salesmen fail because when they came up to closing, they became unsure. They either talked too much, or suddenly went silent, holding their breath and trusting to their luck. Tony believed this was the moment to be bold. He liked closing. It was a matching of wits and far more exciting than selling bologna over the counter in his father's store.

"Let's face it," he once said, "there's some actor in all of us. We like to hear our own voice. I know I do; I'm a big ham. As a kid, I won third prize in an amateur contest at the Capitol Theater, and I'll never forget the whistling and clapping I got just for doing a reading. Well, the kind of selling I was doing gave me a chance to be a ham in someone's living room, I liked this, and when I was going good I liked the salesman's life, too."

He liked everything except the loneliness. On the days when he didn't make a sale it seemed to trail him. Generally, he would quit early, only to find himself facing a strange city, alone. Although he had grown up as an only child, he had been alone only infrequently. There had always been the store, Uncle Bruno's parlor, Michael-Angelo's and all the Saints. It had been easy to find companionship. Here it was different, and he couldn't handle it. He was incapable of spending any length of time by himself and had neither a desire nor capacity to use leisure time constructively. If the solitude of Tarawa was a boon to Roger Brooks, the loneliness of Buffalo, New York, was anathema to Anthony Milasi.

After a week during which he continually was lonely, and had thought a great deal about his brother, Tony drove home to Binghamton and went directly downtown to the Bureau of Vital Statistics. As he mounted the wooden porch steps that led to the bureau offices he told himself he was finally going to find answers to his questions about his twin, for he knew his adoption papers were on file in this building.

"What I really need to know," he told the pleasant, heavy-set woman behind the counter, "is whether my adoption records have all the information about my brother. Nobody in my family seems to have the full story. All I get is bits and pieces. I want to know things like who adopted him? What his name is now. Where he's living."

As Mrs. Jane Buckland, the registrar, listened to his story, she thought: "Suppose one of my two boys was looking for his brother? Oh, God, I hope someone would help him!" Yet, there was nothing that she could do for Tony Milasi. She explained that under the law his adoption file was sealed, and could only be opened, even to him, by a court order from a justice of the state supreme court. Mrs. Buckland talked to him as she would to her sons. She said he was fortunate to have had good parents and a fine home. As to his brother, "I'm sorry," said Jane Buckland. "I'm truly sorry. I know how you must feel. But there is no way I can help you."

Tony left not knowing what to believe. He thought hard about this confrontation and concluded ". . . my brother must be dead, otherwise Mrs. Buckland would have given me some hint to keep up my hopes. I couldn't believe that a law was going to keep a person from telling me about my twin brother. I felt sure she would look in my file after I left and that if my brother was alive, she'd find a way to tell me. When I didn't hear anything, I became depressed. I decided that my mother knew the truth and all these years was only trying to protect me. When I figured it was useless for me to do anything more. I gave up. But a couple days later, I came back to the idea that if my brother was alive, we would meet; it was bound to happen. This was my personality taking charge. I've always been a dreamer, an optimist, a big planner, and as Mrs. Buckland said to me, I've been lucky in life."

Four months after he joined the Great Books Company, Tony was promoted to division sales manager. With the new title came the trappings, an office suite that "looked like a movie set." Tony remembered, "It had drapes all across the back window, wall-to-wall carpeting, a wall cabinet with a television set and a complete stock of liquor. It also had an intercom system and two secretaries who were knockouts. I know. I hired them."

As division sales manager, Tony was responsible for training new salesmen and saw this as the perfect opportunity to eliminate future loneliness. His first move was to telephone Binghamton and hire two former Saints. John Russo was chosen to become his sales ace, and for sales trainer he singled out Dino Pirozzi, the one-time Il Duce.

"This job had better be all you say it is," Dino told him, "because I'm giving up a good opportunity here."

"What's that?"

"I'm working for Danny Affatato, in his shine parlor."

"Doing what?" Tony asked.

"What do you think? Shining shoes and tips have been good."

Dino Pirozzi had matured into an engaging and inveterate nonconformist. He lived alone, saw no good reason to work steadily or hard and was an aggressive if inconstant faddist. One month he was a vegetarian, an art fancier another and in a third he became a crusader against water pollution, lamenting that the Susquehanna was no longer safe for swimming. He was also an unbeliever, having come home from the army in 1958 to renounce the Catholic Church and God. This act had a traumatic effect upon several of his boyhood followers.

"They were completely shaken when he left the Church," said George Tomaras, the Saint who became a social worker. "Some of them aren't over it yet. They still sit around Michael-Angelo's and complain, 'Can you imagine that goddam Dino saying there ain't no God!'"

Despite generally antithetical thinking on most serious subjects, Dino and Tony had become close friends. Pirozzi continually mocked Tony's strivings to make money, yet when he arrived in Buffalo and saw the setup, he was impressed.

"The executive! Well, Milasi, you finally made it."

"Damn right," Tony answered. "Expense-account living, too. Health club in the afternoon, then a couple Scotch highballs, a steak dinner and a little date with an airlines gal. But wait until you see where I'm living."

It was a $250-a-month hotel suite, with bedroom, sitting room and kitchenette, directly across from the Great Books offices. Dino and John Russo moved in with Tony, made good use of the hotel's health club and shared his credit cards for meals and new suits with which to launch their sales careers.

Another newcomer on whom Tony made an impression was a chatty, eighteen-year-old Bostonian named Mark Frattalone. He presented himself during the early summer of 1962 and was hired. "I liked him," Tony said, "and he was Italian." Frattalone did well for about six weeks and then left. He explained to Tony that his father had insisted he return to college. He was going back reluctantly.

"Where do you go to school?" Tony asked.

"Florida," Mark said. "The University of Miami."

"Sounds great," Tony said. "My last year in the navy I made some great liberties in Miami. If I ever get back down there I'll look you up."

"I'd like that," said Mark Frattalone. "You've been a good friend, Tony. I'm not going to forget you."

14

Roger and Tony

"I've got it," Roger called, as he went to answer the kitchen phone.

Bessie Elman asked, "Is it for me, Roger? Who is it?"

"Hello, rabbi," said Roger, and to his grandmother he yelled, "It's your favorite boy friend. He wants me this time."

Roger had known Rabbi Skop would call. He also knew that he would bow to the rabbi's will.

"Do her this one favor," Morris Skop said to Roger now. "How much longer does she have to live?"

With the coming of September 1962 and the Tishri, Bessie Elman began to prepare for her ten days of repentance. She was eighty-two and weakening, yet she eagerly looked forward to Rosh Hashanah with her rabbi in his new temple,

Beth Shirah. In her enthusiasm, she approached her grandson to ask two favors. She wanted Roger to take her to temple on Rosh Hashanah and begged him to sing with the choir.

"You know," Bessie Elman said, "how I love to hear you sing the prayers."

Although it hurt him, Roger refused his grandmother, explaining he already had made a date for Friday, September 28. He felt confident, though, that this wasn't the end of the discussion. Knowing Bessie Elman as he did, he anticipated this call from Rabbi Skop.

"Roger," Morris Skop was saying, "you can't refuse your grandmother and your pal the rabbi!"

"Okay, okay," Roger said. "I'll sing, but only this one time."

"I knew you wouldn't let your rabbi down," said Morris Skop.

When he hung up the phone, Bessie Elman came out of her room. "What did the rabbi want?" she asked, innocently.

Roger had to smile. "I am going to sing on Rosh Hashanah." This was all he said. After a pause, he added, "Just for you."

"Bless you, my grandson," Bessie Elman said and, searching for something more, something to measure how she felt toward him in this moment, she faltered and then said, "God will one day reward you."

There were close to a hundred persons sitting on folding chairs in the humble Temple Beth Shirah, a rented hall above a supermarket, when the Shofar was sounded and the rabbi stepped into his pulpit. Bessie Elman was in the front row, in the twenty-five-dollar complimentary seat to which Roger, a choir member, was entitled. Morris Skop began his Rosh Hashanah sermon by reminding his congregation it was a time for introspection, forgiveness, and understanding. He was soft-voiced, as always a cerebral rather than an emotional leader.

"This is our most dramatic moment," he said evenly. "These are the solemn days, a time when all the world is judged before God's throne. Yet, it is not a somber time. 'Be not sad, for the joy of the Lord is your strength.' "

The choir sang three songs. Tenor Roger Brooks sang out loudly and beside him, Ray Skop smiled. The rabbi winked at Bessie Elman. After the service, Roger made certain that his grandmother had a ride home with one of her temple auxiliary friends and then took Ray aside. He saw this night as an opportunity to spend some time with Ray and his new bride; only Alva Skop had a headache. She preferred going straight home, but proved no match for Roger's good humor.

"Come on, it's Rosh Hashanah," he coaxed. "No one has a headache on Rosh Hashana. We've got to celebrate."

"Well, where will we go?" Alva asked, still hesitant but no longer unyielding.

"What difference does it make?" Roger persisted. "We'll find a nice place. You pick one out, come on!"

This then is how the three happened to drive out U.S. Highway 1 in Roger's Ford, headed in the general direction of Miami University in Coral Gables. When Alva saw the Pancake House up ahead, she decided this was where they should stop, and fifteen minutes later busboy Mark Frattalone was standing beside their table, staring wide-eyed through dark, horn-rimmed glasses at Roger Brooks.

Shaking his head as he spoke, he persisted, to ask a second time: "Are you sure that you're not Tony Milasi?"

Roger Brooks was correct and polite, yet equally persistent. So Mark Frattalone tried again and again. "I don't know," he said finally, "I'd swear you were Tony Milasi!"

On the ride home, Roger asked his friends, both of whom knew he was a twin, what they thought of the encounter.

"I'm not sure," offered Ray, the student psychologist. "He's young, and did you see how excited he was? He doesn't seem a reliable type."

"I think," Alva remarked, "that he wants to get you to buy some of those books that he and his friend sold in Buffalo."

This skepticism was understandable. However, Roger had wanted to listen to Mark Frattalone again, and in their second meeting, twelve hours later, he discovered a genuineness about this exuberant busboy. He sincerely wanted to help, and after Mark had established that Roger and Tony had the same birth date and had shown Roger the photograph of Anthony Milasi, he declared, "If I bring you two together, it will be the greatest, most exciting thing I've ever done in my life!"

Once he had seen the photograph in the Great Books Company newsletter, Roger felt sure that Tony Milasi was his twin; yet he was determined to go forward deliberately, cautiously. For a full week, he met every evening with his confidante, Aunt Mildred. They talked of the discovery, and they planned. On Monday, October 8, Roger walked into the Miami Family Service office to ask for an appointment.

"I remember that afternoon very well," said Miss Catherine M. Bittermann, casework supervisor. "I was filling in for someone who was out sick. I was doing my own and this other job, too. It was late in the day, and Mr. Brooks was the last thing I needed. I took him into one of our small interview rooms and candidly, my first impression was his story was highly unlikely. I told myself there must be a *hangup* in here someplace. You know, it was too good to be true."

As Roger Brooks continued, speaking of the expectations he hoped for from the relationship with his twin, she had a second reaction. Catherine Bittermann was reminded of her beginnings as a social worker seventeen years before in rural West Virginia, where she had seen classic, textbook cases of family suffering. Nothing she had learned at Columbia University Social Work School had prepared her for regularly serving families where the mother had died in childbirth, or the father, in this coal mining region, literally had vanished, being trapped in a mine cave-in or lost in a gas explosion. Still, some of her most poignant memories of family pathos involved brothers and sisters separated during the depression, when oftentimes compassion moved parents to give their youngest children for adoption.

"I would get them years later, as grown men and women," she said. "They would come in a fervor, anxious to reestablish ties with some brother or sister only dimly remembered. Occasionally, they were even able to relocate the relative, only to discover the adoptive parents were against the reunion. These parents refused to give up the married name, the address or the telephone number—that one bit of information that was the key. Oh God, you never saw such confusion, disappointment, despair then!"

The casework supervisor warned Roger Brooks that he was romanticizing about someone who was still a stranger. She gently tried to blunt his enthusiasm, pointing out that he and his twin as yet had no shared experiences, no bond of common interests and, quite possibly, came from entirely different backgrounds. She finally sent him home, counseling him to be patient. She knew that even before she could write the Binghamton Family Service and ask their cooperation, she must read through the Roger Brooks file. It was three inches thick and "just too heavy to drag home."

She began her reading the following day and in the first hour, Catherine Bittermann saw the story told her by earnest, naive Roger Brooks was, in all probability, incredibly true. For he was a twin, and his brother had been adopted in 1938 into an Italian Catholic family in Binghamton, New York. The family's name, however, was not recorded.

"Apparently, in 1948," said Catherine Bittermann, "there had been some thought of legally adopting Roger. So at Mildred Brooks' urging our office got up an entire history on him. This is how the information about his twin happened to be in the file, but even luckier than that is the fact that the record was still intact. We only keep files six years, but on Roger's folder someone had written 'Do Not Destroy.'"

Roger returned four days later, on Friday, and Miss Bittermann reported her positive, but still incomplete, findings. She added that now she would write to the Family Service in Binghamton and the Milasi family would be interviewed. If their son, Tony, proved to be his twin, the question of a reunion would then be up to Mr. and Mrs. Milasi.

"Suppose Tony doesn't know that he's adopted?" asked Roger.

"Then, I imagine the Milasis won't want any reunion."

"What do I do then?"

"You must decide that question for yourself," Catherine Bitterman said.

She let him absorb her answer, turning it over in his mind, before continuing: "You would have a very difficult ethical decision to make; only let's not worry until we're faced with the actual situation. Hopefully, it won't ever come to this."

"And how long am I going to have to wait now?" Roger asked.

"A week, maybe ten days."

"That long?"

"You've already waited twenty-four years," Catherine Bittermann said.

In her letter to the Binghamton Family Service director, Miss Bittermann wrote that "Roger's own experiences with his foster family have left him with a lack of family identification, and he feels somehow that his twin brother is a part of him. He is terribly eager to meet with his twin and, to date, has shown admirable restraint.

"What he most wants is to telephone his brother and say, 'This is your twin brother, Roger.'"

She was, of course, a career professional. Still, Catherine Bittermann felt herself becoming emotionally involved in this case. She understood that Roger Brooks needed this break, and deserved it. Reading through his file she had seen where he first came to Family Service in 1947, when he was nine. She concluded that if the agency had had funds enough then, it properly should have placed him in another, more adequate, foster home.

"One of the tragedies of Roger's story," she was to say years later, "is that he was allowed to grow up where he did."

As he climbed the stairs to the second-floor apartment, Zev Hymowitz, at thirty-one the youngest of nine Binghamton Family Service workers, told himself this should be an easy case. Coming from Brooklyn, New York, he knew about volatile Italians; he understood that when you discussed family with them you had to go gingerly, only this was such good news. He already had read through the adoption history of Anthony Milasi; he knew that he was Roger Brooks's twin, that both boys were born to a Maria and Jules Brooks.

It was 10:30 on Tuesday morning, October 16, and Pauline Milasi was in her kitchen. When she heard the knock, she called out, raising her voice above the noise of the television, "Door is open!"

Zev Hymowitz introduced himself and began by announcing, "I've brought good news. It's about your son, Anthony."

Pauline Milasi thought, "Strangers call him 'Anthony.' To friends, he is 'Tony.' And strangers never bring good news." So she said, "Tony not home. You come back. Maybe home Saturday."

"As long as I'm here, I'd like to tell you the story, Mrs. Milasi. It concerns you, too."

It suddenly came to Pauline Milasi why this man was here. "Mother of God," she thought. "He wants my Tony. He's come to take him back."

Hymowitz saw the confusion, then the terror in her small brown eyes and said reassuringly, "It's a wonderful story and

I'm sure you'll agree, very good news. Can we sit down first?"

"I have papers," Pauline Milasi said. "Adoption papers, from the court. You wait, I get."

"Oh, no. That isn't necessary," the Family Service worker said. "This is about Anthony's brother. His twin brother. He's been in touch with our Miami, Florida, office and wants a reunion with Anthony."

"He's alive?" Pauline Milasi put her hands over her throat and her voice seemed to catch on the words. "Santa Maria."

"Oh, yes, very much so."

Pauline made the sign of the cross and turned to stare into her dining room, where a three-foot statue of the Madonna stood on a radiator cover. "Hail, Mary, full of grace," she said softly and once more blessed herself, repeating, "Hail, Mary, full of grace."

Turning back to face Hymowitz, she said, "You wait, please. I get my niece and we talk."

Lilly and Memo Saraceno and their four healthy, heavy-footed children lived in the apartment directly above, and since Tony had moved to Buffalo, Lilly often helped her aunt in business conversations. Now the two women sat on the Milasi living room couch and listened to the account of how Roger Brooks, with the help of a busboy who had known Tony, had found his brother. With Lilly repeating the story in Italian, Pauline Milasi understood; she had difficulty concentrating, though, because her mind kept going back to that spring day in 1938 when she first saw the twins.

Pauline Milasi stood up and walked to the side window to look down on the very house that twenty-four years ago was Vince Maddi's home and medical office. It was here that she first held the infant twins and initially chose the "red-face baby," the one of whom they now spoke. To Zev Hymowitz, she said: "Tony wants to see his brother, Mr. Zev. Tony asks me about him, many times."

This was what the worker had been waiting to hear. "That's wonderful," he told the women. "I'll pass this right along to Miami."

"You tell Roger," said Tony's mother, "that Pauline and Joe Milasi say he come here and live. Just like our son."

The understanding was that Mrs. Milasi would relay the news to Tony in Buffalo and, once the Miami Family Service office had a complete report from Binghamton, Miami was to arrange for the brothers to *meet* on the telephone. At a specific time on a prearranged date, Roger Brooks would call Tony Milasi.

Driving back to his office, Zev Hymowitz thought this was the type of case you needed to strike a balance, to hold up against the almost mind-boggling misery and deprivation you experience day after day. If these two brothers met and built a relationship, it would be a good thing on which to look back. A social worker could take pride from having played a part in bringing separated monozygotic twins together.

15

Roger and Tony

Although they had been friends since Christopher Columbus Junior High School, Dino Pirozzi had never known Tony Milasi was an identical twin. This was largely because Tony was chary of talking about his past, fearing that the conversation might turn on the fact he was illegitimate and his father was Jewish.

On the night of October 16, 1962, while lying around in their hotel suite in Buffalo, and for reasons that in retrospect excite him, Tony chose this time to introduce the fact of his twinship. Dino Pirozzi was unresponsive. An indiscriminate as well as a constant reader, he was occupied with a copy of *Mad* magazine.

Tony began with the inquiry, "Did I ever tell you about my twin?"

"No."

"Well, I am a twin, you know."

"Hooray. For both of you."

"Honest to God," Tony protested.

There was no response. Tony continued, "Somewhere in this old world, there is someone exactly like me."

"Can't be."

"Why not?"

Without turning his head from the magazine, Dino said, "Two fat asses like you? I won't believe it."

"I don't care what you believe," Tony said, becoming impatient. "I was adopted—"

"I'd heard."

"—and my twin was in a foster home. There was a fire. I think his crib, or bed, caught fire, and Mom says he was burned. She thinks he might have died because of the fire or after it."

"Uh huh."

"Is that all you've got to say, damn it?"

Dino nodded his head, signaling yes. Tony paused before trying again: "Do you think I'll ever find him?"

"Who, Judge Crater?"

"No, my twin."

There was another pause, longer than the first, and Tony again said: "You want to hear something horrible? Suppose my twin and I were on two planes that passed in midair. We'd never see each other. It could happen on buses, even, and we might just be looking the other way."

Dino dropped the magazine on his chest. "Why don't you advertise in the *Binghamton Sun?* 'Twin, come home! Bring money! Your brother, Tony.' "

"Boy, I can see talking to you is useless," Tony said disgustedly.

"Try me again later."

Tony walked to the television set and turned it on. It was almost ten o'clock. For the next twenty minutes he watched television in silence. When the phone rang, Dino answered it.

"It's your Mom," he said, holding out the receiver. Tony got up from his chair and turned down the television volume. As he approached the phone he asked himself why was she calling? At this hour? He knew it was serious, because his mother disliked long-distance calls. The operators never understood her and having to repeat everything two and three times embarrassed her.

Tony could think of only two reasons for this call: she was sick and wanted him home or there was a buyer for The Block. Real Estate values in the old ward were skidding, and Joe Milasi wanted to sell 47 Carroll Street.

"Hello, Mom. What's up?"

"Guess, Tony. Guess what?"

"Mom, c'mon. You didn't call long distance to play games."

"Guess what happened?" Pauline Milasi repeated.

"How am I going to guess, Mom?"

"It's what you always talk about."

"You sold the building?"

"No. Better news. Guess."

"Ma, I don't know. I can't. I'm tired."

"Tony," she said in a remote and almost grave tone, "you find your brother!"

"Mom, what do you mean? What are you talking about?"

"Your brother. You find him," she said a second time. "The man was here. He says so."

"Holy Christ!" Tony screamed now. "Ma, that's fantastic. You can't mean it!"

"Yes, yes, it's true, Tony."

"But what man says so, Ma?"

"From agency. A nice man."

"What agency?"

"Tony, I don't get the name. But it's true. Your brother find you."

"Where is my brother?"

"Florida. Miami."

"How does this man know all this?"

"Tony, it's long story," Pauline Milasi said. "You come home and I'll tell you everything."

"Okay, Ma, but wait, I want to tell Dino." Turning from the phone, he repeated the news, and from this point it became a three-way conversation. Pauline spoke to Tony; Tony repeated the news to Dino; Dino answered, whereupon Tony asked his mother another question.

"Ma, how did my brother know where I was?"

"You look like him. Some boy sees him, thinks it's Tony Milasi."

"Beautiful, Ma."

Dino asked Tony, "What is his name?"

"Ma, what's my brother's name?"

"Roger Brooks."

"Roger Brooks?" Tony repeated.

"What kind of an Italian is that?" asked Dino.

"Ma, he's not Italian?"

"Who knows, who cares?" Pauline Milasi answered. "He's your brother, your blood. I say he come live with us, be our son, too."

Tony thought, "Wow, that's just like her," and he told his mother, "You're beautiful, Mom. Hey, what's his phone number? I'll call him up. Tonight, right now."

"No good, Tony. Your brother has to call you."

"Okay, Ma. I'll come home Thursday night. I want to hear the whole story, and we can work everything out then."

"Tony?" his mother interrupted. "I'm happy for you. I pray Saint Anthony that everything be okay. Everybody happy now."

Tony laughingly assured his mother that everyone would be happy now, and forever, and said goodnight. He put the phone down gently and turned to face Dino. "I told you," he suddenly shouted. "Oh, you're such a smart ass, Pirozzi. You wouldn't believe I had a twin. Well, what do you say now?"

"You said he lives in Miami?"

"Yeah."

"It's a wild town. You want to pack or should I?"

"Oh, you front runner," Tony said. "I'm going home Thursday. My brother is going to call me."

"Maybe I'll come, too," Dino said, smiling.

"I wonder what he's like? And what he does for a living? Man, isn't this fantastic! Hey, suppose he's rich?"

"If he is," Dino answered, "no more doorbells for us."

"You mean we'll help my brother spend his money?"

"It's an idea."

"But suppose he's not rich?"

"Then maybe he can fit in here. He's your twin, so he ought to be a good peddler, too," Dino said.

"You know," Tony said, "I hope he looks exactly like me. What's the fun of having a twin unless you both look alike?"

The two got ready for bed and then lay there, smoking and talking about the discovery. The longer they talked, the more excited and wide-awake they became. Dino confessed he definitely wanted to go home with Tony. He didn't want to miss any of the new developments.

"I haven't been this worked up over something, since my father wrote the White House asking President Kennedy for the grounds keeper's job."

Tony said, "You know what's going to happen? I'll bet some of the other guys aren't going to believe me when I tell them."

"*Some* of them? None of them will believe it and I don't blame them!"

In the morning, Tony found it was impossible to concentrate on business, and so at noon he and Dino packed a suitcase and hurriedly left for Binghamton. They continued to discuss Roger Brooks during their drive home, for in their minds, he was an enigmatic figure.

"What a hairy coincidence," Tony said. "I just told you about my twin and wham: my mother calls! While I was thinking and talking about my brother, he must have been looking for me. Both at the same time. Do you understand what I mean?"

"Yeah. ESP."

"Could be, Dino."

"And it could be a mistake, too. Maybe this Roger Brooks is a phony. Maybe he only looks like you. Did you ever think of that?"

"It's no mistake," Tony replied. "And I'll tell you how I know he's my brother. My name when I was born was Roger Brooks. This is in my adoption papers and was in my navy jacket, too. I used to pull the jacket out, stare at the name Roger Brooks and then think about my twin, wonder what his name was. Now, how do you figure that?"

"I can't," Dino said. "Only I thought of something else. It's bad."

"What's bad?"

"Suppose you do look like your brother, and he's a fag! There goes your ladykiller's reputation. You know, the girls won't know which is who."

"Stop it! For God's sake, he's my brother. My twin!"

"Only trying to help," Dino weakly protested, and they both had to laugh at the idea that Tony's twin brother could be a homosexual. Tony understood that with this laughter he was releasing some of his tension. He realized, too, that he was filled with anxiety. There were so many things he wanted to know. He held inside himself a score of unanswered questions and not only about his twin. He wanted to know about his natural parents. Did his brother know them? What were they like? What had become of them? Did they have other children, his brothers and sisters? His anxiety forced him to drive faster and faster. . . .

When Roger Brooks parked in front of his house on the Monday night that was October 22, 1962, it was already past ten o'clock. He had come from a voice lesson and was sitting there listening to a Richard Tucker recording on his car radio when he heard his mother calling excitedly from the porch.

"Come quick, Roger. Miss Bittermann wants you. She's been talking to your brother."

Since the previous Friday, when she had received the letter from Family Service in Binghamton, Catherine Bittermann and Roger had been trying to speak on the phone with first one, then the other being out of reach. Tony Milasi, meanwhile, had impatiently called Miami Family Service and learning that Miss Bittermann was at home, called her there.

"I've been waiting six days and the suspense is killing me," he complained. "I'm smoking a pack of cigarettes a day."

Miss Bittermann explained to Tony that it was his brother's place to make the first call, and through no one's fault, she had been unable to give Roger his good news.

"Well, if you won't let me call my brother," Tony answered, "at least tell me if he looks like me."

"I wouldn't be much of an authority on that since I've never seen you," Catherine Bittermann replied. "However, I can tell you that your brother is well-mannered, good-looking and a sensitive young man."

Roger hadn't tried to phone Miss Bittermann at home before, not wanting to disturb her. But this time he was returning her call, and he listened closely now as she gave a deliberate and unemotional account of all that had taken place in the ten days since they had last met. He made no comment at first, for the reality that it was all over, that he had found his twin, was suddenly overwhelming.

"Well, Roger, your brother wants you to call him in Binghamton as soon as possible, preferably tomorrow night."

"Why me?" he asked. "Why do I have to make the call? Can't he call me?"

She knew that he was particularly vulnerable in this moment and so again Catherine Bittermann was gentle. "Well, you were the one to find him."

"Yes, but what will I say?"

"Oh, I hardly think that's important. The moment will be so big for both of you that words aren't going to be important. You'll find things to say, and they'll be the right things."

"I hope so," Roger said. "I want my brother to like me. I'd like to start off with something really clever."

A few minutes before 6 P.M. on Tuesday, the twenty-third of October 1962, Roger Brooks locked himself in his room, alone. Changing his mind then, he called to his mother to join him. He told her, "C'mon, I want you here."

"For God's sake," Mildred Brooks said, slurring her words as she often did when excited, "Hurry up. I've got goose pimples."

He picked up the receiver and told the long-distance operator that he was making a person-to-person call to Mr. Anthony J. Milasi. He spelled out Milasi, gave her the number, RAymond 4-5207, and then took a deep breath. He waited while she placed the call, and he felt the excitement over his whole body. Nearly 1,500 miles away, the telephone rang inside apartment two, second-floor right, in The Block at 47 Carroll Street. Sitting in his mother's square, brown stuffed chair, the one in which Pauline Milasi said her rosary, Tony Milasi grabbed the receiver on the first ring and lifted it to hear the operator's voice. "Long distance for Anthony Milasi."

"That's me, operator."

Then he heard, "Hello, Tony?"

"Roger?"

"Gosh, Tony. I don't know what to say."

There was the smallest of silences, a dead period that both twins filled with the same small laughs. Roger then asked, "How tall are you?"

"How tall are *you?*" Tony asked.

"I asked first," Roger said childishly, almost petulantly.

It was such an absurd impasse that both broke into natural and relieved laughter, and although neither of them noticed it, the uniform sound seemed to be coming from one throat, out of one pair of lungs. This was, of course, the laughter of monozygotic partners.

"I'm just over six feet, three inches," Tony said, relenting.

"So am I," Roger quickly said. He was pleased; Mark Frattalone had told him Tony was shorter than he was.

"How much do you weigh?" Tony asked, assuming the conversational lead.

"Right now I'm 208".

"I'm about 210," Tony said. "What color are your eyes?"

"Blue."

"So are mine. What color is your hair?"

"Brown, dark brown," Roger said.

"So is mine. . . ."

With both brothers behaving as schoolboys, the conversation richocheted between Binghamton and Miami, and they established, to their eminent satisfaction, that, in addition to being of large and almost equal proportions and having the same color eyes and hair, they both parted their hair on the left; both wore size 13 shoe and 16½-35 shirt; both were high school graduates but neither was a scholar; both enjoyed "all kinds" of music, except western; both loved all sports but were more spectator than athlete; both favored Italian food; both had been in the service, entering separate branches only eight days apart for four-year enlistments, and that each had girl friends but no thought of marrying. Tony then asked Roger what work he did.

"I'm an expediter, which is a big title for a factory job," Roger answered. "We make aircraft engines and parts."

Tony said he was a salesman, and doing pretty well.

"I know," Roger said, "Mark says you're a big wheel. He was really impressed."

Tony laughed. "I'll never be rich. I spend it too fast."

Roger explained then that he really disliked his job and was taking voice lessons and studying opera.

"My brother the opera star," Tony said.

"No, I'm not much good yet, Tony. I'm only a beginner. But someday I'll be able to do something with my voice."

"Rog," Tony asked. "What about our parents? What do you know about them?"

Roger hesitated, "Well, I'll write you something about our father, but I'd rather leave that subject for when we meet, okay?"

"Okay," Tony replied, "But do you know our father?"

"Yes, I lived with him. I knew him for two years."

"What's his name?"

"Jules Brooks."

"What about our mother? Her name was Maria and she was Italian. I know that much."

"Tony, I know almost nothing about her. But let's leave all that."

"Okay, Rog, when am I going to see you?"

"Well, do you want me to come up there, or would you rather come to Miami?"

"I'll come down there. Your weather is better," Tony said.

"Great, Tony. When can you come? Soon?"

"I'll be there within three weeks, at the latest."

Tony told Roger that as soon as they hung up they should immediately write each other, chronicling their lives and enclosing snapshots, especially baby pictures. "I want to see if we always looked alike." Tony added he would get busy right away with plans to drive to Florida.

"Make sure," he instructed Roger, "that you send your letters air mail special."

"Tony," Roger said, "I can't believe it's happening."

"Neither can I, *brother*."

During the following week, Roger Brooks telephoned Miss Bittermann to report that everything had gone well, and he and his brother were planning a vacation together. In her case report, Catherine Bittermann noted, "Mr. Brooks seems to have a new lease on life."

Tony Milasi made a similar call, completely voluntary, to the Binghamton Family Service office. He wanted to thank Zev Hymowitz and bring the bureau director, Perry Gangloff, up-to-date. At the bottom of the file report the director summarized: "First contact October 15, 1962. Case closed this office October 26, 1962."

Perry Gangloff was to say later, "After these boys were apart twenty-four years, they were brought together in just eleven days. In those eleven days a small miracle was accomplished."

16

Roger and Tony

Researcher James Shields has reported on separated twins who, when they were thirty-five, learned of each other's existence. Immediately, they began a correspondence, exchanging photographs, locks of hair and even clothing. Shields commented that this correspondence "supplied something in their lives which they had felt lacking."

They began then by writing, but more important than their hurried, incomplete letters were the snapshots they enclosed.

"Both pictures of me are bad," wrote Roger Brooks. "The purpose is to show my mother and, if you look hard, you will notice a scar on my left elbow. This happened right after I was born."

"This is me at eleven months. Dig the curls!" Tony Milasi wrote in one of his captions.

Researchers of twins explain that after long separations identicals have an almost irresistible urge to make up for the pleasures of twinship denied them and will therefore approach each other with great curiosity. This was clearly the case with Roger and Tony.

"This is when I was about six," Roger had written on the back of a wallet-sized snap that showed a scrubbed and serious-looking boy holding an unsmiling pose. He was wearing a blue shirt with a rounded collar, green tie and inexpensive brown suspenders. "My mother is an artist and she colored me," he added.

Tony sent one of himself as a seven-year-old. The striking thing about this picture was his dress. He had on a white linen suit with short pants, double breasted jacket and a white shirt with a large floppy bow. His shoes and knee socks were chalk white, and he was posed with his feet and knees together, holding a missal and rosary beads. On the back he had written, "Don't I look holy! (Ha, ha.)" Here was little Saint Anthony, with the soft, unworried face of an only child who intimately knew comfort and easy laughter.

Both families intently studied these pictures, marveling at the likenesses, particularly the oval shape of the large heads; the coloring and thickness of the hair; the wide-set, narrow eyes; the long, virile noses. Still, there was something that set them apart. It was more than just Tony's happy grin and that he was neatly groomed, his hair combed back in a perfect pompadour. Mostly, it was in Roger's eyes and the set, serious line of his mouth. His earliest years had marked him; still, it was more shading and shadow than scar, and Tony suspected nothing at first. Moreover, Roger tried hard not to play for his brother's sympathy. He described his beginnings as though they were common among adoptive children.

Tony wrote in a light and candid style:

> Well, where do I start? I can't say at the beginning because that would take 24 years, 4 months and 23 days. So I'll try and brief you on some of the high points of my life. I was adopted when I was five days old by Joseph and Pauline Milasi, two of the sweetest and greatest human beings that Italy ever produced. I could write about them forever, Rog, but I'll tell you more when I see you.
>
> My life has consisted mostly of helping my Dad in his grocery store (he is retired now) and of leading what I guess you'd call a normal, everyday life. I grad-

uated from high school in June, 1955, and in August entered the navy. I did quite a bit of traveling (I was on three ships.) and for the most part, Uncle Sam and I got along pretty well. I was discharged May 27, 1959, a day before our 21st birthday. (Where were you that day?)

Since that time I have run a snack bar, gone to California (six months), worked for IBM, sold real estate and am now a book salesman. Although I'm a fairly good salesman I don't really know what I want to be. I'm still searching and hope that I won't have to wait forever to find what I want.

Some of the bad characteristics of your twin brother are as follows: 1) not a hard worker; 2) does not know how to manage money; 3) too soft-hearted. I'm an easy touch; 4) girl crazy. (I don't know if you classify this as a bad characteristic.)

I've got a million and one other things to say but would rather wait until I see you. If it's possible, I would like to have you come to Binghamton for a visit later on. I would also like to work something out so that we can see more of each other. We can talk about that when we're together, too.

I still can't believe that all this is happening and I am perhaps the happiest man alive at the present time. I'm really looking forward to coming to Florida. I don't know exactly when I will be there but I'll definitely come before the 15th of November. Meanwhile, take care of yourself, BROTHER.

Although it was to be only three weeks, Roger found the waiting hard. It was made more difficult when Tony telephoned to apologize that he couldn't possibly get there by the fifteenth. Two more dates were made, and broken. Tony had to have a cyst removed from his back; he couldn't get time off from work, and in late December Pauline Milasi was hospitalized with another of her heart spasms. Tony wrote that it was out of the question for him to leave Binghamton then.

Roger, meanwhile, had room in his mind for little else besides thoughts of Tony Milasi and so let his voice lessons and theater work lapse. Around the house he was unnaturally cranky, and his mother complained he wasn't the Roger

Brooks she knew before he found his brother. She suggested that he have an hour's session with a psychologist with whom she was friendly. Although Roger was hesitant, he nevertheless went twice. The doctor told him to relax by focusing his thoughts on the good time he and his brother were going to have.

"This will be an experience that obviously you are to have only once," he said. "You owe it to yourself to unbend, to enjoy it. And you shouldn't let money be a consideration."

This is precisely what Roger needed to hear. He drew two hundred dollars out of savings and borrowed another two hundred dollars—half from the bank, the rest from Uncle Lou Brooks.

He was determined to buy all new clothes and asked Alva Skop, whose father was in men's wear, to help him shop. In the past, Alva was forever poking fun at the way he dressed, but on this day she took Roger to a Miami Beach haberdasher and selected an entire wardrobe for him: socks, underwear, shirts, ties, gray slacks, black blazer with gold crest and brass buttons and a red silk ascot with white polka dots. Standing before a three-way mirror, Roger wasn't confident these clothes suited him. Alva was delighted.

"Now you're sharp," she said. "You don't look so nineteen-twentyish, like you usually do. Everything matches, too. Why you're a king-size Cary Grant."

Roger was flattered and reminded himself that Mark Frattalone had pictured Tony Milasi as a New York swinger. He wanted to be prepared to keep up with his brother, whose enthusiastic telegram reached him New Year's night and promised: THIS IS IT. HAVE RESERVATION JAN. 10. ARRIVE MIAMI INTERNATIONAL 10.40 P.M. WILL STAY AS LONG AS MONEY LASTS. YOUR BROTHER.

Roger quickly put in for a week's vacation. So that he and Tony could be alone whenever they chose, he made motel reservations. Watching him now and apprised of all the logistics, Aunt Mildred commented that her own preparations to welcome her husband home after two years in the Pacific during World War II were shabby compared to Roger's activities.

On the evening of Thursday, January 10, 1963, Roger began to dress around seven o'clock. He had allowed himself two hours. He visited with the Skops next, permitting Alva to approve of her fashion creation and then checked his suitcase into the motel. He arrived at the airport forty minutes early. He bought a *New York News,* believing this a cosmopolitan thing to do. He was much too nervous to eat and decided to have one Scotch and water in the airport cocktail lounge. It was the first time he had ever been in a bar alone; this was to be a night of firsts.

Seated next to the window about midship, Tony Milasi had a middle-aged man and his wife for seat companions. He was tempted to tell them whom he was to meet in Miami only he was afraid they would ask him too many questions. He wanted to sit back, relax and let his mind drift. All around him other passengers were reading, talking, sleeping, having a drink. He felt estranged from them, even superior, because he was someone special. It was the same feeling that used to come over him when he was an altar boy. On those mornings, he would rush into the church, coming in out of the dark and cold of Hawley Street to become a special person, privileged because he walked on God's altar. Now, he and Roger Brooks were a special pair, with a special secret.

When the stewardess brought his dinner he ate it all and then dozed off; the plane was already in its descent when he awoke, and out his window he saw the Miami Beach skyline, bright against the black night. He knew that strung along the shore were the resort hotels, which at this hour were pulsing with the action of people spending money. Tony hoped he and his brother would be a part of this scene, for at least one night. That would be about all he could afford, since the only money he had was the two hundred dollars that Joe Milasi handed him as they said goodbye.

The plane rolled to a complete stop at 10:50 P.M. and the mobile stairs were pushed up against the fuselage. Roger Brooks and Tony Milasi now began a game. Each was anxious to see his twin before the twin saw him. Roger stood in a cluster of people, craning his neck and fixing his eyes on the plane door. Tony stayed in his window seat, having decided he would be one of the last to exit. In this way, he was able to see—and to study—his brother.

"He looked nervous," Tony remembers, "and a little scared."

"I *was* nervous," Roger later would admit. "Especially when I didn't see my brother getting off the plane."

Tony continued, "When I saw my brother in that blazer with the crest and polka dot ascot, I thought: 'Oh, no!' "

As Tony Milasi started down from the plane, Roger Brooks quickly moved across the concrete apron; he wanted to greet Tony right at the foot of the stairs. Roger looked up then and saw that his brother was wearing dark slacks, a blue shirt with a black tie and a bluish-green tweed sports jacket. "Oh, no!" he thought, realizing how wrong his own dress was.

Roger stood waiting, trying now to meet Tony's eyes, but his brother continued to look past him until they were almost close enough to touch each other. Then Tony looked directly at his brother: "Hi, I haven't seen you in twenty-four years."

Both knew at once this was the right line and, more relaxed because of it, Roger answered simply, "My God, Tony! I still can't believe it's happening."

Roger had wanted to reach out and grab his brother, only was afraid of embarrassing him. So instead, he shook hands with Tony and each then put an arm around the other; linked in this way, they walked happily toward the main lobby to wait for Tony's luggage.

Roger asked the standard questions. "Was it a good flight? Did you have dinner?" Tony replied in the accepted cliches.

Neither was completely at ease, but once they stood before the baggage counter Tony made a move designed to remedy this. Seeing two stout and graying women, obvious vacationers wearing wide-brimmed straw hats from the Caribbean, he nudged Roger. "Watch this."

"Excuse me, ladies," he said politely. "Do you think we look like brothers?"

One of the women answered, "Are you crazy? You got to be twins."

"That's right," Tony said, "but suppose I told you we just met, that I'm seeing my brother for the first time in twenty-four years?"

"What fool would believe that?" the second woman said.

"Two nice boys, only a little crazy," said the first woman.

Roger was pleased by his brother's prank, and he told Tony that he had reserved a motel room, explaining he felt they should be alone to talk and do as they pleased, at least

on this first night. Roger wasn't ready to share his brother—
not with his family, and surely not with Mark Frattalone,
who had wanted to be a witness to their first meeting.

It was 11:30 when finally they were settled in their room
at the Green Mansions Motel, Tony lying on one of the twin
beds with a pillow propped behind him and Roger facing him
in a cushioned wooden chair. Roger knew it was his place to
begin and wanted desperately to have the disclosure behind
him.

"Tony, what I have to say is difficult. I don't really know
how to begin. It has to be talked about, though. . . ."

Tony cut him off: "You mean that we're illegitimate? I
know all about it. Big deal! What's so bad about that?"

"Then you know?" Roger said, obviously surprised.

"Sure, I know. As a kid I heard people saying Tony Milasi
was different, and I knew it wasn't only because I was adopted. When I got out of the navy I asked my mother, and she
told me the truth."

"Boy, am I relieved that you know and that I didn't have
to tell you," Roger said.

"Well, it's nothing to be ashamed about," Tony continued.
"God knows, it wasn't our fault. It was an accident of birth,
which is something that just happens. I'll bet there are
100,000 illegitimate children born every year in this country."

This was Tony's best reasoning and was adequate for the
moment. Roger had no desire to prolong the discussion and
Tony saw no reason to. He asked Roger about their father.
"What's he like? How come you went to live with him?"

Roger went back to his beginnings with Mildred and Jules
Brooks. He moved forward slowly, telling the story as his
mother had once candidly told it to him. When he came to
his two years in Schenectady, he exaggerated Jules' positive
qualities—his reading, his facile way with words and people,
his salesmanship, his love for fine restaurants. He described
their father as he would have wanted him to be.

"Well, he's not my father," said Tony. "Joe Milasi is my
father." He paused, studied his brother's face and asked if
Jules wasn't a gambler. Tony said his mother had told him
that Jules played cards and bet the horses. Roger admitted
this was true. He dropped his head and quietly added, "He
should have been a pigeon."

Tony laughed. "A pigeon? Why a pigeon?"

Roger was serious. "Because a pigeon has no worries, no responsibilities. He flies around, and when he wants to eat he comes down in a park and someone feeds him. That's the way Jules has wanted to live, with no responsibility to anyone. He couldn't handle it, Tony. He ran from it every time. That's why he never was much of a father, to me or to Rodney, either."

"Rodney?" Tony said loudly. "Who the hell is Rodney?"

Roger explained that he was their half brother, of whom they had a right to be proud. In Roger's words, Rodney was a genius. He was working for his doctorate in physics at Harvard.

"A brother at Harvard!" Tony said, elated by this revelation. "Fantastic. Wait until I tell my buddy Dino." He explained who Dino was and then told Roger of the night in Buffalo when his mother had called him with the news. "And when I told Dino you were studying opera, he said we couldn't possibly be twins because I can't even carry a tune."

Tony explained that though he wasn't a singer, he loved music and had played the trumpet all through high school.

Roger said, "I played the French horn. It's like the trumpet; they're both valve instruments."

"Hey," Tony remarked, "that's something else we have in common. Were you any good?"

"No. I was terrible."

"I was bad news too," Tony said. "But I had the best trumpet in the band. My mother bought it for me.

Tony waited as Roger laughed and then, in an unnatural, sober voice, asked, "What do you know about our real mother?"

"Not very much, Tony. I only know her name was Maria, because it was on my birth certificate, which I lost in Japan."

"I brought mine with me," said Tony. "Her name isn't on it, though, because it's an adoption certificate. But my mother described her to me as tall, blond and nice-looking. She also said she was sickly for a young woman."

"I know she had two other children before us, which means we have stepbrothers or sisters we've never seen."

"Do you care about finding her?"

"No," Roger answered, hesitated, then said, "Not really. The only one I cared about finding was you."

"Me, too. I'm the same way. Still, I would like to see her once. I'd want to see her from a distance, without her seeing me. To see what she looks like, and whether we look at all like her."

Tony shook his head and added, "All those times I asked my mother about my twin. But I almost never asked about *her*."

This was a strange and poignant scene. The brothers, together after twenty-four years, spoke now of their biological mother as *her*. She was the outsider, a mystery, and an unknown quantity to them. The two women who had reared them were their mothers. The other, who gave them life and deserted them, could not, even in conversation, be considered *mother*.

They both sensed that this night, which they had meant for laughter, had become too sober. Roger accidentally ended the sobriety. He broke wind. Tony jumped up from the bed, feigning anger. He strode the door, pulled it open and with his hands cupped to his mouth, called: "Oh, dear! My brother farted! Yes, my brother did it!"

Roger flushed; he was mortified, a circumstance that only encouraged Tony to repeat his catcall. This time, however, he wore a pained expression and added: "He got me from Binghamton, to gas me. My own brother. First time I meet him and phew-e!"

Roger again was pleased by his brother's ridiculous antics. Wanting to show his pleasure, he suggested they have something to eat and explained that this was his treat, as well as the motel room, for however long Tony stayed.

"I'm a big eater," Tony warned and ordered a double hamburger with "the works" and a vanilla milk shake. Roger rang up room service and he too ordered a double hamburger with "the works" and a vanilla shake.

When the food arrived, they both ate hurriedly. Tony said, "Don't mind me, I'm a fast eater. Too fast."

"So am I," Roger added and, after finishing his hamburger, offered Tony a cigarette. He held out a pack of Lucky Strikes.

"That's my brand, too," Tony said, taking out his own cigarettes to show Roger. It was like the first firecracker in a string; when it went off, so did all the others. They took turns asking questions to discover neither was a beer drinker, nor did they have a particular fondness for alcohol. A big night was two Scotch highballs.

"Do you like to play cards?" Roger asked.

"You name it, I've played it," Tony answered ."Poker, hearts, pinochle, scuba, blackjack. I love them all. Many a time we've played all night."

"I like cards, too."

"Have you ever played the horses?"

Roger said, "Only at the track, and I've only been a few times."

"I've never been to a track, but I've played with a bookie a few times. Nothing big," Tony said.

"We'll go to Hialeah while you're here," Roger said, and wondering if Tony was tired, asked, "Do you like to sleep? I do."

"At least eight hours," Tony answered, "and I always wrap one arm, the right one, around the pillow."

"So do I," Roger added.

"I hate to get up in the morning," Tony continued. "It was the thing I hated most about the navy. You got up so early."

"That and the calisthenics," Roger added.

"Right. I agree. But you know, I've always loved sports."

"Me too."

"What's your favorite?"

"Baseball."

"Me, too," Tony said, but they were divided in their loyalties. Tony was a Yankee rooter. Roger was a Dodger fan, principally because of Bessie Elman's passion for Jackie Robinson. Later, he was especially proud of Sandy Koufax, who once asked to be excused from a World Series pitching assignment because it fell on Yom Kippur.

"Are you right-handed all the way? asked Tony.

"I bat and throw righty," Roger answered, "but I kick lefty."

"I do everything righty," Tony said, and now he was restless. He got up to pace. Roger also stood and started for his bed, to stretch out. For a second, both images were in the mirror. Tony shouted, "Stop!" Pointing to the mirror, he said: "When I look in there, I can't see that you're my twin. I don't think you look like me. Yet, sitting across from you and listening to you talk, I know we're twins. I can sense it. I was sure of it the moment that I saw the first picture you sent me."

Roger said he never had any doubts, and when Tony mailed some recent pictures of himself, he took them to work. He asked his friends, "Who does this look like?"

The response always was, "Who're you trying to kid? That's you."

They both were still standing, and Tony said, "Let's get back-to-back." They quickly proved they were identical in height, and in the width of their shoulders and hips, which made Tony laugh. "My friend Dino said there couldn't be two fat asses like Moon Milasi."

Next they compared right hands. They were a perfect match. Each hand had the same broad back, the same long, thick fingers; even the coloring of the fingernails was alike.

"Can you do this?" Tony asked, bending his right thumb under to easily touch his wrist. "I'm double-jointed."

"So am I," Roger answered, duplicating his brother's trick.

"Let's see you hold this," Tony said, handing a pen to his brother. Roger gripped it awkwardly between his right thumb and forefinger, holding the pen nearly in the middle.

"Same as I do," said Tony, taking it back to show Roger. "And did you ever have any trouble with your teeth?"

"Just a wisdom tooth."

"Which one?"

"Lower right."

"Rog, that's amazing," Tony said. "That's the same one that has been bothering me lately." Tony opened his mouth wide and held a finger in front of the troublesome tooth. Roger looked into his brother's mouth and nodded, but there was really nothing to see.

It was 2:30 in the morning, and though neither of them admitted to being the least bit tired, they decided to get ready for bed. They could then talk themselves to sleep.

Tony started to unpack; Roger began to unbutton his shirt. They continued to talk, searching for more similarities. Tony asked, "Have you had your tonsils out?"

"Gee, I don't know, Tony."

"I had mine out," said Tony; then lurching off in another direction, "Were you afraid of thunder as a kid?"

"No."

"I was. Thunder and bats."

"I don't like snakes," Roger said. He was in his T-shirt, and when Tony saw the scar on his left arm he said, "Wow! That's a bad one."

Roger bent his left elbow and then held the arm up toward Tony. The pinched and scared tissue ran along the top of the forearm from just above the crease to three inches below it. Tony took off his own shirt. He held his left arm down. Beginning just below the crease, the ribbed line of a four-inch scar ran down the center of the forearm.

"When I was a little kid," he said, "I fell off my bike with a soda bottle in my hand. The bottle head broke and tore the arm. I had eighteen stitches and my mother was afraid I was going to lose the arm."

Roger considered the closeness of their scars an astounding coincidence. Tony was not as impressed. He explained, "I was accident-prone," and then described all his calamities—the time he fell down a flight of outdoor stairs and broke an arm; the afternoon in the movies he panicked because he had lodged a dime in one of his nostrils; the time he fell in the bathroom and was in traction for a week.

"I was combing my hair," he said, laughing as he spoke, "and I climbed up on the toilet seat to see myself in the mirror. I slipped."

Roger said he didn't believe he had been accident-prone, but he twice had fallen off his bicycle, injured himself and was left with scars. One of these, strangely, followed the crease line of his right arm and was in the same area as the scar on his brother's left arm.

"Now that is plain weird," said Tony, his voice rising and announcing his excitement. "You know, maybe it's a good thing we didn't grow up together. We would have driven our parents crazy." He returned to his unpacking then and disappeared into the bathroom with his shaving kit. A moment later he was back, holding up Roger's Canoe after-shave lotion, "What are you doing with this?"

"I use it."

"So do I," Tony said, and challenged, "Okay, what kind of hair tonic do you use?"

"Vitalis, mostly."

"So do I. How about toothpaste?"

"Well," Roger said, "my Aunt Mildred told me about a Swedish brand. You've probably never heard of it."

"Vademecum," Tony said, with finality. "It's the best and I use it."

"Amazing!"

Since neither Tony nor Roger had any understanding of monozygotic twins, they were unaware the taste buds of one-egg partners react similarly and that among the tests to establish monozygocity is one for taste. The fact both favored the highly concentrated pink Swedish paste, therefore, was additional evidence that they were identicals. They also were unaware, as they stripped to the waist to wash, that they were about to pass a second test, the hairline test.

When Roger turned suddenly and saw his brother's chest hair, he was dumbfounded. He said nothing, but he pointed, first to Tony's chest, then his own. On each expanse the scruffy black hair began about an inch below the collar line and extended to the middle of the chest, being centered between the pectorals. There was a second furry crop at the belt line and then another swatch on the lower back.

Tony insisted that Roger join him before the mirror where they both stood, pointing, laughing and scratching themselves like a pair of orangutans.

"Tony, it's weird."

"Strange and peculiar," answered Tony. "That's what it is. We're a couple of freaks."

From this moment of high hilarity, they drifted now into a quieter period. When both finally were in bed, dressed alike in T-shirts and jockey shorts, Tony lit a cigarette. Roger then lit one. Neither said anything for a time and the only sound in the room was the noise of their deep, rhythmic breathing.

"I was just thinking," Roger said, without looking at his brother, "that the only way we're different is our religions."

Tony replied that to him this was an unimportant difference. He admitted that while his mother was a good Catholic who had raised him in the Church, he no longer worked at his religion. He explained that he rejected much of Catholicism, "but as long as my mother is alive, I'll never leave the Church."

Roger answered by saying that he surely was not a good Jew. He hadn't been Bar Mitzvahed, and when he analyzed it, he realized that he followed Judaism out of love for his grandmother and loyalty to Rabbi Skop.

In his own way, each was assuring the other that his religious commitment represented no threat to their future relationship. Roger later would say, "Finding each other was such a beautiful thing that nothing could take away from this. I didn't care what Tony's religion was. It didn't matter to me, and Tony didn't put my religion down. He admired it; he said he liked the idea we didn't have priests whom we put on pedestals and that there was no confession. But it wasn't any big discussion. It was a touchy subject, at least I thought so, and Tony got us off it."

"Tell me about your love life, Rog."

This was a poor subject for Roger. For two years he had been going with a girl, who suddenly had decided they weren't right for each other. Four weeks ago she had broken off their relationship, leaving Roger hurt and, he confessed, still very much in love.

To distract his brother and ease his embarrassment, Tony began telling what he said was a funny story. On New Year's Eve he had met a blond. They were drinking and dancing. He decided he "loved" her and so gave her his friendship ring.

"She's a Slovak whose mother warned her never go out with an Italian. I told her that it was all right. I was only half Italian."

Roger asked, "You're not going to marry her are you?"

"Oh, hell no. This was New Year's Eve. I lost my head."

Roger knew it was foolish, yet he couldn't help being jealous of this girl. The idea that his brother might marry soon after they had met was threatening to him. From the moment that he first saw Tony in his tweed jacket with the leather sleeve patches, he knew that he was sharp, that he'd been places and was worldly. The more Tony talked, the prouder Roger was that he was his twin.

"Do you know how I always thought I was going to find you?" Roger asked. "I planned on going to Binghamton and disguising myself. I would put on glasses and a moustache and a big overcoat. Then I would go around looking for you."

"It wouldn't have worked," Tony quickly said.

"Why not?"

"Because too many guys would have spotted you and said, 'Hey, Milasi, how come you're dressed up funny like that?' "

It was now four o'clock in the morning, and having momentarily run out of stories and questions, and confident their new life together had successfully begun, they slipped easily into sleep. Three hours later, Roger was first to awake. He rolled over quietly, hoping to take a long sneak-look at his brother. In that instant, Tony opened his eyes and said, "What the hell are you staring at?"

There was a pattern to all their days. They were up early, despite their late hours, and then off to sight-see, to shop, to the beach or the races at Hialeah in the afternoon. But the largest share of these daylight hours was for visiting. Roger took Tony to meet his family. They were at Uncle Lou and Aunt Mildred Brooks' every other day, to meet the Ray Skops and the Rabbi Skops and a number of his mother's friends. Then, with darkness, the tempo changed. They dressed leisurely, more to Tony's pace and tastes. Roger never again wore his blazer and polka dot ascot when he was with his brother. Instead, both wore dark suits or similar sports outfits that called attention to their likenesses.

For dinner, they chose the expensive and well-known restaurants, and afterward they went to jai alai or the harness races. Still later, they began a second pursuit of excitement in the clubs and late-hours bars popular with the "singles" crowd. Like the majority of tourists, they were searchers, restless for the good time. Unlike most others, however, they were also content to be alone and never tired of each other's company.

"It seemed that we had known each other all our lives," Roger said. "What I suggested, Tony agreed to, and when Tony wanted to do something, I wanted to do it, too."

That first morning they began at Roger's home with Tony meeting his mother, grandmother and dour Florence. Mildred Elman Brooks showed them photographs of Jules as a young man. He was tall, thinner than they were and in his courting days had a small moustache. "As you can see," she said, "Your father was a handsome man."

"He's not my father," Tony corrected.

Mildred let the remark pass, but said, "I think you look more like him than Roger."

"In what way?" Roger asked.

"I don't know," she said, "he just does. Maybe it's more an impression than something physical."

In late afternoon, after Tony had taken a sunbath in the backyard, which was to be a part of his routine, they walked across the street to a neighbor's. Roger introduced Tony to Mrs. Eleanor Bak, saying, "Tell him; go ahead, tell him what I said."

Mrs. Bak said it had happened the day before Roger went into the air force. He had come to say goodbye and "we got talking. Roger said he believed two things would happen to him: before he turned twenty-five he was going to find his brother and then someday he was going to make a lot of money."

"How do you like that?" Roger asked.

Tony said, "Brother, I'm pulling for you to make it two-for-two, and when you make your pile, I'll be right beside you to help you enjoy it."

Both twins shared this anticipation that one day they were to have money enough to live well and expensively. But theirs was an open-ended dream. Neither knew how they were to come into wealth unless it was a derivative of a show business career, because a second life's desire they had in common was to "be in the public eye, preferably as actors." Talking deeply of what they wanted to do with their lives, they discovered each other's secret. Tony said then that he had a friend from Binghamton in show business and what you needed was a *break*. Roger was more of a pragmatist. He thought study, hard work, good story material and direction were also considerations. Still, he was willing to give it a try, with Tony.

"Maybe we could get started as a twins act," he offered.

"Anything is possible, but since I don't sing, dance, whistle, juggle or play piano, we're sort of limited," Tony answered.

They did work out an act, though. It was strictly for their own amusement and consisted of Tony being Roger, and vice versa. In their first days together they had fooled Roger's mother once, Bessie Elman and Florence repeatedly and and made hapless victims of the neighbors. After these early successes, the boys scouted new targets. Roger discovered one while reading a newspaper. The restaurant ad said, "All the spaghetti you can eat, $1." Dressed in an open-necked blue sports shirt and black chinos, he walked into the small, neighborhood restaurant at the supper hour. A red-haired waitress served him the spaghetti in a bowl, topped with three tiny meatballs. Roger finished the meal and asked for seconds; he came back for thirds, too. By now, the chef was looking out from the kitchen and smiling. Roger wiped his mouth with his napkin and picked up the check, which was left with the first serving. The waitress stood over him.

"Ooops, I left my wallet in the car," he apologized.

So Roger Brooks walked out of the restaurant and Tony Milasi walked in, holding his brother's check in his hand. He was wearing an open-necked blue sports shirt and black chinos.

"You know," he said to the unsuspecting waitress, "I think I'll have one more bowl."

Tony then ate what the restaurant counted as a fourth, fifth and an incredible sixth bowl of spaghetti. The little chef, the Cuban dishwasher and the cashier were all watching in astonishment. The red-haired waitress said nothing, but as she set down Tony's third bowl her eyes were uneasy and she shook her head in disapproval.

Since he had timed his own eating, Roger knew when Tony would be midway in his last portion. At this point, he walked back into the restaurant, sat down at a table close by his brother and picked up a menu. The waitress walked over, looked at him hard, then over at Tony, and smiled. Before she could say anything, Roger held up a dollar bill, explaining, "We wanted to see if someone else thought we looked like twins."

"And we happen to like spaghetti," Tony added.

These were their charades, little shadow plays in which they reveled. Another favorite ploy was to make up words and use them in nonsensical conversation. It amused Tony and Roger but completely distracted anyone around them. Roger's mother continually scolded them. "Stop that baby talk. Someone will hear you!"

"It isn't baby talk," Roger corrected. "It's perfectly plain *shinagawa*. Any grown, reasonably intelligent *dippernoose* can learn to speak it in thirty days."

Tony picked it right up. "Or his money is cheerfully refunded, because our motto is *chennango franastan*. We aim to please. *Iya Taka Err*."

"*Iya Taka Err,*" Roger repeated.

Tony had made up *Iya Taka Err*. It became their favorite, a code phrase to mean anything they wanted. They said it most often when things were going especially well. Tony told Roger that if he became rich he was going to build a skyscraper office building in the center of Binghamton. "I'll name it the IYA TAKA ERR Building, and people will look up and see that sign, ITA TAKA ERR. They'll want to know what it means. Newspaper reporters will ask, and I'll say, 'It means, The Greatest, me and my brother.' "

17

Tony and Roger

There was a clearly identifiable pattern to the relationship as Roger Brooks and Tony Milasi drew close. Since Roger had the greater need for a sense of family and the attention of a twin, he readily submerged his will. So when the brothers went shopping for shoes, Tony picked out black ankle-boots for nine dollars. Roger thought his were tight on him; Tony said no, and they each bought a pair. But the boots did prove too small and they both later gave them away.

From the shoe store, they went for haircuts. Tony had already decided they would go to a men's hair salon that catered to show business people. "This is no ordinary haircut," he had explained. "Your whole head is sculpted. It makes you look like a movie star."

Never asking himself whether he wanted to look as a movie star does, Roger sat down in a chair alongside his brother. It was the only time in his life he would pay $4.75 for a haircut.

Tony's leadership did not necessarily result because his was the stronger, more versatile personality or even from his being the more intelligent, although he believed then that both were the case. Largely, it was because Roger encouraged this order, and Tony, the more aggressive, had wanted to be in command from the moment he got off the plane in Miami. This was why he had sat in his seat waiting and studying his brother out the plane window.

He explained a long time after that first night, "I don't understand it, but I just had to be in control."

Roger only wanted his brother to be proud of him, but he also felt a compulsion to be genuine with Tony, and in their first hour together confessed to being emotional and sentimental. Tony remarked: "I hold my emotions inside. I guess I'm a little harder than you."

As he had talked on, Roger further exposed himself as dependent, conservative and uncommonly loyal. He neither rationalized his failings nor faulted his home life. He was gentle in references to his mother and charitable toward Jules Brooks. Tony listened unquestioningly, reading nothing into his brother's presentation, taking him at his word when Roger said of his boyhood, "I was happy; or at least I thought I was."

Tony, however, was to catch insights into a much different past during the ten days they were together. The most important of these came when Tony least expected it. On a brilliantly sunny afternoon the brothers drove to south Miami Beach to visit Roger's grandfather, Sam Elman. This was not like the ordinary social call, because Sam, who was ninety-three, was the family character. He had earned a fortune with his pants and vest business in Syracuse, but it remained his secret just how large this fortune was. Asked straight out if he had made a million dollars, the old man's face wrinkled in a smile and he responded, "I had a good nibble—a good nibble out of a million." Yet, he now lived alone in a residence hotel where oftentimes there wasn't enough hot water for showers, the halls were filled with sour cooking smells and down in the lobby, long rows of metal folding chairs waited before a giant television set, ready for Saturday night and Lawrence Welk, the finale to another week of routine, tedium and hypochondria.

Through its retelling, Sam Elman's story had lost its extraordinariness for the family. However, it is a remarkable history and, in minuscule, an account of the persecution of the Jews in eastern Europe, later becoming a classic tale of a Russian immigrant who built himself a new life in America.

Roger's feelings toward his grandfather were ambivalent. He had heard his mother and grandmother rebuke Sam as cheap and incompatible, yet was a witness to the hypocrisy of inviting him as a dinner guest several times a year. And during the Jewish holidays he and Rodney were expected to court Grandpa Elman's favor. Their solicitude generally resulted in a twenty-five-dollar Hannukkah gift for Rodney and a ten-dollar present for himself. When he was old enough to analyze his emotions, Roger decided that although he didn't love Sam, he greatly admired his independent spirit and respected his business acumen. But he was afraid now that Sam would say something to offend Tony, and as they started up in the slow-rising elevator of the Hotel Simone—Mildred Brooks called it "Coney Island with palms"—he warned Tony.

His brother shook him off. "He sounds like my Uncle John. He's a ball-buster, too."

They found Sam Elman sitting on the edge of the double bed that filled nearly half the small, cluttered room. He had on colored undershorts and a pajama top that hung open, showing a tiny mat of white hair on his tanned chest. He had been reading a Jewish newspaper through a magnifying glass. As he stood to his full height, Tony realized that Roger's wealthy, erratic grandfather was a stooped, shrunken figure. The left sleeve, and the stub of his arm, which following an automobile accident had been amputated above the elbow, hung pathetically loose.

"Grandpa," Roger said, "this is my twin, Tony Milasi."

"Who remembers last names," said Sam Elman.

"You remember, Grandpa," Roger went on, "Mother called and told you how we found each other."

Sam Elman nodded. He remembered, he knew. "Men die, babies are born and brothers find each other. Life goes on. So, sit down and have a drink."

Roger's balloon of enthusiasm burst. "Couldn't he have found something nice to say?" he asked himself. Tony took no offense. He was laughing politely.

"It says in the Good Book," Sam Elman said, inching toward a kitchen chair, "there is nothing new. Everything has happened before."

As the old man lowered himself into the chair, Tony looked around the room. There was an old photograph of what he presumed were the five Elman children and two oil paintings which he later learned Mildred Brooks had painted for her father. Otherwise, this largely impersonal hotel room might have belonged to an overnight guest. The single arresting feature was a picture window that looked out on the beach, the ocean and an infinity of blue, cloudless sky. Sam Elman paid his view no mind; he wanted to hold court.

"I think," he began, "that Malthus was right. Why produce so many children? We can't feed them all. All over the world, they're hungry and too many are starving."

Roger looked at Tony. His brother was nodding his head, pretending he followed Sam Elman's line of thought.

"I'll tell you," Sam said, "we were all against Mildred adopting that boy. She couldn't even support herself, and then she wanted still another mouth to feed. Do you understand what I'm saying?"

For Tony's benefit, Sam Elman was explaining why he and the other family members had opposed Mildred Elman Brooks when she first took Roger into her already troubled home. He shook his head, "It's a miracle, a miracle how she brought up this boy." He was looking at Roger as he spoke.

"Mildred is like her mother, you know. Money? Ha, what's that? Her mother and me were from different worlds. I was a penny-pincher. Economy, thrift—that's why I was a good manufacturer. For two people who made each other miserable, we produced some wonderful children. But that Mildred," he said, again returning to his daughter, "she wasn't able to manage her own affairs, and here she was taking this boy. It's a wonder, a marvel that they made it."

Thereafter, it was almost stream of consciousness. The brothers stayed nearly two hours and the old man used up most of it talking. It was a performance remarkable for endurance, sagacity and the recall that this ninety-three-year-old demonstrated. It was only at the end that he drifted into melancholia.

"I found this little room," he said, "and I'm in love with it. Some mornings I hate to get out of my warm bed. I can't go out in bad weather anymore. So I walk in the hall, back and forth. People complain—when the weather is good, I go out and still walk three miles."

In the car going home, Tony celebrated Sam as a tough old bird, adding, "Only what a way to end up! What good is his money? What does he do with it?"

"I don't know," Roger answered. "Sometimes he buys Israel bonds or gives money for trees in Israel. Other than that, I don't know. Nobody does."

Roger had been afraid of this afternoon, afraid that Sam Elman would show himself as a cheapskate, and Tony would come away with a poor opinion of his family, believing them too tight, too much the stereotype of Jews as seen through anti-Semitic eyes. He was thrilled when Tony declared: "Holy cow, does Sam remind me of my Uncle John Milasi! What a tight-ass he was! He used to charge me for penny candy. His own nephew, can you imagine?"

And later when Roger found the courage to ask Tony if he had any anti-Jewish feelings, which he said he could understand, Tony replied: "Are you kidding? I'm the same as you. I'm half Jewish, too."

Moreover, the longer Tony thought about it, the more parallels he saw between Sam Elman and his uncle. He told Roger that old John was full of superstitions, one of these being that a family was shamed when a member became tubercular. When his own daughter fell seriously ill he was enraged at the suggestion she had TB. He even forbade that she be hospitalized. Tony said the full truth has been lost through the years, but the girl, Dolly Milasi, a beautiful young woman of twenty-six, died, and the account of her last night is a family legend. According to the story, a doctor pronounced Dolly Milasi dead, at which point her mother became hysterical.

Dolly then opened her eyes and, looking straight at her mother, whispered, "Don't cry, my momma. Where I've been is the most beautiful place in all the world." She next made the sign of the cross and once more closed her eyes.

Tony explained that the older women in the family simply will not be dissuaded that Dolly Milasi came back from heaven to console her mother and asked his brother, "Is it any wonder I feel the way I do about my religion?"

Roger asked how the death had affected John Milasi.

"Oh, it tore him up," Tony answered. "They buried Dolly

from the home and it was one of the biggest funerals the ward ever had. So many people crowded into the house the cellar beams started to split. Then, John built her a ten-thousand-dollar stone tomb in Calvary Cemetery. It even has her photograph set into it. You'll see it when you come to Binghamton."

Vague references, similar to this one, were as close as the brothers could bring themselves to talk of a second meeting. They were incapable of discussing it for two reasons. It was a subject that could lead to disagreement; for example, Roger might be unable to come when Tony wanted him, and neither wanted to disappoint his twin. Secondly, they didn't want to acknowledge that their present time together could end. So, they depended upon a silent understanding that Roger was expected in Binghamton within a reasonable time.

Originally, Tony had announced he could stay a week. Later, he said, "I'll stay a few more days." On their tenth day together, he remarked the time had gotten away from them, and their money as well. They were broke, having spent six hundred dollars between them. Roger then had to borrow another twenty dollars from Uncle Lou to lend Tony. That night they drove to the airport and Roger waited until his brother's plane was long out of sight. He felt proud and satisfied. Everything had gone well. They had begun as strangers and in ten days had grown to be brothers, and twins. He knew that nothing again could ever change this.

There was talk in the Elman and Brooks families about how Roger had changed. "It's Tony," said the female whisperers. "He has to comb his hair like Tony, tie his tie like Tony, wear Tony's jacket, buy his pants tight like Tony, he has to be exactly like Tony."

Roger was aware of the talk, knew it to be accurate, yet didn't care, because he had come to idolize his brother. Moreover, he had the support, if not the complete approbation, of his Aunt Mildred, and this was a strength to him.

Mildred Jordan Brooks was too happy for Roger to be dismayed because he was, at the moment, following Tony's lead. "You can't see anyone that happy and not be happy for him," she said. "There was unmistakable joy in Roger's eyes. It was almost enough to bring tears."

From the first, her only apprehension had been that the

twin would be more educated or well off financially and summarily reject Roger. "Because his twin was the answer to so many needs," she said, "this might have been a shock Roger couldn't survive."

On five of the ten days they spent together, the boys had stopped in to see "Aunt Millie," and so she learned that Tony wasn't a threat to Roger and, importantly, "was capable of returning some of his tenderness." She watched Roger imitate his brother; she also believed that Roger would in time work his own effect upon Tony.

"When Roger talked about music, or something that required sensitivity," she explained, "I saw Tony studying him. I came to understand that actually they needed each other, though not in the same way nor to the same degree. I also concluded that in many ways they are the same person, and it would have been cruel to keep them apart."

18

Roger and Tony

A raw wind blew down from the Appalachians. It swept across the dark Susquehanna, her winter currents made swift by melting snow and ice, and then on toward the inner city. Overhead a low sky pressed down, adding to the bleak and punishing quality of this noonday. But Roger Brooks was untouched by this dirge of nature, just as he was also oblivious to the industrial grime, weather stain and Victorian grayness that marked much of Binghamton, New York, on March 6, 1963. He knew only that Tony Milasi had pledged him a holiday and now, after six weeks, he and his twin were together again.

He followed Tony into the hallway, past a baby carriage and tricycle, up the wide stairs and through a half-opened door. He was in a living room then, rectangular, with a high ceiling and crowded with people and heavy furniture. Standing before him, like a committee waiting to greet him, were three silent men in deep black suits. None of the three smiled.

"Roger," he heard Tony's voice saying, as from a distance, "these are my cousins, Memo and Frank Saraceno and Gabe Romeo."

The three masks spoke dully: "Hello . . . I'm glad for you and Tony . . . Pleased to meet you."

Roger was unconvinced. Something was very wrong. What he didn't know, because in his own excitement Tony had forgotten to tell his brother, was that the cousins were mourners. Tony's favorite Uncle Bruno Saraceno had died and had been buried just the day before. Only their infinite respect and love for Pauline and Joseph Milasi compelled Bruno Saraceno's two sons and son-in-law to group for this welcoming party.

Memo Saraceno stepped forward now and took Roger's two hands in his. Recognizing Roger's confusion, he quietly explained the reason for the dark suits and the restraint.

"The family has lost one life," he said, "but in you, Roger, we've gained another. Welcome. Welcome to our family."

"Yes, yes," Gabe Romeo added with force. "You are one of us, Roger."

Most of the memories of this first day in Binghampton are mottled. They come back as leafy shadows. Roger remembers in patches of light and dark, and hears broad sounds. Only a few individual voices are recalled. However, he was so stirred by this expression that he is able to recite the exchange and remembers how when it was over he vowed that he would earn this family's loyalty, so freely given.

He was aware next that all around him people were talking in Italian. One voice impatiently called in English, "Let him go. Let us meet him."

As Tony began to introduce him in a great counterclockwise circle, Roger suddenly remembered that in the air force he had been absolutely incapable of retaining Italian names. He couldn't even pronounce most of them.

"This is Mom's niece, Frances Marano," Tony was saying,

"and I want you to meet Lilly Saraceno, Memo's wife . . .
You met Memo already. . . . Tita Romeo, Gabe's wife. . . .
Vincent and Josephine Russo. Josephine is Memo's sister.
You just met Memo, remember? . . . and this is Bruno, one
of Memo's brats. I mean kids. There are three more around,
too. . . . Here's cousin Paula and . . . over here . . ."

Behind them someone said, "Wait until he has to meet all
the Stillitanos." Everyone laughed. Another family wit added,
"What about the Ruffos!" They laughed still harder.

Roger was trying. He smiled and he nodded, nodded and
smiled and later would say, "I felt like a new automobile. I
was on display."

He stayed close to Tony, believing he was safe alongside
his brother but without him would instantly drown in the un-
charted social sea. In the next moment, his worst fear was a
reality. The phone rang somewhere in the apartment and
Tony went to answer it, leaving Roger *alone*. Lilly Saraceno
rescued him, taking his arm and ushering him into the kitch-
en, with its warm, spicy aromas.

"Here," she said, "is Tony's mother."

Roger had expected a "fat, jolly woman, my idea of the
typical Italian." He was unprepared for small, thin Pauline
Milasi, who seemed closer in age to his grandmother than his
mother. But as she reached up and gave him a quick, powerful hug Roger understood this tiny woman of seventy was far
stronger than she appeared.

"You come live with Tony?" she asked.

Roger was too surprised to answer immediately, and before he could find a reply Tony was there to plead, "Mom,
he just got here."

"Rog, come here." It was Memo, calling from the living
room. "Someone wants to meet you."

Tony whispered, "It's my Dad."

Roger walked toward Joe Milasi, instinctively holding out
his right hand. Tony's father simply pushed it aside to em-
brace Roger and kiss him high on the cheek.

Afterward, Roger was to say, "I never knew that men
hugged and kissed until I walked into Tony's family that
day."

Now this front room was noisy with conversation and
laughter, enlivened by the examples of open, virile affection.

In the background, the phone was ringing. This time Memo answered it and reported to Tony, "Dino and Sharon are coming tonight."

"Who is?" Roger asked.

"Everybody," Tony said. "All my friends. This is just for family, and it's only my mother's side. You still have to meet my Dad's people."

Frank Saraceno handed each of the brothers a glass of wine, and Tony put an arm over Roger's shoulder, saying: "Didn't I tell you it was going to be like this? And every day you're here is going to be a feast."

Toward evening they sat down to the dining room table, and the immense meal that followed was not in courses, but rather in stages, each lasting a half-hour. First, there was antipasto. Next came ravioli served in soup bowls, which allowed adventurers to top their portions with Pauline Milasi's nonpareil, miniature meatballs.

Pushing the platter toward Roger, Tony announced, "No one makes meatballs light and fluffy like my Mom."

Lilly Saraceno leaned over to explain that Tony's mother had been cooking and preparing for two days. Hearing this, Roger felt obligated to eat everything, and in abundance. When the "main course" arrived, he chose several veal cutlets, two chicken breasts, built a castle of rigatoni, apologized for passing up the eggplant parmesan and eventually worked around to the green salad. He knew his trencherman's reputation had preceded him. (At his suggestion, he and Tony on several nights each ate two dinners in Miami.) It became obvious that the more he ate, the happier he made everyone. The four Saraceno children gaped. Joe Milasi encouraged him, refilling his wine glass each time he took a sip. Pauline Milasi smiled, the sound of his knife and fork working the only praise she asked. And Tony celebrated his performance as noble.

"Didn't I tell you, Ma?" he said. "Roger can eat!"

Throughout the meal, which also included a dessert of fruitcake, Italian coffee, apples, grapes and tangerines (Joe Milasi insisted on peeling an apple for Roger.), the telephone continued to ring. Most callers wanted to know when they could meet Tony's brother. One of these was Dolores Manni Augostini, who as a girl had clerked in the Milasi store. Her husband, Lou, was a reporter for the *Binghamton Press* and wanted to interview the boys. "Is it all right," she asked, "if we stop in Sunday after Mass?"

Tony imposed only one condition for the interview, that Lou Augostini not disclose he and Roger were illegitimate. This of course was agreed to and in all the March 11 editions of the *Press,* the story of the Binghamton twins spread across five columns, with four pictures completing the layout.

The following day, the Associated Press and United Press rewrote the *Binghamton Press* story and transmitted it to radio and television stations and papers across the country. In New York, the *Times* carried it; the *Pacific Stars and Stripes* printed it in all its Far East editions, and in Miami, *The Herald's* story appeared under the headline: "He Asked For A Cup of Coffee and Got A Twin Brother."

What happened then was predictable. The twins became personalities. They received fan letters, including one to Tony from his navy love, who wrote from Kentucky, "You always said I would be reading about you someday," and when they walked downtown teenagers called, "Hey, which twin is the Toni?"

They were both excited by this attention, and Tony became convinced the publicity would see them break into show business. Here then was the dramatic last act to their dream of the rich life. Wasn't it possible, even likely, that Hollywood would write their story into an ambitious movie with Tony Milasi starring as himself, supported by Roger Brooks as played by Roger Brooks?

In Michael-Angelo's restaurant, where such weighty matters were discussed at length, Tony heard numerous assurances that he had it *made.* Roger, however, was even more pleased by another development, his acceptance by his brother's friends who were fascinated by the likenesses, particularly their mannerisms: the voice tone, the way they held and turned their heads, folded their arms, each crossed the right leg, and their laugh.

"You hear that?" Tommy Giorgio exclaimed, pointing to Roger. "He even laughs like Moon."

"Jesus, we're stuck with two Moons," said Johnny Visconti.

Because the brothers were physically alike, it was readily assumed they were alike in all ways, and Roger must therefore be an extension of Tony's personality. No one thought then to ask him what his youth had been like. This didn't matter to Roger. He was conscious only that he was accepted warmly, totally, enthusiastically. "They showed me a friendship I'd never known. Here they were, grown men, some of them with families even, and they took me into their circle because I was Tony's brother. And it wasn't only his friends. It was all his family, everyone I met. I found friendship, acceptance and an all-around warmth everywhere. I hadn't known people could be this friendly and generous. Those first two weeks in Binghamton were something beautiful to me."

As Tony had promised, they traveled in an orbit that kept them close to the family, and its dining tables. They also managed one side trip to Cambridge, Massachusetts, to introduce Tony to his professorial half brother, Rodney, and on their way back to Binghamton they stopped in Boston to visit Mark Frattalone, who was home from Miami University on spring vacation. Several times they double-dated with Tony's Slovak girl friend, Shirley Gaydos, and her sister Joyce. Generally, on these nights they took the girls for dinner, which confounded Tony's father.

"Eat out?" he asked defiantly. "What for? Your mother no good?"

"It's not that, Pop," Tony tried to explain. "The girls would rather eat out."

"Eat better home," Joe Milasi insisted. "I'm butcher. I know."

Roger quickly came to love Joe Milasi. He saw beyond the gruff façade; he enjoyed the swagger walk and the incorrigible accent and grammar. He was seeing the retired Joe Milasi, relaxed and good-humored, eager to tilt with Roger and to suffer gentle derision.

"You're from the old country, Mr. Milasi? Which old country?"

Tony and Roger shared a bedroom with Joe Milasi, and this helped Roger to understand what his brother had meant when he first described his father as "the funniest man alive." Roger remembers how they would keep Tony's father awake nights with annoying guttural noises, mostly grunts. "First Tony grunted, and I'd answer. We might keep it up, adding one more grunt each time until we were up to six—uhnt, uhnt, uhnt, uhnt, uhnt, uhnt!

"In the morning, Tony's father had his revenge. He either swatted us with a broom or he stood over us with a teaspoonful of water, dripping it on our noses. He was always up at 6:30, and his favorite torture was to turn up the radio loud and dance around our bed in his silly long underwear with the hole in the seat. All this time he would be singing: 'Lazy bum sleep in the sun, don't know where the money come from.' What a sight that was. We'd have to get up and have breakfast with him then, which is exactly what he wanted."

Roger wasn't envious of Tony's home and family. At least he told himself that he wasn't. He was, instead, grateful. Yes, that was his feeling. He was grateful to be a part of this family.

"It would have been good fun growing up in Binghamton," Roger thought, and once or twice he and Tony talked of how it might have been. They improvised on their basic fantasy, pretending that Tony was a Catholic and Roger a Jew and both lived under the same roof.

"Suppose," Roger offered, "that I was a rabbi and you a priest."

"I'd try to convert you," Tony said.

Roger said nothing. He continued, "Suppose we were baseball stars, who had to face each other. Maybe in a World Series."

"I'd probably strike you out," Tony answered.

This time Roger reacted. "I don't think you would," he said. "I was a pretty good ball player, Tony. Ray Skop and I used to pitch to each other for hours. Some days we never even stopped for lunch."

"We'll never know," said Tony.

Roger was standing before the front windows in the living room. He looked down across Carroll Street into Christopher Columbus Park and the Little League baseball field. It was an unseasonably mild day in March, one of those bonuses that sometimes occur as winter begins to give up some of its strength.

"Let's go hit some," he said.

"You can't. The park's too small."

"I'll bet you can't hit one out on me," Roger challenged.

"You're not serious."

"Sure I'm serious."

"Five dollars worth of serious?"

"We don't need to bet money."

"Well, a steak dinner then, with a shrimp cocktail."

"Whatever you say, Tony."

They borrowed a bat, two old balls and a glove much too small from one of Tony's Amadeo cousins who lived close by, and for the next forty minutes they batted against each other. They took turns hitting ten balls apiece with the winner being the one to hit the greater number of "home runs."

Tony hit first. He had watched many a game here and had the advantage of being familiar with the park. Since the fence was only two hundred feet from home plate down the foul lines, he squared off his stance and tried only to meet the ball, punching at it with a little half-swing motion. In the ten times he connected, he slapped two over the waist-high fence in shallow right field.

Then Roger confidently stood deep in the batter's box, his feet well spread and took his full cut. He managed to pull only one ball out of the little park and when Tony declared himself the winner Roger accused him of cheating, of violating the spirit of their bet.

"Who said anything about having to take a full cut?" Tony answered. "I'll give you a break though; we'll hit ten more for double or nothing."

They went another round, and with the same results. Tony again dumped two into the right field corner, barely clearing the fence. Roger persisted on his big swing, sending his one homer far beyond the barrier in deepest left center. Afterward, he boasted, "At least mine was the best shot of the day."

"That's got nothing to do with it," Tony argued.

"Sure it does. I'm the real power hitter in the family," Roger maintained. "That makes me feel better."

"I'll think of that when I'm eating your steaks."

They had now spent a total of three weeks together, and Roger's aggressiveness was clearly indicative of the growth of the relationship. He had become so confident of Tony's love that he felt secure enough to challenge his brother and then play to defeat him.

In Miami, they had avoided direct competition, and even though they had watched each other swim, shoot baskets, drive a car and play carpet golf they were too intent on discovering new likenesses and sparing each other's feelings to declare that one was a winner and his brother only second-best. Whenever they had been asked, "Who is better?" they had answered, "We're about the same in everything."

On the Little League field, though, it had been different and Roger understood that he and his brother were gaining what Miss Catherine Bittermann had called "shared experiences." Tony had given him a fine vacation and even volunteered to drive him home to Miami, promising to stay over a few extra days as well.

On their last night in Binghamton, Joe Milasi refused to allow the boys to eat out. It was to be spaghetti night, and so neither of them resisted. After the meal, Tony's father unexpectedly cleared the dishes while Tony's mother stayed seated. She slowly folded her linen napkin and, looking at Roger, began her own account of the day nearly twenty-five years ago when she had chosen between the Brooks twins. It was difficult for Roger to understand her words, but he had no doubt she was apologizing. She was very close to tears. Her face was downcast, and the rigid lines around her thin lips quivered as she spoke haltingly. "Believe me, Roger, I was old woman—sick, tired, no good take two babies. Dr. Maddi tell me no good."

Roger knew this whole story. Tony had told him the first night, and his reaction then had been, "Oh, God, if only she had taken us both!" Still later, Roger's family interpreted Pauline Milasi's act as selfish and unthinking. Of course, he was influenced by their judgment, but he characteristically forced the story from his mind, fearing it might somehow jeopardize his relationship with Tony. And after having lived in Pauline Milasi's home for two weeks he told himself that he understood and forgave.

When she was finished, Pauline Milasi said simply, "I'm sorry. Roger, so sorry."

Joe Milasi was standing behind her chair. "Should take both babies," he said.

"Yes, both. I make mistake."

"Ah, Ma! You were sick," Tony said, wanting to help her with this guilt.

"Still, I make the mistake."

Roger answered that he understood. "It's all right," he said. "Please, don't apologize." There was a long moment when no one said anything. The room was perfectly still. There was a strangeness to the silence. It was incomplete; everyone sensed that something was coming, and then Joe Milasi broke the quiet to say, very rapidly, "We make it up to you. Live with us, Roger. Here, with your brother."

So, there it was. If he and Tony were to live together, which they both wanted, then one of them was going to have to make a move. It was a subject that neither brother had wanted to open. When the reporters had asked, they explained, "It doesn't matter where we live, Miami or Binghamton. The important thing is that we're together."

Now the decision largely was Roger's burden.

19

Roger and Tony

When Roger and Tony reached Miami, Bessie Elman was dying. Cancer had shrunken her eighty-three-year-old body and taken her voice. Still, she forced a smile when she saw the boys together.

"Don't try and fool me," she wrote on her bedside pad, "I know my grandson."

Sixteen hours later, she was dead. Her last words, literally her dying words, were to her rabbi. "Thank you," she wrote Morris Skop, "for everything you've done for Roger."

Bessie Elman had been sick several months, and the family had understood that it was terminal, but this fact did not lessen their grief. In the weeks following her death, and after Tony had returned to Binghamton, Roger was held by lassitude and morbidity. He had never openly confessed it, but he was closer to his grandmother than to Mildred Brooks. In temperament, in philosophy, in his desire to be well liked and with his gentle, good manners, he was Bessie Elman's child. This thought, which kept crowding back, slid him deeper into his depression and filled him with guilt. He wanted to make amends, to give his mother more love; he also wanted to live with his brother. Yet, how could he possibly obey his impulses and Tony's urging and pack and run *now?* He simply was unable to declare that he wanted to move to Binghamton.

He said nothing of his desire in April. In May, Rodney came to Florida on vacation and resolved his dilemma. He counseled Roger: "Go now, mother will manage. Make a life for yourself while you're still young. Or you'll never go."

This was all the encouragement Roger needed. He eagerly gave notice at the factory, sold his car, drew out his savings of six hundred dollars and, to assuage his conscience, gave his mother one hundred dollars. Mildred Brooks was convinced that he was making a poor life choice. She told him he was forfeiting everything and wondered if he wasn't giving himself over to the Philistines.

Tony, meanwhile, was building word pictures of a golden life. He wrote Roger, "Don't worry about a job; just hurry up! We'll celebrate our birthday together."

Roger left Miami in such a state that he forgot his mother's picture, an oversight Mildred Brooks immediately interpreted as proof she was being consigned to a second-class relationship. Despite his big rush, he was still nine days late for his birthday and so the party was delayed until his June 6 arrival. Tony's mother had a steak and spaghetti dinner and a two-foot-long single layer cake with one candle. Across the icing was the message: "This is The First."

Pauline Milasi proceeded to treat Roger as a favored son. He was given half of Tony's closet and the single bed in the men's bedroom, which meant Tony and his father had to double up in the oversized bed. He also took Joe Milasi's seat, opposite Tony, at the kitchen table. From the first hours in the crowded, five-room apartment, his life was secure and carefree. Outside this home, however, it was troubled and often alien to him, not at all what he had hoped.

There was no job waiting. In fact, Tony himself was out of work. When the Great Books Company had refused him time off to visit Roger last January, he had quit. He was drawing $50 a week in unemployment insurance and to his surprised, discouraged brother, Tony explained: "I just don't enjoy breaking my back working."

Their idleness made Roger uneasy, and after seven weeks he took a job selling perfumes, household brushes and spices door-to-door. The newspaper ad had said the job's potential was $40,000 a year. Roger was paid $50 a week and quit when he was required to buy his own free samples, a $78 expense.

"See," said Tony, "I told you that ad was a phony."

Roger continued to be upset over their situation, though his brother talked bravely of things being better in the fall. Tony lived confidently too; he bought a new car, a $2,700 Pontiac Grand Prix with leather bucket seats. Roger drove a used Ford, for which he was paying $1,400.

As Roger studied his brother in these weeks, he saw that Tony was also restless, but his discontent manifested itself in different ways. For one thing, Tony was almost manic about getting out of the house. Once dinner was finished, he was gone, off on a date with Shirley Gaydos or to "see the guys" at one of the diners and later back at Mike's. Some nights Roger didn't want to run after Tony. Other nights Tony never asked him along. So Roger helped with the dishes and then played cards with Pauline and Joe. He loved to hear them argue in Italian, accusing each other of stupidity. Then, after nine o'clock, Mrs. Milasi would make a pitcher of fresh lemonade with cut-up orange slices, and there was always a platter of homemade Italian cookies.

Tony's behavior around the home generally dismayed Roger. At times he was uncivil, and he usurped all authority. He fixed everyone's mealtimes and menus and demonstrated that he was equal to or slightly above his father in command. Yet, he contributed almost nothing. He paid no board and did no work, not even troubling to make his bed. Roger wasn't like this; he was used to doing his share of the work, of being a contributor. Years before when he had stayed overnight at the Skops' home he always took out the garbage and voluntarily scrubbed the kitchen floor for Ray's mother. But when Roger tried to fix his own bed, Pauline Milasi grew angry: "You guest, stop!" Then he understood one reason why Tony was a noncontributor.

Roger let no one sense this disappointment in his brother,

though, and told himself that nothing, or no one, would ever stand between him and Tony, and whenever they were alone they talked only of how much alike they were, closing their eyes to their differences. Roger loved to hear Tony call him "brother" or refer to "my brother" and Tony enjoyed the nights when they went out dressed alike and people gaped.

"Look, look," he would whisper, "those girls are staring."

"I hate that," Roger would answer.

"Stop it, you love it. You know you do."

Roger's mother had sent them an article on twins from one of her *Today's Health* magazines and they read how they had started life as one being. This fact excited them and prompted Tony's weak joke, "No wonder we're the same in everything. We began as womb-mates."

This was the side they showed to Binghamton, that they were alike in every essential way, and they truthfully told questioners they had yet to have an argument. There was no cause to disagree. To be with his brother, to please his brother, Roger was ready to make any adjustment—and nearly any sacrifice.

Tony had told him he ought to move to Binghamton; so he did. Tony said then that he should sleep late, they would hang around Affatato's shine parlor in the morning and do something, maybe catch a movie in the afternoon. So they did. Tony told him he was a simp not to file for unemployment; he never had, but he did now. Tony told him not to worry about his car payments and getting a job. Roger tried, but not even his brother's reassurances could unfetter his conscience. Roger still continued to equate responsibility and maturity. A boyhood spent within earshot of three women who were quick to excoriate Jules Brooks had conditioned him. And to make a poor situation worse, in September Tony was hired as a salesman by a local radio station. Roger saw his brother less often then, and before he was able to completely adjust to this, Tony and Shirley Gaydos surprised their families by announcing they were engaged.

Roger took the news hard. Damn, he thought, life is always playing this trick. It gives with one hand, and then takes away with the other. Now, he had found his twin only to lose him. He was to marry a giddy, affectionate blond who was forever kissing him on the neck and in a little-girl voice calling him "Pumpkin," "Baby" and "Honey." Even his own mother thought Tony an elephant, not a pumpkin. Pauline Milasi had looked at Tony and Roger sleeping together one morning and said, "Hey, two elephants? Get up."

Roger liked Shirley well enough, only he doubted his brother was ready to marry. Tony's parents believed marriage would make him settle down. He wasn't so sure. At least once every two weeks Tonny came running with some idea or notion of what he *truly* wanted to do with his life. Then there was the selfish matter of how Tony's marriage would affect him. Roger tried to convince himself that nothing was going to change, but he knew that from here on, his brother's first loyalty must be to Shirley Gaydos. He told himself he had no right to be jealous, yet couldn't help himself. There was also another dimension to this new equation: there had been no room in his life, or his imagination, for a new loyalty. There had been in Tony's. So, as strong as their bond was, his brother obviously loved less profoundly than he did. He had suspected this was true, only it hadn't mattered before. But he suddenly began to feel that he was a stranger and an intruder. He was in Tony's town, in Tony's home, surrounded by his family and friends, and without his brother constantly beside him, he felt alone. Tony was his catalyst. Tony made things happen. Tony was his family, his security, the closest to him.

The result was that Roger fell into an unrelieved depression. Through September and October he was without a job. He ate more, gaining fifteen pounds, a circumstance that only further disturbed him. He slept later in the morning, sat around the apartment longer and was drawing out of savings to keep up his car payments, which compounded his melancholia. The one break in his narrow, bleak day came toward evening. He would be sitting on the second-story balcony, waiting. When he saw her soft, earthy Italian figure coming toward him, he felt better at once. She was Nancy Milasi, a brunette with beautiful green eyes, and of all the family, this bright nineteen-year-old, a cousin to Tony and granddaughter of old John Milasi, understood what was happening to Roger Brooks. She was sorry for him. On her way home from work each day, she stopped to say hello, to smile and talk and listen.

Roger liked Nancy; he took her out a few times but made it abundantly clear that, as he had just found his brother and didn't have a decent job, he was going to stay unattached. This was fine by Nancy. She had only recently broken off an engagement and shared his feeling. Moreover, Roger impressed her as "another Tony—friendly and easy to talk to, but I thought of him as a cousin."

Nancy lived just around the corner on Tudor Street, and Roger liked to walk her home and sit in a wooden rocker on her narrow front proch. As she got to know him better, Nancy thought him the most sensitive person she had ever met. She understood then that he was terribly homesick.

Weekends were the hardest, because Roger knew that if he were home in Miami, he would be out doing something interesting. There weren't even places you could drive to and sight-see in Binghamton. There was a sameness, a tediousness to the city and Roger was nostalgic for Florida. He had found it exciting in Miami just to get dressed up and drive around. Usually, he went over one of the causeways to The Beach and walked through the lobbies of the big hotels. He strolled among the expensive furnishings, the imported statues and the well-dressed people, and it gave him a feeling of well-being. He would finish his routine by staring into one of the darkened cocktail lounges. This moment was always the same. He would slowly light a cigarette and stand there, listening to the band play a love tune. All of this was a signal, releasing the actors in his mind to play out the cliché scene from a thousand movies of his past. A girl with a Marilyn Monroe figure would come to him from the smoky lounge and in a Lauren Bacall voice invite him to follow her back inside, telling him, "You look interesting."

"I was a little coward," he confesses, remembering these nights. "I never went into one of those lounges and naturally, no girl ever came out."

In Binghamton there was no Collins Avenue or Lincoln Road with its gaudy, pastel-colored hotels and, as far as Roger could see, all anyone did was attend weddings and funerals and watch television. The set in the Milasi home played from early morning until bedtime. It even stayed on when no one was there to watch, playing to an empty room.

In November, Tony helped Roger find a job. As a shoesalesman in a highway discount center, Roger worked a fifty-two-hour week for $67.50, after taxes, and for six nights of the week he wasn't finished until ten o'clock. On Sunday night, his free night, he took Nancy Milasi to dinner and tried to introduce her to frogs' legs and baked potato with sour cream. Sitting on her front porch after dinner one Sunday, Roger again told her how clean and beautiful Miami was and confessed that if it weren't for her, he would go home.

"But you mustn't tell anyone this," he said, lowering his voice. "I wouldn't want to hurt my brother's feelings, ever."

The neighbors on Tudor Street began to whisper that Nancy Milasi was kissing on the front porch with her own cousin. Roger himself was too confused to understand that he was in love, so when Pauline Milasi teased him, saying that he was going to marry Miss Nancy, he denied any such intention.

Borrowing Milasi syntax, Roger Brooks protested, "Too young; she too young."

20

Roger and Tony

The weddings were in February, a year apart. Roger was Tony's best man on February 8, 1964, and Tony was Roger's best man on February 27, 1965. Both were Catholic ceremonies in the Milasi parish, St. Mary's of the Assumption of the Blessed Virgin Mary, a small dark Gothic church where Rosie Finelli had had a vision and Tony had clumped about as an altar boy.

In all of Binghamton, but particularly in the Seventh Ward, weddings keep to a pattern, and the Milasi and Brooks happy affairs faithfully adhered. They began with the marriage Mass at 10 A.M., followed with a wedding breakfast and proceeded inexorably to the social climax, the reception. For the bride and groom their day was eighteen hours long and required they be marathon performers at standing, sitting, smiling, eating, drinking, embracing, kissing, dancing, posing, hand-shaking, laughing and being gracious. The experience was part ecstasy and part nightmare but immensely profitable. Including children, there were more than six hundred at each reception at the St. Michael's Greek Catholic recreation center in Johnson City. Along with the toasters, blenders, water goblets and electric carving knives, the couples gathered a packet of small white envelopes, each with a $5, $10 or $50 gift. When totaled, their sum in each case was close to $1,800.

Naturally, many of the same guests attended both weddings, but at Nancy and Roger's there was one newcomer. Considerable attention and thought had been given to his presence, for he was Jules Brooks, the boys' natural father. At Uncle Lou Brooks' urging, Roger some weeks before had written him. It was strictly a courtesy, but as soon as he received the note, Jules telephoned. He was eager for details and asked Roger to visit him in Schenectady.

Ten years had passed since they last saw each other, yet they again acted as if there had been no break in the continuity of their relationship. They were like long-time friends, except that they talked only of the present and future. Their past was walled out of the conversation, although it was never far from their thoughts.

Roger saw that his father was heavier and older. When he got up to walk across the living room he moved ponderously, almost as though he were in pain. But he was still a drummer, selling kitchen items and housewares out of the back of his car.

When it was Roger's turn he talked too fast, racing on out of nervousness. He began with the story of his finding Tony and his settling in Binghamton. Jules nodded. He had read several of the newspaper stories. Roger mentioned the wedding and a little shamefacedly explained that Nancy was a Catholic. Jules smiled, "So? I'll have Catholic grandchildren."

Roger was more at ease talking of Tony and knew Jules wanted to hear all there was to tell. He related how close and how much alike they were and boasted of Tony's new job as a salesman with a Binghamton television station.

"What line of work are you in?" Jules asked.

Roger answered that he recently had gone to work for Nancy's uncle, Jimmy Rotella, who owned a market and wholesale beer distributorship. "Uncle Jimmy is teaching me the business." Roger saw no reason to mention his $44.44 salary for a fifty-hour week.

Jules nodded again, adding that family businesses often were very good. When they both were silent, Jennie came into the room to announce lunch. She had a favorite of Roger's, lox and fresh bagels. As they sat to the table, Jules started what sounded to Roger like a speech, and as he listened he understood that his father was selling; he was selling himself.

He said he would come to the wedding knowing that people were going to talk. Some surely would say he didn't belong there. He didn't care. What harm could they do him?

"I'll be sixty this year, Roger, and we don't live long in my family. It's too late for anyone to hurt me and it's too late for regrets. I've gotten into my share of trouble and I've been in and out of debt most of my life. I've not worked as hard as other men. Still, I've been able to make good money with less effort. I don't know why I've lived this way; I just know that I'm too old to change or to seek explanations. Sure I feel bad about some things in the past and I don't know how you look at it, but I think it's fantastic that you and Tony found each other. Somehow, it has all worked out okay. I'm happy for you both. I hope you have happiness now, or at least long moments of happiness. God knows, you deserve them.

"You've had it rough, rougher even than I had it and my childhood was nothing to speak about. Maybe if I was a different kind of man you would have had it easier; but I wasn't. I was the very opposite of my father, who was a pious, hard-working Jew—a tailor and pants-presser. I was unconventional, a radical sometimes and I suppose some people will say that I did what was expedient.

"So, I'm not the best guy in the world and neither am I the worst. Can you understand that?"

Roger said yes, he did understand, only he didn't want to have to make a long answer. He wasn't sure what he wanted to tell Jules this day and was glad when Jennie interrupted, complaining this talk made her edgy. Why didn't they find a happy subject?

"All right," Jules said, seizing a new idea, "tell me more about Tony. Is he curious to meet 'the heavy' in the story?"

"The what?" asked Roger.

"The heavy," Jules repeated, enjoying his own wit. "You know, the villain."

Roger said when they had met in Miami, Tony's first questions were about his father. He was positive Tony very much wanted to meet Jules.

"Then why not bring him here?" Jules said, and was excited at the prospect. "Let him bring his wife, too, and you bring Nancy. Come for the day, and have dinner. We'll make it a big celebration."

It was all agreed and then later, as Roger got ready to leave, Jules walked him to the street to ask would they be coming in Roger's car? "No, we'll probably come in Tony's Grand Prix," Roger said, realizing that Jules was worried about being able to distinguish between him and Tony.

Driving over from Binghamton the following Saturday, the two couples wondered aloud about the meeting. The girls were anxious to be well received. Shirley had her long hair teased and borrowed her sister's leopard-skin coat. Nancy was dressed simply but tastefully and kept her thoughts to herself. From everything Roger had told her, she had grown to hate Jules Brooks. As the time for her to face him came closer, however, her hatred gave way to reason. When Roger so obviously loved his father and needed his approbation, Nancy understood she would be of no help to her fiancé if she scorned him.

Roger and Tony strained to be relaxed. Tony feigned indifference, but behind this screen were deeper, truer emotions. "I was nervous, so I put on a front. I kept asking myself, 'Well, are you going to hate him? Punch him? Or maybe like him?' For my brother's sake, I thought I better not hate. If I had known that Roger didn't love him I'm pretty sure I would have hated him.

"It wasn't that I condemned him. I didn't. What I felt, my bitterness, was because of everything I learned from my brother. I mean, the way Jules acted toward him when they lived together."

When they pulled up before the two-family frame house, Jules was standing on the porch, dressed neatly in a tie and white, short-sleeved shirt.

"Hiya, Jules," Tony said, as he started up the walk. "Are we in time for the first race?"

Jules's face relaxed in a calm smile at this thrust and when Shirley came forward he took her hand and asked, "Can I kiss you?"

"Sure," she said, and his smile broadened. He kissed her cheek and quickly said, "Come on, Jennie's waiting."

So, this anxious moment was behind them, and upstairs in the second-floor apartment they found Jennie in an effervescent mood. She had made a pitcher of Manhattans and after cocktails served a luncheon of scrambled eggs and bacon, using her best china and linen napkins. Although he said nothing, Jules was obviously elated over the physical similarities between Roger and Tony. Both caught him staring at first Tony, then Roger, then back to Tony. When he seemingly could no longer control himself, he suggested they all pose for pictures and produced a borrowed Polaroid camera.

"I knew he would have a Polaroid," Roger later would say, "because he couldn't bear to wait until his pictures were developed."

Jules took shots of the boys, of Nancy and Shirley, and finally he jumped into the picture himself between first the girls and then the twins, his sons. Jennie was trusted to work the camera. The host next made sure that everyone had at least one souvenir picture. He was like a child in his joy, and everything was going so well that the two couples agreed to stay for dinner. After their second meal Tony told Jules he had some questions. He suggested they take a ride.

"All right," said Jules, and to Jennie, he explained, "I'm going for a ride *with the boys.*" Jules plainly liked the ring of this line and turning to Roger, said, "I'm ready."

It was Tony's idea. Roger wanted no part of the interrogation but was willing, indeed, he wanted to be a witness. He climbed into the back seat. Jules sat up front, relighting a cigar as Tony steered the Grand Prix away from the curb.

"I want to know," Tony began, and he wasn't asking, he was telling Jules, "about our real mother."

"What do you want to know?"

"Look, I know what happened, but I want to hear what kind of a woman she was. Was she—you know—a whore?"

Jules answered at once, "No. She wasn't."

Roger couldn't see his face, but he knew from the way Tony's shoulders relaxed that his brother was satisfied. He was sure this is what he had come to hear.

"No," Jules continued, volunteering, "she was a good woman, who had a lot of poor luck."

"What did she look like? Was she pretty?"

"Well, she was tall and blond. She was nice-looking, in fact she was something like your wife, Shirley. Her face was thin, like Shirley's, and she had nice eyes, only they weren't dark like Shirley's."

"Where is she today? Do you know?"

"No, I don't," said Jules, "and I think it is best for you to get her out of your mind. There is nothing more to be gained. As I told Roger years ago, it's all over and done with, and best forgotten."

"You're probably right, only I had to know this much," Tony said.

They drove in silence for a while and then Jules directed Tony back to the house. It was after ten o'clock when everyone said goodnight. Jules promised he would see them all at the wedding.

"Well, what do you think of him?" Roger asked his brother.

"He's okay," Tony said. "He's a nice guy. I could get to like him . . . only Joe Milasi is still my father."

Roger let the matter rest; he said nothing more. He was well satisfied. The day had been a success. He and Nancy later agreed that Jules and Tony had "hit it off."

Tony saw no reason to voice it then, but he thought that in a number of ways he and Jules Brooks were closely alike and when he knew him better was one day to remark, "It scares me, how much I'm like Jules."

Jules not only kept his word and appeared, but he walked through the long wedding day of February 27, 1965, holding his head high. He played the role of the groom's father as though born to it, and Tony and Roger were impressed. He sat in the first seat in the front pew in St. Mary's Church; in late afternoon he strode tall and proud into the gymnasium-sized St. Michael's Hall, where he was at once the object of sidelong glances and whispers. Some even regarded him as an interloper, and as he stood on line before the makeshift bar he overheard two men.

"I understand their father is here," the first said. "Hasn't he got a nerve!"

"Well, you don't know the whole story," the second said. "Besides, I understand Roger and Nancy wanted him to come."

After the first speaker had moved away, Jules tapped the second man's shoulder. In a big voice, he announced, "I'm Jules Brooks, father of the twins."

Strangely, the most outspokenly critical reaction to Jules' wedding attendance came from his ex-wife, Mildred. No sooner had Nancy and Roger debarked from their plane in Miami, where they were to spend their honeymoon, than Florence Dwyer informed Roger exactly how angry his mother was.

Roger understood that his mother's latest displeasure traced to his original decision to move to Binghamton and, secondly, his marriage to a Catholic. He had received a long and bitter letter to this effect. Already troubled with certain guilt feelings and apprehensive over the inevitable confrontation with Rabbi Skop, who he knew was disappointed, Roger was understandably upset by the letter. The irony was that his mother had no faith. Time and again he had heard her exclaim, "When you're dead, you're dead." She had rejected all religions, yet during her lifetime put her trust in the power of the stars, the healing power of psychologists and physicians and, for a time, followed the individual preachings of a Congregational minister. But never had she given obeisance to a formal religious creed; how could she objectively and intelligently judge what he now chose to believe?

If only she would give him a chance, Roger wanted to explain that for him religion was *feeling*, that when he was sitting in church he felt good, and a little noble. It didn't matter so much what church. It happened now to be the Catholic Church. This was because of Nancy. She had a strong faith, the product of her lifetime. He didn't. How could he then ask her to sacrifice her Catholicism when he had nothing to give her in return?

He wasn't truly a Catholic and probably never would be

one. At least not a good one. He didn't know the rosary; he couldn't accept the infallibility of the pope or the concept of mortal sin, and he believed in birth control. But when Sunday came he looked forward to seeing the family and others he knew in church and on the steps outside after the Mass. He looked forward to sitting there and praying, thanking God for his good health and especially for good eyesight, which he had always felt was a God-given, precious gift. He prayed too for the GIs in Vietnam and wherever else they were fighting and dying and he always remembered to pray for the souls of the dead. Bessie Elman had once told him that the dead know when you're praying for them; he hoped this was true. He liked the idea that here he was, the convert, praying in St. Mary's Assumption for the soul of his Jewish grandmother.

He would arrive early, before the Mass, when the church was very still. It was dark then; the only bright lights were those above the altar. He would sit straight up in the hard wooden pew and let the thoughts come, deep thoughts that were beyond him except during this one hour in the week. By the time he had said all his prayers and the Mass was over, he would feel that he was a better person and maybe the world was a little better place, too.

Was there anything wrong with any of this? Why couldn't his mother understand the important thing was to have experienced these feelings, not that they came to him in a Catholic Church in Binghamton, New York.

There were other reasons for his turning. The most important, unquestionably, had to do with his brother. Even though Tony seemed to be running away from his religion, Roger believed they were closer both being Catholic. Another thing, there was little doubt that through his marriage and conversion, he had become a member of the inner family. Tony innocently made the point with his wedding toast.

"Today is a very special event in my life," he had said. "For today my cousin becomes my sister-in-law and my brother becomes my cousin."

As the husband of Nancy Milasi, Roger no longer called Tony's parents "Mr. and Mrs. Milasi." He rightly called them, as did Nancy, "Zia and Zio." They were now his aunt and uncle. Moreover, by his marriage, he had moved closer into the Saraceno, Stillitano, Rotella and Amadeo families. He held significant new credentials in the ward.

He was closest, of course, to Tony's parents, for in the year between Tony's marriage and his own he stayed on in the apartment. And to Pauline and Joe Milasi, it was like having another, more attentive Tony all to themselves. Roger was there at mealtimes to give tribute to Pauline's cooking and be a conversational partner. He was there to do dishes, make his bed ("I'm no guest anymore.") and take his turn scrubbing the kitchen and bathroom floors. He was there to suggest to Tony they buy his mother a new self-defrost refrigerator, and it was Roger who had insisted Pauline buy a new dress and hat for Tony's wedding.

At night he was there to flatter the Milasis with his skill as a listener and, importantly, he never tired of their stories of Tony. In a way, they were all partners. Each of them had lost a piece of Tony and to fill the loneliness they leaned on one another.

Maybe he wouldn't live in Binghamton all his life, but he could always go back and be comfortable. For in the river valley city where he had been born, where he had found his brother and then a wife, he had over the last twenty-one months put down roots. Binghampton was rightly his home town and now that he and his brother were both married, both of the same religion and both shared the abiding love of Pauline and Joe Milasi, Roger believed they were even closer as brothers.

"Did you speak to your mother?" Nancy asked him one morning. "I mean, about your turning?"

"No, we've agreed not to bring it up," he answered. "I think it's best."

"I don't."

"Nancy, I don't want to argue, not on our honeymoon," Roger explained. "Not with you, not with my mother, not with anyone."

Nancy persisted, "Roger, I think you owe her an explanation. She'll think it was all my doing."

"Do you know that Tony and I are the same? We want to be happy all the time. We don't want to hate, or hold animosity toward anyone. I never let out my hostility and—I just realized—my brother is the same way."

21

Roger and Tony

In October of 1965, Roger Brooks became a salesman and was able once more to tell himself he was "just like my brother." He was hired then to sell invoices, receipt books and other business aids and had so impressed the Sturgiss-Newport Company recruiter he was allowed to chose his assignment area. He selected Miami, making a separation from his twin inevitable.

"But why?" Tony asked him. "Why do you want to go?"

Roger explained that he was twenty-seven, married eight months and he had to think of the day when he and Nancy had children. Besides, they had given up on Uncle Jimmy Rotella and his $44.44 a week job, they simply couldn't live on that little money. Still, there was more to the decision. Roger wanted to compete with Tony, to do as well; Tony had continued to improve himself, and as a salesman of Smith-Corona office copiers his monthly salary was $550. So when Roger had been asked what salary he expected, he told the Sturgiss-Newport man, "Five-fifty a month."

On the day that he and Nancy were to leave Binghamton, Tony was around early to help pack and load the car. In the moment to say goodbye, the brothers turned unnaturally silent. Neither was able to look directly into the other's face and they hurriedly shook hands. Tony later remarked, "We found that we were both lousy at saying goodbye."

This was only the beginning. Over the next nine months, they were also to discover that apart each did poorly and missed his twin far more than he had believed possible.

At first, it was an exciting new start for Roger Brooks and he began his days confidently, calling upon a succession of restaurants, bowling alleys, offices and factories. But his failures always outnumbered his triumphs by more than ten to one and he arrived home in the evening bruised by repeated rejection.

"Why are people so rude?" he asked Nancy. "Does it cost any more to be polite? Does it take that much more time to be decent?"

The poorer he did, the deeper was his depression; the deeper the depression, the less he tried, and so the following week was a little worse than the previous one. He started later in the morning, took a longer lunch at his mother's house and quit earlier. Nancy would come home from her job as an insurance company secretary to find him watching television.

"Let's talk about it, Roger."

"There is nothing to talk about. I just had a bad day, that's all."

"But yesterday was bad, and the day before."

"Yes, and all last week, too. Is that what you want me to say?"

"Roger, what I'm trying to get at is that maybe you're not meant to be a salesman. It isn't everyone who can sell. I see some in my company and—"

He cut her off. "Tony is a good salesman. You said so yourself. Well, I'm his twin; I can sell because we're both the same."

Nancy loved her irresponsible cousin, but she could not accept that he and Roger Brooks were *the same*. She knew, for example, that Tony Milasi was able to accept rejection and respond in anger. Everyone in their family knew Pauline and Joe Milasi argued every day of their lives, yet never held their anger. They were Italian and this was their way of venting frustration. Well, Tony had profited from his environment, but Roger had not. Even though he grew up in a home where three women were continually bickering, accusing one another of some thoughtless act, he was incapable as an adult of articulating anger. He lacked the security to give way to a loud, intemperate outburst. He had never stood his ground to scream at someone, "I'm right. You're wrong. Go to hell."

Nancy Brooks further recognized Tony was quite willing to reassign blame. He could fix responsibility for failure on those around him, or a bad break. Her Roger instinctively turned inward, making each failure personal. In self-examination, he asked: "What is it about me that people don't like?"

She understood that following a childhood filled with rejection Roger was incapable of enduring any more. Faced with unpleasantness, particularly a setback, he withdrew and turned silent. But she knew it was useless to try to explain these differences because he saw any critical comment about Tony as either groundless or an attempt to put enmity between his brother and him. Lately, any conversation about Tony led to an argument, and so Nancy was forced to watch her husband struggle, powerless to help and afraid to suggest he and Tony weren't *the same*.

Roger gave himself six months in the Sturgiss-Newport job and the following spring, with things no better, he finally quit. He had no new job waiting and fell into a period of almost complete inactivity. To Nancy, the pattern of his days became familiar and painful. She would reach home to find him in his Bermuda shorts stretched out on the couch. Two empty soda cans were on a coffee table and the newspaper, folded back to the want ads, was on the floor. One evening he was deep asleep, and since it was her seventy-five dollars a week salary that sustained them she found this galling.

"For God's sake, Roger," she screamed, "do something. Get a job—any job—until you find what you want."

He accused her of not wanting him to be happy. He said he had pride, that he couldn't take just any kind of work. To keep peace, though, he became a shoe salesman, only his flat feet swelled from the hours of standing and pained him until he grew faint. He lasted four days.

A worried Nancy Brooks now turned to Roger's mother and Aunt Mildred and Uncle Lou Brooks, yet none of them had a solution. When his mother had rebuked him, Roger had answered, "Well, I'm just like my father, aren't I?"

It was plain to Nancy that only his brother was going to be able to reach through the fog of Roger's depression and help him recover the motivation that he unaccountably had lost by returning to Miami. Since neither of the boys was a good correspondent, their contacts had been infrequent. But two of them had been unusual and, considering the brothers were monozygotic twins reared apart, revelatory. The first of these had come last Chrismas when they surprised each other with identical gifts. Both had selected Banlon, turtleneck shirts with matching socks. Roger chose black for Tony; Tony picked blue for Roger.

Standing before the haberdashery counter in the discount center, Roger had first held up the blue, asking Nancy's opinion.

"I don't think Tony will wear blue socks," she had said.

"You're right. I'll take the black instead."

In Binghamton and Miami, the families regarded this exchange as bizarre. Shirley had at first suspected her husband of playing a trick. Nancy remembered, "I couldn't get over it, and neither could my mother. Tony had opened his present at her house and she telephoned us right away."

Oddly, the principals were only momentarily excited. Their attitude was, "Well, we have been saying all along that we are close."

The second incident had occurred in March. This time both brothers were impressed. It started with Roger losing his paycheck. He had just cashed it and after tucking the bills into his money clip, he went to slip the packet into his right-hand pants pocket. Apparently he dropped the money.

When Nancy saw his face, she was sure someone in the family had died. He felt so poorly they decided to call Tony, and over the phone Roger said, "Wait until you hear what happened! I lost my pay."

"How much?" Tony asked.

"The whole thing—One hundred thirty-seven dollars. In cash."

"Rog, you're not going to believe this, but maybe you'll feel better."

"What's that, Tony?"

"I lost my wallet two days ago with fifty dollars in it. Does that grab you?"

Nancy had realized that night when they compared losses

that although she didn't fully understand the bond between Roger and his brother, it was truly unique, and she had no other choice now but to draw them together again before her husband lost all his confidence and self-respect. It wasn't only for Roger's sake either, because she knew from Shirley's letters that Tony was also doing poorly.

Shortly after his brother had left Binghamton, Tony became restless and quit his job. He had wanted a big city with major league baseball and basketball and a night life. He set out for Philadelphia, believing he was to become the Great Books Company sales manager in that city, only there had been a misunderstanding; he never got the first job and had refused a lesser one. For the next three months he could find nothing, until he joined the Royfax Company, again as a salesman of copiers. This is where he was working when in the late spring of 1966 Nancy suggested to her dispirited husband that he have a talk with Tony.

Roger placed the call then, and from the quick smile that came over his face, Nancy knew this was the correct therapy. "Good old Tony," she thought. "To hear him tell it, half the world is his with the other half under negotiation."

She was reminded of a time two years ago when Tony had magically gotten the brothers a television show in Binghamton. He had announced unequivocally: "This is it! We're made!"

Called "Double Vision," it was a ten-minute interview show three evenings a week following the "Mickey Mouse Club." There was, however, one drawback. The hosts were unsalaried and dependent on new sponsors for a budget.

After their third show, a desultory interview with the local Secretary of the Year, who declared Binghamton was the capital of Dullsville, Tony and Roger walked into Michael-Angelo's to find critic Dino Pirozzi.

"How're we doing?" Tony asked him.

"Stinks."

"That bad, huh?"

"Next week organ music."

"A lot of kids like our show," Tony added.

"They think you're the second half of the 'Mickey Mouse Club.' "

Dino was wrong, though. The show lasted *two* more weeks

before being replaced, trammeling Tony and Roger's hopes of seeing their program develop into a Binghamton fixture.

On the phone from Philadelphia now Tony described his job with Royfax as the best he'd ever had and his boss as the finest he had ever known. "I told him about us, Rog. He said that if I made my quota this month he would hire you and pay part of your moving expenses. How about that for a deal?"

When Roger hung up the phone, he was shaking his head. All he could say was, "What a brother! He's a lifesaver."

Nancy Brooks believes she knew from the start that when she married Roger she had also married his twin. Yet, until July 1966, when they moved into the White Horse Apartments in Somerdale, New Jersey, a twenty-minute commuter drive from Phildelphia, she hadn't even begun to understand the completeness of her involvement in this consuming, oftentimes inscrutable relationship. For now the twins worked and lived, literally, side by side. The Anthony J. Milasis were in apartment 110 and four doors away, in Number 106, were the Roger D. Brookses. The husbands and their working wives drove into Philadelphia each morning and home again each evening. Both couples shopped in the Somerdale Market and read the same newspapers. Tony took the morning *Inquirer* and told Roger to get the evening *Bulletin;* at night they swapped. They watched the same television programs, frequently all four together, and as they had in Binghamton after their marriages, they went out socially and always ate Sunday dinner together. They had the same neighbors, friends, landlord, doctor, priest, tax accountant, dry cleaner, gas station attendant and mailman. Nancy and Shirley readily borrowed eggs, sugar or detergent from each other and each considered the other's apartment an adjunct of her own.

The brothers, meanwhile, wore each other's clothes and often bought duplicate or similar items, particularly ties. Nancy said she was able to sort her husband's ties into two categories, those bought before Tony and those bought after Tony. The latter group was "louder, flashier and definitely *not* Roger's personality."

The most notable feature of this living arrangement, at least to Nancy's concern, was that during their waking hours, Roger and Tony seldom were apart.

Toward the end of an evening that she and Roger had decided to spend by themselves, her husband would suddenly get up from the couch, yawn, stretch and move cautiously toward the door.

"And where are *you* going?" she would ask.

"Down to my brother's."

"What for?"

"I want to see him."

"You saw him all day."

"I know that. But I want to see him now."

"Can't it wait until the morning?"

"No, it can't."

"Well, call him up."

"I don't want to call him when I can walk down the hall."

"Then go walk down the hall but will you please tell me what is so important at eleven o'clock at night?"

"I just want to find out if he wants me to drive tomorrow."

"Oh Jesus, Roger. Go ahead—"

"You know what, Nancy? I think you're jealous of my brother."

"For God's sake, Roger. If you didn't find your brother then I wouldn't have met you and we wouldn't be married."

Nancy didn't believe she was jealous; rather, she was protesting they had no life of their own. They had no secrets and there was almost no corner of the day that belonged only to themselves. She too had looked forward to rejoining Shirley and Tony, only she hadn't envisioned it like this. "They couldn't be much closer if they were Siamese twins," she wrote her mother of Roger and Tony. "I don't know what I'm going to do with him; I mean *them*. Shirley and I call them Ike and Mike."

On too many nights to please her, Nancy sat home with Shirley while the husbands were at a Phillies' baseball game, and after someone in their office told them that at 220 pounds they were too heavy for twenty-eight-year-old salesmen, they spent two evenings a week at a health club, a privilege that cost them two hundred dollars each.

"We could use the money for any number of things," Nancy explained in a letter home, "but I wouldn't mind if only Roger lost some weight. One of these days I'm going to get tired of sacrificing."

This is precisely what happened. Nancy ran out of patience one evening. In going through her husband's pants pockets she had found a note from Tony to Roger describing a plan to sneak off to the races on, of all nights, Saturday.

"I was boiling," she remembers. "I stormed down to Shirley's and we decided to confront them separately. Well, they told us two different stories, neither of which could hold water. We wanted to punish them and so announced we weren't going to cook for them and didn't plan on talking to them again, ever."

What followed then was ludicrous, yet instructive, for the twins seemed to suffer only a minor inconvenience. While the wives commandeered one apartment, they retreated into the other and took turns cooking for each other.

"They tried to make us jealous," Shirley said. "We were content with a sandwich, but they cooked spaghetti or veal cutlets or eggplant."

Aside from the mess of pots and dishes, the dust and soiled laundry that accumulated, their routines were seemingly unchanged. The ostracism continued into a third day and ended with the husbands feigning repentance, ostensibly apologetic. But despite their brave front, both Tony and Roger greatly depended upon their efficient and resourceful wives. They depended upon their salaries, their sense of organization and their patience. While the two women were not at all alike, they shared a common purpose: each kept her husband solvent and content.

To an outsider, the couples in apartments 106 and 110 appeared to be leading parallel lives. Behind the two doors, however, there were pronounced differences in the comparative life styles, just as there were in the personalities of the brothers and their wives. To begin, there was a major difference in their handling of and regard for money.

Tony and Shirley made a little more than Roger and Nancy, and they spent more. Though they earned less, Roger and Nancy saved more, because saving to Roger was as much a part of the living process as spending. Tony found saving inimical and, from every evidence, impossible.

Nancy Brooks explained, "If the boys both got a forty-dollar monthly gas and oil bill, Tony would pay twenty dollars and the following month he would owe sixty dollars. Roger always tried to stay current. He's very good that way. He knows when everything is due and I've had to learn to budget from him.

"With Tony and Shirley, it is the opposite. Shirley was the careful one when they were first married. As time went on, she got more and more like Tony. Actually, Roger makes Tony nervous when he pays his bills and even manages to save a little. Tony can't understand how he does it, and of course, he knows what we make because Roger tells his brother everything."

Shirley Milasi accepts a share of the blame for her husband's poor budgetary habits because, she explains, she spoils him by letting him have his own way. "He simply loves to charge things," she said. "So if we have one credit card and someone sends us another, he has to go out and buy something. I should tear them up as they come in the mail only I can't deny him anything."

"Now," Nancy continued, "if they should both get a check, something they weren't expecting, like a sales commission, well, Tony gets excited right away and wants to go out and celebrate. Roger will use his to pay off whatever bills we have and then maybe we'll go out for dinner. And when they go to the races together, Roger figures out beforehand how much he can afford to lose. Tony is already mentally spending the money that he figures to win."

By the time the Brookses joined the Milasis in New Jersey, Tony had accumulated more than one thousand dollars in debts, which he insisted to his brother would all get paid "No one is going to get stuck," he told Roger. "It may take a little time until we get rolling, that's all."

They never did get rolling, though. Professionally, nothing went smoothly for them. Tony hadn't misrepresented the Royfax job. It did seem to be a good opportunity, and they started at six hundred dollars a month plus a twenty-five-dollar commission for every copier they placed. But after less than three months a memo came down rescinding the bonus agreement and fixing monthly quotas. Their salary became a "draw," and unless the quota was met, they were unpaid. With a rush in the last days of his months, Tony reached the quota. Roger never did.

In the fourth month, their sales manager quit in disgust. Tony and Roger followed him. They filled in for six weeks selling Florida real estate at night until Tony got them jobs with an insurance company, selling an accident-sickness policy to dentists and doctors. Again they started off resolutely, talking of turning a corner in a solid industry. Even the wives caught their enthusiasm. Nancy sent out hundreds of company postcards informing the prospect, his name copied from the Yellow Pages of the Philadelphia directory, that he was to be called shortly by Representative Brooks.

"I tried hard," Roger remembered. "Those first months, I really tried. But I couldn't get used to having the phone hung up on me. I never thought professional men acted that way. Then, I didn't always blame them, because we used a little trick, telling the nurse we wanted to speak to the doctor about his income.

"I got so I didn't want to pick up a phone. I felt that I had to get out of the office and pretended I was going for coffee. I would walk the streets, looking up at the buildings, wondering if the people in those offices were doing as poorly as I was. I knew you were supposed to be hard-nosed and thrive on the pressure; I just couldn't. A few times, when I had actual appointments, Tony went with me and tried to help. He coached me, 'Be tough, sell hard, push for the sale.' "

Nancy Brooks looks back upon this segment of her life as unreal. When she was a little girl of ten her Grandpa John Milasi had locked her in his cellar because she had refused to work in the grocery store. She had the same helpless feeling living in the White Horse Apartments in Somerdale that she did that long ago afternoon in her grandfather's pitch dark, musty cellar. She believed herself trapped, and nearly everything about her life displeased her. She was homesick for Binghamton, for her sister Angela and her infant niece. The noise of the traffic from the highway that ran past their building unnerved her, and she hated the cooking smells from the other apartments. They made her sick. Still, it wasn't just the cooking odors that upset Nancy, for finally, happily, she was pregnant.

All her frustrations she visited upon Roger, and when he stared blankly at her, wondering what to say in reply, she cried, just as she had done in that cellar under John Milasi's market.

"Roger, I'm not going to have my baby here," she said, and it was as close to an ultimatum as she dared. "I want to go home. I want to be near my family and to have my own doctor."

"Okay, okay. I'll talk to Tony."

"Don't talk to Tony," and now she was screaming. "He has nothing to do with it. Just do something! Let's *us* go back to Binghamton!"

But between her own discontentment and *his* struggles with the job, Nancy saw that Roger needed Tony's companionship. The best and most relaxed moments of his day came when he was with his brother in the gym or off to the harness races. This wasn't, however, helping her loneliness—or their marriage. For the first time, she wondered if he wouldn't have been a stronger, more complete personality had he not found his brother. And without Tony, wouldn't he be better able to cope with his problems? These thoughts didn't stay with her very long, for suddenly Roger became sick.

It happened at three o'clock one morning. She rolled over in bed and her arm touched his body. He was cold and clammy, and the sensation caused her to wake.

"Roger, what is it?" she asked.

"I don't know," and he began to moan, "Oh, oh, oh, my back."

She got out of bed to turn on the light and what she saw turned her anxiety to pounding terror; his face was ash-white and contorted by pain. As she stood watching him, fumbling in her mind for their doctor's name and phone number, he screamed: "Don't touch me, don't touch me! Get my brother. Get Tony!"

Tony dressed quickly and rushed his brother to the John F. Kennedy Hospital, where doctors discovered Roger had a stone in his kidney. Four days later, however, he was completely well again. With treatment and medication, the stone was passed and Nancy appreciated that she had witnessed another and dramatic example of how much her husband and his twin meant to each other. She knew then that if they returned to Binghamton, Shirley and Tony would have to go with them.

On a clear and very warm morning in early May, a week after Roger was home from the hospital, the boys were moving slowly through the Philadelphia rush hour traffic in Roger's Ford. The girls already were at work, Shirley at her bank and Nancy at the insurace company. Roger chose this moment to test his brother, who was reading the baseball news.

"You know, Tony, I still haven't found myself."

"What do you mean?"

"Well, most of my life I've worked hard and never minded it. Now, I dread going to the office and I'm not much good at this job. I want to find something where I can work hard and be happy. And if I can't be completely happy, then at least I want to be in a job where I can get up in the morning and not hate going to work.

"Do you realize that in the last three years I've had six jobs," Roger continued. "I don't know what has happened to me. I want to settle down in one thing."

Tony nodded and asked, "You think we're in the wrong business?"

"I know I am," Roger answered quickly. "I think Uncle Lou was right. He told Nancy that I belong in a business where the public comes to me, not where I have to go out and sell them. In my own business I would be more relaxed and I know that then I could sell. I'm positive of it, Tony."

"Rog, I feel the same way. I've felt this a long time, too."

"Why haven't you said something?"

"I was afraid you would think we've done too much jumping around."

"We have. Only we still haven't made the right move."

"Do you want to go back to Binghamton?"

"Yes."

"Where people already know us."

"Yes."

"And start our own business?"

"Yes."

"Something that will make us a lot of money!"

"And something of which we can be proud," Roger said. "Something that we can build."

"We can open a market, Rog."

"Why not? We both know the business."

"We'll sell fresh meats, cheeses and fruits—"

"Your dad will be our butcher."

"And the girls can help out until we get going."

"Tony," said Roger, turning to face his brother, "we've got to make it go. This is it for us."

"We'll open at eight in the morning, and we won't close until ten o'clock at night," Tony answered. "And we'll be open seven days a week."

"Good, that's good," and now Roger couldn't wait to tell Nancy this good news, that he and Tony—at age twenty-nine —were about to become business partners.

The Twin Market opened for business July 22, 1967, a sunny and hot day, which boosted watermelon and ice cream sales. In a vacant lot alongside the store, which had been decorated with red, white and blue rented bunting, was a mobile van from radio station WNBF, and every half hour a disc jockey announced the location south of Binghamton on a four-lane approach route. He concluded each commercial with the imperative, "Come on out and meet the twins."

Meanwhile, inside the low, cinder-block building were the proud storekeepers giving away souvenir note pads, pens, balloons and jug milk at three cents below cost. At the butcher's block was Joe Milasi, and behind the checkout counters were the retired secretaries, Nancy and Shirley.

The grand opening was the culmination of an exacting, often frustrating campaign that had begun eight weeks before with Tony and Roger borrowing a produce truck to move themselves. There were three round trips to complete the transfer, and this time the families settled in apartments removed from each other by a ten-minute drive. Tony had found a modern, carpeted three-room unit in Johnson City, close by Shirley's parents. Roger chose an older, five-room apartment in Binghamton, pleased that there was a room for the baby, due in October.

They had pushed hard to get ready, first securing the location, then taking a bank loan, hiring a lawyer and accountant, buying a cash register and a cooler for the fruits and vegetables, painting the store inside, laying a tile floor, lining up wholesalers, deliverers and, finally, stocking the shelves. Yet, neither of them minded their long hours, because they were always together and building something entirely theirs.

So, their beginnings were impressive and self-satisfying. By summer's end they showed a small profit, but because their debts plus overhead were substantial, this net was never realized.

To escape a rent that they realized too late was unfair, the brothers now decided to reopen in the Seventh Ward, where the old Italians complained they no longer had a delicatessen catering to their singular tastes. In the final week of October 1967, the Twin Market sign, a gift of the Pepsi Cola Company, was hung above 115½ Susquehanna, at the corner of Carroll and Susquehanna Streets.

There were a number of romantic ironies that tied the twins to this corner. Here, over sixty years before, John Milasi had had his first business; here, in his brother's store, Joe Milasi had learned his trade; and here, too, Tony had suffered the indignity of having to pay for penny candy in his uncle's place of business. Then, just across Carroll Street at Number 47, Tony had spent the best of his boyhood years, and each day now he and Roger would eat a hot lunch there, set for them by an invigorated, smiling Pauline Milasi.

In this location, with its storehouse of happy memories, the brothers absorbed the good will of a neighborhood that still remembered the "old Milasi's," and they easily trebled their weekly receipts. Roger was sure his good furtune had begun back on October 18 at 4:15 A.M. when Stephanie Ann Brooks made him a father. She was born normally, if noisily, at General Hospital where twenty-nine years before, when it was the City Hospital, an uncomfortable Jules Brooks had learned he had fathered twins.

Now further lengthening the string of unlikely events, Jules Brooks elected to return to Binghamton and become part of the boys' excitement. Shortly after Roger had relayed the news of the business partnership, he and Jennie had moved from Schenectady, taking a walkup apartment on Hawley Street in the ward. He explained his curious relocation by saying it brought him closer to his best sales territory. Whether this was the truth is immaterial; the fact is he became a daily caller at the market, pulling up in an old, two-tone green Dodge. He would sit in the car until one of the boys came out. He didn't want to go into the store, he said, for fear of offending Joe Milasi. But once, when Tony came out to talk, Jules said, "Look, you've got a father, and he's a good one. If anything should ever happen to him, though—well, if you feel then you want to call me Dad, that will be all right with me."

They had all come full cycle. Pauline and Joe Milasi again had the store as the central force in their lives, and Tony as they always had hoped, close by, with the stability of a good marriage and business.

Shirley and Nancy were near their family homes and among girl friends from their high school years; moreover, for the first time, the two couples had a future to which they could look expectantly. All agreed that one day soon the store would provide a comfortable living.

It was Roger, though, who secretly considered himself the biggest gainer. All about him now he had security and the "sense of family" of which the social worker Catherine Bittermann had spoken. There were Pauline and Joe, his in-laws (Nancy's father was the landlord of 115½ Susquehanna), his father and his own wife and child.

He was standing there one morning, in the aisle between the vegetable bin and the soap powders, and the smell of the fresh meats filled the store. He liked the aroma, and he liked these early morning midweek hours when he and Tony had time to make a pot of coffee on their hot plate and talk. Ahead of them were the Thanksgiving and Christmas holidays; their confident accountant assured them this was bonanza time. It was all a good feeling, and he agreed with Tony.

"All we have to do," his brother had said, "is put in the hours. The business is here."

But the hours were torture. They already were working a ninety-hour week with no days off, and Roger made Tony laugh when he said, "Anybody who suffers this way has got to be rewarded. It's God's way, Tony. He is testing us!"

There were others, even some members of their family, who also believed they were on trial. Several negative voices had warned Roger against a business alliance with Tony. This had happened back in the spring when each of them had driven home to Binghamton alone, to sound out a few relatives and friends on the idea of a market. What Roger heard had first shocked and later saddened him.

"Don't do it! Don't go into business with Tony," these voices counseled. "You don't know him, Roger. You only think you do. You're blind because you love him. But he won't work hard—he doesn't know what hard work is. He was that way in his father's store and in his own snack bar and whatever else he's gone into. Why should he be any different now?

"For your own good, don't do it! Be his brother, but don't be his partner. You'll both go broke. But even worse, Tony will break your heart!"

On his drive back to Somerdale that night Roger hadn't been able to tune out the terrible sound of the incriminating words. The accusations played over and over in his mind. He asked himself, who do they think they are? Telling me I don't know my brother! And because he had listened and hadn't argued with his brother's critics, he lapsed into guilt. He knew Tony never would have submitted as he had. Tony would have defended his twin.

When she saw him come through the door, Nancy knew something had gone poorly. "What happened? What's wrong, Roger?"

"They are," he said. "They don't know him, and so they make up lies."

"What do you mean? Who're you talking about?"

"Relatives. Troublemakers. God, you Italians are excitable!"

Saying this, he put his hands up to his face and began to cry softly. Nancy saw his thick shoulders slump and his upper body shook as he fought to hold back his sobs. He was defenseless against his tears. They slid down his face, proof of his disappointment. Standing there—confused, ashamed, feeling helpless—he suddenly began to retell the story. Typically, he told it not so much in anger or from a spirit of vindictiveness, but more in sadness and incredulity.

"Why do they tell *me?*" he asked, "And why don't they leave us alone? Why don't people want Tony and me to be together? My folks, your relatives and the others, why do they try to make me think that I shouldn't have found my brother? How can they even think it would be better for me, for us to be apart? Isn't that stupid!

"They don't understand us, Nancy. They don't know us: not at all. They don't have any idea what it means to be a twin, to share a life with your twin, to have his love. God, they are so stupid and small. Do they really expect me to believe that Tony will hurt me? He just couldn't. It simply is not in him to hurt me.

"Nance, we aren't like that. We're different. You know that, don't you? You have seen us—and how we are. You see that we are not like other brothers. We are both the *same*.

And if Tony is all that bad, then so am I. You don't believe that I am all those things they said Tony is, do you?

"I'm going to tell Tony what they said. We'll show them! We will make that store go. Then they'll see how Tony is, how he really is. Won't they?"

As he stood there rearranging the lettuce, Roger realized this was to be an easy day, because Tuesdays usually were slow. Knowing it would be light, Tony had told Mitch Pirozzi, a barber now with his own two-chair shop, to come around. They would go down the cellar where John Milasi once kept chickens and goats, and while they sat on packing cases, Mitch would cut their hair. Later, that evening, they had the Sons of Italy induction.

Since someone always had to mind the business, there were separate ceremonies. Roger went first, and his was in English. Tony's was in Italian, naturally, and at its completion the president of Principe del Piemonte Ereditario Lodge No. 487 shook his hand and handed him a twenty-three-dollar check for the cold meats that were the meeting refreshments.

Back in the store, Tony held the check up and told Roger, "See, and we'll get this every month they have a meeting."

"The business is here, Tony."

"Sure it is, Rog."

They both laughed, and in unison they said, "All we have to do is put in the hours!"

Ringing up the Sons of Italy check on the register, Tony had another thought. "Hey, Rog."

"What?"

"You close up tonight."

"Right. You open tomorrow, Tony."

22

A Summing Up

In any investigation directed toward measuring the effects of heredity and environment, the observation of twins affords an almost indispensable source of information.

—*James Shields.*

While the personal histories of Roger Brooks and Anthony Milasi are both unique and compelling, they provide more than just a human interest story. As dossiers of thirty-year-old separated monozygotics they represent an addition to the literature of twins and, more specifically, to the available evidence on the effects of heredity and environment. Indeed, a measure of the intrinsic appeal to their story comes in the challenge to first identify, and then seek causes for, their similarities and their differences, particularly those disparities in personality. Yet, even for the scientific investigator this is not a simple procedure, because both heredity and environment influence development. From the very beginning, forces within a child work together with forces outside to develop a personality. The question, therefore, becomes one of degree.

Consider the observation by Tony Milasi that he is "harder" than his brother, that he rarely cried as a boy and is better able to hold his emotions in check. Roger Brooks remembers that he often cried. He cried during movies, and almost any suffering or cruelty upset him. When his cousin Ray Elman aimed his air rifle at birds, Roger instinctively winced and had to turn away. And his Aunt Millie remembers that Roger was absolutely incapable of looking at a cripple in the street.

Since none of these latter examples sound as though the boy, Roger Brooks, was an identical twin to Tony Milasi or a son of Jules Brooks, what is the explanation? Is this a triumph of the environment? The answer must be a qualified yes. But even as I submit this evaluation, I am reminded that Tony once took the better part of a week to nurse a stray cat he had wounded with a BB gun, and though he was drawn by the excitement of a street gang he also sought out Ernie D'Aristotle, an intelligent and serious-minded friend, to be his homework partner. My point being that had Tony Milasi grown up close to Bessie Elman and with the ethical example set by Rabbi Morris Skop, he would have become a different man.

Ashley Montagu, the Princeton anthropologist, has said that living things are not results of action but rather of *interactions*. "Neither genes nor environment alone can produce development," Montagu said. "Both are necessary in interaction for development; it is the *interaction* that is the important part of the process, for the genes and environment are not simply parallel processes."

So, while the combination, or interaction, of Roger's genes and environment was producing a child who was emotional and sentimental, Tony Milasi was learning in his home and on the streets that the display of raw, unchecked emotion was a sign of weakness.

And yet, despite their dramatically disparate environments, these monozygotics at thirty years of age share a number of similar traits, characteristics and patterns of behavior. Born of the same egg and possessors of identical genes, they are, foremost, physically alike, even to their both being double-jointed and having identical cranky lower-right wisdom teeth.

Their voices too are similar, they share similar tastes in food, are temperate drinkers and have the same musical preferences, although Roger is alone in his appreciation of opera. Both are fond of sports, with baseball and professional football their favorites. Moreover, both are long sleepers, enjoy playing cards and going to the race track, and frequently they will share a Sunday football bet or a State Lottery ticket.

Since their meeting they have been obviously influencing each other, but it is nonetheless interesting that recently they both decided to give up smoking, suffer dieting together and allow their hair to grow reasonably long.

In adolescence, both brothers were followers rather than leaders, and neither was motivated to prove himself physically. But both played on organized basketball teams and spent many summer afternoons in a batter's box striving to master the curve ball. While Roger was with Ray Skop in Miami, Tony in Binghamton was hitting against Ernie D'Aristotle or Johnny Visconti; and the likelihood is that though far apart, these two scenes were played out on the very same afternoons.

Significantly, while neither twin thought of himself as an athlete, each judged himself to be a fair baseball player and was willing to argue the point with his brother.

Further, they both enjoyed the excitement of performing before others. After school Tony used to run errands for a local disc jockey and occasionally they would talk on the air. Roger was a GI master of ceremonies and later joined an amateur theater group. Both enjoyed being with people and, in describing their feelings, use similar language.*

In addition to their being closely alike in all these ways, they have virtually identical intelligence quotients, a fact that surprised them both, since the brothers had assumed Tony was the brighter by far. Their equality was confirmed when in the summer of 1967 they volunteered to take a full series of intelligence and personality tests. Following James Shields's injunction to "investigate and record" all cases of separated monozygotics, Tony and Roger had agreed to this

---

* Shields believes there is "something distinctive about the personality resemblance of certain twins that is almost diagnostic of monozygocity . . . a close similarity in many aspects of how they talk and in the rapport they make."

testing experience, but since someone had to mind the store, they took turns traveling to New York City for two days each. Their examiner was Dr. Solomon Machover, the chief psychologist at Kings County Hospital in Brooklyn, a 2,600-bed city institution said to be the second largest general hospital in the world.

Although Dr. Machover's background included thirty-eight years' experience in psychology, during which he had practiced, taught, lectured and done research in his field, he was examining his first pair of monozygotics reared apart. His initial surprise came on two early subtests of the Wechsler Adult Intelligence Scale, a standard intelligence examination.

In arithmetic, Roger scored a ten, an average grade. Tony, however, scored a fifteen, a mark that is equaled or bettered by only five in a hundred adults. Then, in digit retention, Tony again scored well; he repeated eight numbers forward and six numbers backward, a mark that is reached or bettered by only ninety in a thousand. But here, Roger's score was phenomenal: he repeated nine numbers forward and eight in reverse, a performance that is matched or bettered by only *one in a thousand* and, according to the physchologist, "is normally beyond the competence of any but quite superior intellects."

Analyzing these results, Tony's superior arithmetic grade seems easily explained. He sharpened his skills by working in his father's store, having to add long lists of sums and make change rapidly. The reasons for Roger's prowess are not as simple or obvious.

When I asked Roger how he was able to do well enough to rank with "superior intellects," he explained that Rodney had taught him to equate numbers with people. Thus, the successive digits two-four he had associated with Nancy, who was in her early twenties; the combination of seven-three he linked with Pauline Milasi and a set beginning with a nine reminded him that Sam Elman was in his nineties.

Dr. Machover remarked that this last subtest showed that Roger quite clearly "has a greater capacity than Tony to exclude distraction." When he said this, I thought back to the scene of Roger sitting alone in the abandoned automobile in Schenectady, waiting for Jules to come home; of the hours he lay on his bed, alienated, lost in his fantasies and, finally, on peaceful Tarawa. He could credit his environment for this small blessing, for as a boy the reality of life around him was too severe and unpleasant; he had been forced to withdraw, to shut out what he couldn't endure.

On all the other intelligence subtests, the brothers seemingly alternated, with first one, then the other doing better. Tony was the leader in the verbal tests, scoring slightly higher than his twin on Vocabulary, Information and Comprehension. Roger was superior in those requiring performance, such as Picture Completion, where the subject has to discover a missing part, and Block Design, where he must match geometric shapes. Based on these results, the psychologist reported Roger "is the more active thinker and better in reasoning."

There is no mystery to Tony's higher scores in the verbal categories. His was the more stable home life and he had the advantage of a single school system, while Roger was shunted about, attending eight different schools in eleven years and never finishing high school until he entered the service. It is remarkable that Roger was able to keep up with his twin. But then, in the summary grading to determine the whole IQ, Roger finished with a high average score of 109, while Tony graded 108. However, since this one-point difference was within the range of experimental error, their IQs could fairly be considered identical, a fact that Solomon Machover called "remarkable!"

"It was gilding the lily of all reasonable expectation for these twins to score so evenly," he explained. "Their exposure to most dissimilar environments seems to have had no overall effect upon the IQ level. The environment apparently was effective in individualizing their specific abilities—such as these required for arithmetic, digit retention and the like— but the differences then compensate each other, leaving them equal in the level of general intelligence."

Though they had traveled by greatly different routes, Roger Brooks and Tony Milasi had arrived at the same overall intelligence level—and this was unexpected if only because the manifold insecurity in Roger's early environment gave Tony at least a two-year head start on his twin. For on his twenty-four-month examination at St. Joseph's Infant Home, Roger was unable to properly combine words and was judged *retarded* by five months.

It is interesting therefore to speculate on the meaning of these identical test scores. Do they, in fact, represent a signal victory for heredity? Were the twins born with a predisposition for intelligence equivalency, so that not even their uncommon learning experiences could appreciably alter their IQs? Perhaps the scores demonstrate that though Roger Brooks was denied the chance to reach his full potential, Tony Milasi, for reasons of both heredity and environment, has squandered his. As his friend Ernie D'Aristotle said, he wasn't dumb about anything, he "just wouldn't apply himself and wasn't willing to pay the price to be outstanding at any one time."

Following their nearly identical IQ scores, Dr. Machover was at least forewarned; still, he was nonplussed over many of the answers given by Tony and Roger on his Sentence Completion questionnaire. Made up of forty-nine open-ended sentences beginnings, such as "I secretly————" and "My greatest fear————," the test is used to elicit attitudes, fears and desires, and when the psychologist placed the Milasi-Brooks forms alongside each other, he shook his head.

"Some of these similarities are actually hair-raising," he said.

To the sentence stem "If I could live my life over I would . . ." Tony had added, *". . . complete my education."* Roger wrote, *". . . have gone further in school."*

Tony stated, "My greatest fear *. . . is not to succeed."*

Roger said, "My greatest fear *. . . is that I want to be a successful person."*

On some, even their phrasing was alike. "I secretly . . . *would like to be an actor,"* Tony answered; Roger had added *. . . would have liked to been an actor."*

Where Tony wrote he daydreamed about *"being successful,"* Roger answered he liked to daydream of *"success."*

And both completed the fragment "It's not healthy to . . ." with the responses ". . . drink" and ". . . drink extensively."*

Solomon Machover found these *hair-raising* because it would be "absurd to ascribe common attitudes to genes," and their radically different early experiences should logically have produced disparate viewpoints and answers.

"One could be forgiven for suspecting collusion," the doctor told me. "Only this seems out of the question, because

---

* Since Roger's adoptive mother had married an alcoholic, requiring that he be sent to a boarding school at 12, there is some rationale for his answer; Tony's response has no ready explanation.

when Tony was examined, Roger was upstate; when Roger was examined, Tony already had returned to Binghamton."

This, of course, was the case. I had met Tony at Newark Airport on a Sunday night in July two years ago, and he stayed in my home in New Jersey until Tuesday night, the two of us commuting to Brooklyn by car. Roger then arrived late Tuesday and remained through Friday, when he and I drove back to Binghamton together. There was no way they could even have compared their testing experiences until after they both had been examined.

Throughout the four days that I traveled to Brooklyn, first with Tony and then with Roger, and largely followed the same routines with each, I was a witness to an unusual exhibition of their natural affinity and once I had reported my observations to Solomon Machover, the psychologist dismissed his notion of possible collusion. On our very first morning, Tony and I drove down the West Side Highway, following the curve of Manhattan Island south to the Battery and through the tunnel into Brooklyn. As we rode along, Tony stared out the window, occasionally making a comment. He remarked on:

1. *The New York Times* West Side plant. When he saw the sign, he asked, "Is that where the paper is printed?"

2. The luxury liners in their berths. "Before I die, that's what I want to do, take an ocean cruise!"

3. The former Brooklyn Dodgers baseball stadium. Once we had cleared the Battery Tunnel, he asked, "Will we pass Ebbets Field?" I answered that it no longer is standing.

About midway in our trip on the second morning, he began discussing the previous day's tests. He was particularly taken with one of the completion sentences, Number Four, which began, "My hero is————."

"I didn't know who to put," he said. "I don't really have a hero. So I put Frank Sinatra."

It wasn't until forty-eight hours later, after I had made two round trips with Roger, that any of this seemed either noteworthy or meaningful. But on that first morning with Roger he, too, paid special attention to:

1. *The New York Times* West Side plant. "Hey, the *Times*. That's where the paper is printed?"

2. The cruise ships tied up to their piers. "I've always wanted to take one of those cruises."

3. The former Brooklyn Dodgers baseball stadium. "Is Ebbets Field near here? Will we pass it?"

The following morning Roger began to talk about the tests. He said that he had left one of the sentence completions blank.

"Which one?" I asked.

"Number Four, 'My hero is————.' "

"Why?"

"I don't have a hero," he said. "Do you think that's all right, that I left it blank?"

Dr. Machover listened to my account with a bemused smile on his face and then remarked that there were "startling agreements" between these identical twins. He referred to their completion answers regarding money.

Roger had said, "I worry over . . . *money*," and "I do not understand what makes me . . . *worry over money*."

Similarly, Tony answered, "I would like to be like . . . *a millionaire*," and "I hate . . . *to lose money*."

In a later report, the psychologist attempted to explain certain of the almost identical responses. After citing their common tendency toward exhibitionism, with both secretly wanting to be actors, and a preoccupation with success, Dr. Machover pointed to the fact the brothers had now been together four years and recently had opened a business: "these circumstances might suffice for a like concern with money and success."

As to the exhibitionistic leanings, he recalled that at the time of their first meeting, they had been on several radio and television interview shows. "These appearances, plus the feeding of this drive by common experiences could account for their answers about wanting to be actors.

"Among their experiences is that a book is being written about them. It would not be surprising if the twins harbored the fantasy they might be invited to star in a movie version of their lives."

To Tony Milasi this was no fantasy! He talked as though it was a real possibility, and though Roger pretended not to join in this dream-wish, he never discouraged his brother. Still, this was nothing new with the brothers. Tony freely acknowledged that he was a ham, an extrovert who thrived on the challenge of salesmanship. He long had nourished the dream of becoming a disc jockey who would be discovered. He believed performing was his hidden talent, a second nature waiting to be recognized by some director; and Roger admitted he had been thrilled by the applause that he had received in his amateur productions. The newspaper review praising his one lead role was laminated and safely tucked into his scrapbook.

So this common desire, this hope for a chance to claim center stage in a star role, actually predated their meeting and therefore must necessarily be said to have at least some grounding in heredity.

Following the Sentence Completion test, the brothers filled out a long vocational preference questionnaire, titled the Kuder Preference Record. The psychologist again found the results *astonishing! enormously striking!*

He began his evaluation by remarking that apart from musical interests, the last place he expected to find "even traces" of genetic factors was in these listings, since the development of interests is subject to circumstances in the environment. Yet, in ten broadly based categories, the twins differed by one position—or not at all—in eight of their choices. Moreover, they were identical in three positions.

"In light of the extraordinary differences in environmental influences, the degree of similarity in this pattern must be termed remarkable," the psychologist stated. "One can only assume that genetic factors may well be more influential than anticipated, at least with these twins."

Through their answers to the preference questions the twins established these interest patterns:

ROGER	TONY
1. Social Service	1. Musical
2. Musical	2. Persuasive
3. Clerical	3. Clerical
4. Literary	4. Literary
5. Computational	5. Computational
6. Scientific	6. Social Service
7. Artistic	7. Scientific
8. Outdoors	8. Artistic
9. Mechanical	9. Outdoors
10. Persuasive	10. Mechanical

The doctor was fascinated because despite their brief association with music and their limited schooling, both showed a special interest in music and literature. Though neither is a reader, they have as adults had a desire to be better read. When he lived in New Jersey, Tony had joined a book club and read in most of the books he received, yet seldom finished any of them.

Roger's Aunt Mildred recalls, with exasperation, how she had encouraged her favorite nephew to read. She remembers only one time when he was swept up by fine writing. It was shortly after his air force discharge, and she loaned him *Catcher in the Rye*. He read it through in one night and telephoned her to celebrate the J. D. Salinger style.

"Why, Aunt Millie," he told her, "if you could only get me more books like that, I'd read them all."

"I could have brained him," Mildred Brooks said. "He had no appreciation that a book this beautifully done isn't published every other week."

Roger Brooks and Anthony Milasi have similar interests, IQs and preoccupations; they suffer over the same inadequacies, share kindred secret desires and standing side by side they have fooled even canny old Pauline Milasi. Where then are the differences between these brothers whose boyhood environments differed so dramatically?

To begin, though both are basically followers, Tony is the unquestioned intrapair leader. He is the first to enter a room, the first to speak and he works his will over his brother as regularly and nakedly as he once did in his own home. Nancy Brooks is so envious of her brother-in-law's persuasion she has complained, "I can't get Roger to take the garbage out, but he'll do anything for Tony; and there are things he tells Tony but won't tell me, his own wife!"

Tony naturally assumed the leader's role because he is easily the more aggressive. This is true because he grew up not only in a secure family situation but also in the Seventh Ward. It was inevitable that Tony at an early age would become street-wise; so he smoked before Roger, was the first to drink and at fifteen, two years in advance of his twin, experienced sex for the first time.

Moreoever, while Roger as an adolescent was naive and unsure, never dating but one girl at a time, Tony always had several he was seeing and wasn't averse to meeting still another. Nor was he bashful about discussing his companions. As he truthfully wrote Roger in his very first letter, he was "girl crazy."

When the brothers are out together, whether in a stag group or with their wives and other couples, it is Tony who is the storyteller; Tony picks up the check and tips and Tony makes the impression on people. One of Tony's Binghamton friends has said of Roger, "He seems like the younger brother." It is Tony, too, who keeps up with the new rock singers or the latest men's fashions and on New Year's Eve goes to the big, lively party. Roger and Nancy, meanwhile, are at the young couples' dance at the Catholic Youth Organization hall.

Roger doesn't have to hang back, playing the younger brother role, because when he is among close friends and is encouraged, he can be equally entertaining. He mimics well, has routines and does imitations of dim-witted customers who regularly shop in the Twin Market. He is also a good storyteller; his Jewish dialect is natural and excellent and his Italian is laughable because it is so poor.

Tony doesn't consciously or spitefully inhibit his twin, but he does still have a need to be the leader, the *number one*. And even though he wears a white apron behind the butcher's counter by day, he must by night play the part of a swinger and a rogue, the same pretender whom Mark Frattalone met and described to Roger Brooks in 1962. So he buys a more expensive car than his brother (a Chrysler to Roger's Ford), owns three suits to Roger's one and is consistently the better and neater dressed, both in and out of the store. Further, though both are overweight, Tony generally is ten pounds lighter than Roger.

By continuing to be both personally unkempt and sloppy around the home, Roger is still rebelling, being hostile in the only *safe* way that he knows. He is venting his frustration at being unsuccessful, at being too heavy, at not having a college education and, most likely, at not being as aggressive and smooth as his brother.

Once, after he had moved to Binghamton, Roger saw Tony argue with a car dealer for an hour to save two hundred dollars on the purchase price. He described his brother's performance as "beautiful," using one of Tony's favorite adjectives.

My own view is that Tony's strong need to be a braggadocio and to dominate his twin are a result of *his* personal frustrations, while Roger's typically manifest themselves in a more unobtrusive manner. And further, I believe that the same inhibitions and repressions that keep Roger from being Tony's rival as a living room raconteur also prohibit him from temper fits and a release of his emotions through aggressive outbursts.

"If only he could learn to swear," Nancy Brooks once complained.

Another clear disparity between these identical partners is in the pattern of their jobs, which was reflected in the vocational preference test.

Tony grew up close to the store; from his earliest he was taught to wait on customers. By the time he was ten, he was a junior salesman. He knew how to coax another item onto a housewife's shopping list, asking, "Anything else? Fresh tomatoes? Nice young chickens today . . ." Later, he collected bills for his father, then sold real estate, books, insurance. Like Jules Brooks, he was an inveterate salesman and, importantly, believed he could sell anything!

So, on the preference questionnaire the major difference between the brothers was that Tony listed *Persuasive* as his second choice. Roger ranked it last, as rightly he should have. The memory of his sales defeats in Miami and Philadelphia were still fresh with him, and after the rejection he had experienced through his boyhood and into his teen years, he could no longer face the inevitable rebuffing that is a part of nearly every salesman's life.

Roger's first preference was *Social Service,* where he scored a ninety-nine and, in terms of interest in social work, ranks in the top 1 per cent. Perhaps the best way to accentuate this departure is to ask these direct questions:

● Could Tony Milasi ever be a social worker? Surely, not by his own choice.

● Could Roger Brooks sell world knowledge books door-to-door, going from one strange home to another? I seriously doubt it! Roger remembers that he had let several insurance sales slip away in Philadelphia because he actually had agreed with the doctors, that they should take more time to consider their decision.

Though reluctant to acknowledge the fact, Tony Milasi and Roger Brooks are different. As a result of their differing environments, they have diverse personalities. The distinctions are plain and readily identifiable.

Because of the disorganization and the lack of love in his early years, Roger developed compassion and empathy; he also learned great respect for the social work profession. When I once asked him how he was able to look back on his boyhood without feeling bitter, he said he believed the Family Service workers most likely were responsible.

On the Sentence Completion questionnaire he had answered, "I love . . . *life*," and "I hate . . . *no one*."*

"I just don't hate," Roger told me. "Maybe it's a weakness of mine. Anyway, I don't ever get angry enough to hate."

Bessie Elman's example was another contributor to Roger's sensitivity and social awareness. He remembers many times when she consoled him with the counsel, "It is better to pity than hate, my grandson." Further, Bessie was a volunteer at a hospital where she massaged the limbs of crippled children, and on the day that Miami employed its first Negro bus driver Bessie insisted on taking a ride, just to shake the black man's hand in welcome.

Tony Milasi is not a bigot. He grew up with Negroes as his neighbors and enlisted in the navy with a black buddy. Yet, like a great number of other Americans, he does not fully understand the civil rights struggle. During the 1967 summer riots in Detroit he was of the opinion that "all looters should be machine-gunned."

Roger Brooks is simply incapable of holding this view. Moreover, it is impossible to spend time with him and not become aware of his sensitivity.

During our two days together at Kings County Hospital, Roger and I walked the grounds of the huge, sprawling community. Roger continually stared up at the barred windows of the psychiatric section. He wondered aloud at the anguish that was locked away inside those rooms. Unlike his brother, he reacted to all the sights and sounds of this other world— to the police and ambulance sirens, to the indigent patients in their blue cotton pajamas whom we passed in the long corridors and the visitors sitting stoically in the central lobby on wooden benches.

I remember, in particular, one evening. It had been a

---

* Tony had answered, "I love . . . *my wife*," and "I hate . . . *to lose money*."

humid day and was still uncomfortably warm at 5:30 P.M. as we walked toward our locked car. Suddenly, from somewhere above us in one of the buildings, a patient began to excoriate Roger and me, doctors, nurses and any other passersby who came within his line of vision. He unleashed one obscenity after another, halting only to laugh at our cringing displeasure.

His outcries seemed to force everyone to walk faster; everyone, that is, except Roger. He stood in the center of the broad sidewalk and looked up until he found the figure behind the shrill voice. When he saw that it was a boy of eleven or twelve, there was sadness in his eyes. He continued to stand there, shaking his head and asking, "What makes a boy be like that? Why? Why does he say those awful things?"

During the ride home, he spoke of the tormented boy in the window and how he would like to work with disturbed children. He reminded me how much he had enjoyed teaching Jewish Sunday School in the air force and, for the first time, told me of a summer when he had worked as a counselor in a camp operated by his Aunt Frances Elman.

"I've always liked children," he said. "I like working with them, and helping them."

This difference between the brothers in sensitivity, and emotional maturity as well, was also reflected in their psychological tests. Dr. Machover explained there was an obvious correlation between their experiences during early development and their degree of sensitivity. He was impressed then that it was Roger, the product of the unstable home life, who emerged as "the more restrained, realistic and having the more mature attitude."

The psychologist cited certain of the completions in support of his opinion.

Where Roger wrote it wasn't true *all men are dishonest,* Tony said it wasn't true *life is a bowl of cherries.* Where Roger said, "My health is . . . *good,*" Tony answered that his was *excellent.* And when Roger judged himself *average,* Tony said that compared with others he was *tall.*

Asked what he would do if he had a lot of money, Roger said he would *invest.* Tony wrote, "I would *retire.*"

Tony said a husband should be *considerate.* Roger said that above all, he must be *responsible!*

Of course, it is their varying concerns over responsibility

that also sets these monozygotic partners apart. For Roger, being responsible was a way to keep his life on an even plane and to win approbation. To Tony, responsibility was a hair shirt that he flung off whenever it chafed. It therefore is inconceivable to me that Tony could ever have punched a time clock in an aircraft factory for three years—but Roger did. Tony never could have worked a fifty-two-hour week in a highway discount center for eighty-five dollars—but Roger did. And where Roger sent home a monthly allotment of twenty-five dollars all the time he was in the service, Tony periodically wrote home asking for a loan. Until he was married, Roger always had a savings account; Tony never had one.

"Because of his boyhood environment, Roger equated responsibility and conscientiousness with the adequate male personality," Dr. Machover said. "It became for him a prime characteristic, and there is this correlation between his stress on responsibility and the characterization of his father as less than responsible.

"Moreover, he regards the failure of the marriage between his biological father and adoptive mother as largely the consequence of his father's lacking responsibility."

For all these reasons, Dr. Machover believes Roger repressed "powerful trends toward irresponsibility." Tony, however, had neither a need to win the love of his family nor any reason to repress his predispositions and so bears a striking personality resemblance to his biological father in the areas of conscientiousness and responsibility.

Following his first half-dozen meetings with Jules Brooks, Tony himself remarked, "Boy, heredity must have a lot to do with me because I'm so much like Jules."

This was not the first such observation. Several of those who know both men have noted their parallels. Jules Brooks is a glib, persuasive talker; so is Tony Milasi. Both have at times been moderately successful as salesmen and both have a roguish charm appealing to women. Where Jules had told me, "I haven't worked as hard as other men," Tony explained, "I just don't enjoy breaking my back."

Tony hasn't persevered in any job since coming home from the navy. His pattern is the same wherever he has worked: initial success, but when the challenge is increased, Tony leaves in search of something that is easier, pays more and will reward him more quickly. Unlike his monozygotic twin, Tony Milasi has no capacity to tolerate frustration and is incapable of mastering anxiety. His environment has preconditioned him to depend on his family and, should all else fail him, he looks for what Solomon Machover describes as "the essentially magical, unearned and extravagantly happy ending."

Thus, Tony anticipates—he expects—that he will get a new bike, a new car, that at his court martial the chief witness against him will recant, that the girl he pursues will learn to love him and that he will find his lost twin, who very likely will be rich!

Dr. Machover saw repeated evidence of this personality flaw in the various test results, but it was most plain and dramatically represented in the Thematic Apperception Test, where the brothers were required to interpret a series of black-and-white drawings. Tony's responses were conventional and brief. His fifteen stories averaged 85 words—Roger's averaged 202 words—and there was an invariable recourse to the simplistic and indulgently happy finish.

A plate depicting a youth studying a violin becomes for Tony Milasi the account of a boy who listened to his father's advice, gave up his desire to play the piano and became a great concert violinist. In another drawing, he sees a young girl who is determined not to live a life of drudgery, as did her mother. She goes to college, marries an educated man and then helps her parents. A third plate represents a girl exhausted from an examination. Tony explained that after a few days she learns "she not only passed the exam, she got a very good mark."

"It is evident," wrote Dr. Machover, "that Tony has developed little tolerance for frustration, for delay of need gratification, for tension and anxiety. For him the passage between felt need and gratification is a short circuit that circumvents the arduousness of genuine and realistic effort. It substitutes, instead, the hope and fantasy of direct, immediate and extravagant success.

"Whether through maternal overattention or out of fear of reprisal by an authoritarian father, he would seem to have failed to develop security and confidence in the meaningfulness of his own constructive efforts."

There can be no argument that Tony Milasi's boyhood was

marked with maternal overattention. Beginning with Pauline Milasi's insistence that the Sisters at St. Mary's enroll her Anthony while still only five, and continuing with the seven bicycles and the $150 trumpet with *private* lessons, the boy always knew that whatever his challenge, he could look to his mother, his constant support, his advocate, his champion. But because she made few demands of him, he was denied the value of a natural maturing, with all its attendant struggles. He had no opportunity to learn the "meaningfulness of his own constructive efforts."

Oddly, it was Ernie D'Aristotle who first saw this in his friend. He reported that "Tony just wouldn't apply himself."

In comparing Roger's Thematic Apperception responses with his brother's, Dr. Machover begins by stating that both quantitative and qualitative patterns "reflect profound psychological differences." Where Tony's interpretations suffered from "a poverty of ideas" Roger's contained "a richness and subtlety" that quite naturally meant his were the longer stories, averaging more than two hundred words. The psychologist singled out their "white-plate" fantasies to illustrate his point. Each was asked to view a blank white card and describe what he visualized.

Tony set up a simple Frank Merriwell cliché. He saw a baseball game with the home team behind by three runs in the last of the ninth inning. The bases are loaded, there are two out and the count on the batter goes to three-and-two. On the next pitch the batter swings and drives the ball into the center field stands for a game-winning home run.

"Need I say more, doc, to an ending like that?" Tony asked.

Roger, curiously, is no less interested in achievement and distinction than Tony. However, his story takes a strikingly different form. It is told in flashback. He sees a man driven to make something of himself, who decides upon a stage career. He knows the chance for success is small, yet he pushes himself, goes to college and majors in drama. He also works nights, as a bus boy or waiter. He gets his first break in a walk-on part with only a few speaking lines. Fortunately, he has a nice voice, is likable and well groomed. He makes friends with the right people, gets another, bigger break and goes on to become a successful actor.

"From there on, the world is in his hands," Roger said,

"and now he's standing under a marquee on Broadway looking up at his name in the bright lights—that's the white card. He remembers how hard he has worked and he tells himself that it was all worth it."

In his home environment, Roger learned that he shouldn't expect too much from life, surely not happy endings, and if he meant to be even the least bit successful he had better develop a sense of responsibility. To comply, Dr. Machover believes he suppressed "underlying trends toward irresponsibility" and became a harder, more constant worker than his twin.

There is, however, another factor that contributed to this circumstance. Because of the rejection and insecurity that marked his early years, Roger was less sure than Tony of his own worth. Dr. Machover found him "overready to repudiate his views." His goals therefore were more modest than Tony's. He was willing to settle for smaller wages and longer hours. He was ready to be a plodder, taking pride in any advancement. Still, his were more realistic ambitions, and in his Thematic Apperception plates he didn't see anyone overcoming a life of drudgery through marriage or a boy violinist becoming a great concert performer. In fact, his "violin plate" could fairly be interpreted as autobiographical.

The boy had hoped for a trumpet or saxophone. Knowing a violin was the last thing he wanted, his parents nonetheless insisted on the instrument.

"What happened then?" Dr. Machover asked.

"Nothing. The boy never played, he never became a musician, because of that violin."

Implicit in Roger's story, the psychologist explained, are the themes of parental coercion and a rejection of the boy as a talented, independent personality. Roger doesn't remember that he was ever denied a saxophone, but he recalls that no one ever suggested that he join his step-brother, Rodney, in learning to play a musical instrument. He also remembers that he often heard the criticism, "Poor Roger, he doesn't have the Elman brains."

Dr. Machover further described Roger as the realist "who seems keenly, painfully aware of the obstacles on the path to achievement; more oriented toward the confrontation of his weaknesses and doubts. In general, he seems much the more realistically oriented and differentiated personality."

Roger, unquestionably, took the best from his home life, growing up with what a psychiatrist friend, Dr. Milton Gross, has called "good stuff." He survived, the doctor added, "to become a bedrock human. As poor as the environment might have been, he is what he is because of everything that he took from it."

Following a review of my typed notes, totaling 170 pages, Dr. Gross remarked, "Had Roger been brutalized along the way, he might well have been antisocial in a violent manner. I mean, he could possibly have become a murderer."

Yet, with the tutoring and example of a Bessie Elman, the Rabbi Skop family, his Aunt Mildred Brooks, his mother and the influential social workers, Roger absorbed a special sensitivity, a sense of human dignity and of right and wrong. He took the positives that his environment held out, while he walled out and repressed the negatives. They are still with him, though: just beneath the surface and ever-present in his subconscious. The psychologist saw this clearly in Roger's Thematic Apperception Test responses, where rejection and separation were central to ten of his thirteen plots. A third recurrent story line was the lack of a responsible, supportive father. Significantly, Tony made no mention of any of these.

Dr. Machover explained the most impressive of Roger's stories of abandonment was one he created for a woodcut reproduction showing the gaunt figure of a man standing alone among gravestones. It was impressive, the psychologist added, because "it hints at the persistence and profundity of the trauma of early abandonment."

Roger identified the man as a hermit or miser who frequents the graveyard across from his home. He derives a certain pleasure from scanning the names on the stones. On this night, he discovers a stone bearing his own last name. It is actually the grave of his mother, and Roger continued: "He realized that he never had known his mother; he has never had any love, any companionship, any affection, and this is a man about seventy years old. In the picture, right now, he is a little boy crying. He wishes he wasn't such a miserable, unhappy person."

"It is very clear," Dr. Machover summarized, "that Roger's motivating values, as well as his life style, focus around the crucial significance of his early, traumatic separa-

tion. Obviously, it has intensified his need for maternal love
—and made him exquisitely sensitive to its quality."

This surely sets Roger Brooks apart from Tony Milasi, for
there has been no lack of mother love in the life of Pauline
Milasi's only son.

They are alike in so many ways, sharing common interests,
tastes, ambitions, IQs, secret desires, a drive toward exhibitionism and, lending a touch of the bizarre, similar physical
scars. They remain obstinately alike despite their strikingly
disparate experiences but, in the end, it is their differences
that truly give meaning and a particular poignancy to their
story.

The very fact their personalities differ is evidence of the
nongenetical effects, teaching that environment and adult
counsel do matter. This then is the lesson that these case histories add to the literature on heredity and environment: that
a Roger Brooks, having endured abandonment, rejection and
emotional trauma for his first seventeen years, can still become the more mature, realistic and sensitive of the brothers,
the twin with a social conscience and a dedicated enemy of
prejudice.

For me, though, the pathos implicit in Roger's story is the
larger tragedy—what he might have become had he known
the security of a normal home life and the complete, intelligently motivated, natural love of his biological mother.

As I had worked along, piecing together their two lives, I
realized that to complete my story I must somehow find the
biological mother. We all wondered what she looked like,
where she was living and how well or poorly she was doing. I
especially wanted to know whether she was aware her twins
had found each other. I wondered, too, what her reaction
might be if she were to read the psychologist's line: "the crucial significance of Roger's early separation obviously has intensified his need for maternal love."

I began to look for her in northern New York State where
she and her family had lived most of their lives. On my second day, in the cellar of a cramped, heavily trafficked county
building, I found the key to her whereabouts. A patient civil
servant led me to a file that included copies of her marriage
license to Renato; police and children's court correspondence
describing the Binghamton hotel fire, Roger's hospitalization,

his assignment to St. Joseph's Home, subsequent transfer to the foster home and, finally, his release to Mildred and Jules Brooks. In another welfare dossier was the unhappy account of Maria's marriage record, her trial for child neglect and, at the close of World War II, her divorce from Renato. A friend of the family then supplied Maria's present address, esplaining, "She's remarried and has built a whole new life. Around here, her past is dead, if you know what I mean."

When I drove up late that next afternoon I saw her in the side yard, alongside a pastel-colored ranch home. She was wearing a bright orange shift and her arms and legs were brown from the summer sun. Her sandy-colored hair was tied back with an old silk stocking that was close to the color of her horn-rimmed glasses. I'm not sure what I had expected, but I remember that all my first impressions were positive. She was tall, and although in her early fifties, had kept her spare figure.

She was watering down a blacktop driveway that was freshly surfaced, and as I approached she turned off the hose so we could talk. I told her why I had come all this distance and I remember how she just shook her head.

"No, I don't want to talk about that," she said very softly. "It was just something that happened. It was all long ago and is best forgotten."

This answer surprised me. "How can you *forget?*" I wanted to ask. But even more perplexing to me was the indifferent delivery of her little speech. She expended almost no emotion, and seemed to be neither threatened nor ashamed. After twenty-nine years a stranger had stepped from a dust-covered car with out-of-state license plates to ask about her illegitimate, abandoned twins, and from the expression she permitted to register, I might have been a traveler asking directions. She stood perfectly still then, with her hands on her hips, and stared down at the fresh blacktop.

"I'd like to help you," she said, "only there is nothing to say."

"You wouldn't only be helping me," I said quickly. "It's the boys who want you to tell me how everything happened. They want to know; they feel you owe them this much."

"No," she repeated, shaking her head even harder this time. "I don't want any of that to come out. Not many people know and why should they? Am I supposed to go around broadcasting it?"

"You don't seem to understand," I said, and I had become impatient. "The boys are asking you to cooperate. You're not going to turn your back on them again, are you?"

She said nothing; she only tamped at the drive with her right shoe and slowly shook her head. Finally, in a whisper, she said, "There are millions of children who never know their parents."

Since the silence that now surrounded this last remark was particularly uncomfortable for me, I began to talk. It grew to a monologue as I explained how much I already knew about her life. I mentioned her early troubles with Renato, how badly he had always treated her and of his prison record. I touched on Jules and her children's court experience, and said that hers had been a hard life.

"I'm the one who should be writing a book," she said. "You know, years ago they wanted me to write one."

I changed the subject to ask, "Did you know the boys had found each other?"

"Oh, yes. My sister saw it and sent me a newspaper clipping with their picture."

"Had you known where they were before this?"

"Well, yes, I had friends who didn't know I was the mother but used to go over to Binghamton. They told me things."

"You mean about Tony. Roger was in Miami."

"Yes, but I knew he was all right. I knew he was with his father."

"He wasn't with his father," I corrected her. "After they took Roger, Jules and his wife separated a second time. Roger grew up without a father."

She studied me as I said this but then turned to look past me, across the street where a dog was barking. When she answered, she said, "Even still, they had a good life. Better than my kids, who starved half the time."

I again corrected her. "Tony had a good life. Roger didn't. Not at all."

My answer caught her unawares and seemed to straighten her up. She looked me full in the face, our eyes met again, and I knew that she wanted to hear more. So I explained, "As a boy, Roger had a hard life. Yet he turned out fine. They both did. You would be proud of them."

She didn't quite know what to do with this judgment, with its implied flattery, and made no reply. Instead, she began to fill the silence by returning to her cheerless life.

"There were eight of us in my family, and we all worked," she said. "I went to work when I was fourteen and I still work. You know, if I did write a book people wouldn't believe it."

I interrupted to ask if there were twins on her side of the family. "They run in my family," she answered. "Besides these boys, I once lost a pair in my fourth month. I had a miscarriage."

We talked next of her three surviving children by Renato; she told me they were all married, two had children of their own and everyone was well but they had nothing to do with their father. She was filled with contempt for her ex-husband and his family.

"Because of them I had to go to court and I lost my children," she protested. "They were wrong, too. I never left my children. Wherever I went, I took them, but because of their lies my children were put in a home. There is a God in heaven, though, for those people have all suffered."

I said nothing to this and after the slightest of pauses she continued, coming up to that moment in her life that I now believe she wishes she could live over.

"I didn't know what I was doing back then," she said without my prompting or any hint of what was coming. "I mean, can you blame me? I only just lost my children and . . . and what was I supposed to do?"

I thought, for just an instant, she was about to cry. She stared down at her feet again, moved the right one in a tiny circle and repeated, "It was something that just happened, and after all these years, what am I supposed to say? It was long ago, and why should any of it come out now? If there is anything you want to know, ask Jules. Let him tell you. It was all his idea—to give them away."

I was surprised at this, and said so. "Well, he didn't want them," she answered and again reassured herself, "They had a better life than my children. That's for sure."

She bent down and picked up the hose, signaling that our meeting was over.

"I'm on my way to Binghamton," I said. "Do you have

any message for the boys? Is there anything you want me to tell them?"

She stared at me for a second and then gave a shrug. In a voice that was almost a whisper, she again asked, "What can I say?"

I turned and walked across the dandelion-filled lawn until I reached the road. Because of the way my car was headed, I had to walk around it to the driver's side and now I was once more facing her. She said goodbye with a little smile, and as I hesitated I heard her add softly, "Wish them luck for me."

Roger was the more excited, eager to hear details of my encounter with the woman we had all referred to as the real mother.

"You saw her?" he asked, his head cocked to the right, his eyes opened wide. "Is she pretty? What's she like? Did she marry an Italian again?"

Tony asked me the same question he had put to Jules Brooks, "Do we look anything like her?"

I answered that I saw no physical resemblance; the brothers are true copies of their biological father. Yet, when I thought about this, I realized that in Maria's emotionally flat recitations, her use of denial and the way she had insisted that the twins had an easier life than "my children," she reminded me of Tony.

After Roger's small excitement and their few questions, there was nothing more for any of us to say about Maria. The brothers explained they had no desire to see their mother and I was relieved, for Dr. Milton Gross, the psychiatrist, had counseled me against such a meeting. He had said that Maria "has undoubtedly suffered with her guilt. The kindest thing you can do is to leave her alone now, permitting the woman to forget, especially if the twins have no overwhelming desire to see her."

Tony and Roger understood that the woman I found was living a completely new life. They neither wanted to force their way into this life, nor be the reason for embarrassing or, in any way, upsetting her. They were satisfied to know she was alive and well and that she had wished them luck.

There wasn't any prolonged discussion or argument that brought them to this common decision. From the first, they had thought alike on the question, and as I stood aside, listening to them, I was again struck by the force of their disposition to agree. I was reminded once more of Thornton Wilder's Manuel and Esteban.

Wilder wrote of them in *The Bridge of San Luis Rey,* "What relationship is it in which few words are exchanged and those only about the details of food, clothing and occupation?"

I cannot in confidence, say that a communion exists between Tony Milasi and Roger Brooks, but I am convinced their rapport goes far beyond that experienced by all but a very few monozygotics. The mystique of twinship they share is special. Yet, as close as they are, and despite the common genetical grounding that produces their "hair-raising similarities," they remain for me two distinct and most different personalities.

But in the five years during which I have watched them grow close as brothers, I have also witnessed a blurring of their personalities until Roger Brooks becomes, if only temporarily, a mirror twin to Tony Milasi. He is then a reflection of his monozygotic partner, subordinating his will and his life-style in order to share his brother's attention and love.

I am tempted, in a search for an explanation to this personality transference, this subtle and strange metamorphosis, to parallel Roger with Esteban. When Manuel fell in love, the fictional brothers were temporarily divided. Wilder wrote, then "Esteban sat up in their room by a guttering candle, his knuckles between his teeth, and wondered why Manuel was so changed and why the whole meaning had gone out of his life."

Esteban, wrote Wilder, was learning the hard lesson that "there may never be two that love one another equally well." So it is with Roger Brooks and Tony Milasi. It is Roger whose love and need are greater.

Three times before Roger had *lost* Tony: when Tony was first adopted; when unexpectedly Tony married and moved away from Carroll Street, and when Roger felt he must work and live in Miami. To hold onto Tony now, to be always close to him, Roger Brooks is prepared to pattern his life so it is compatible with the life of his twin.

This then is how I left them, sharing each other's day every day. And as I headed south, away from the Twin Mar-

ket and Binghamton, I hoped that the time would never come
when either brother cries out, as did Esteban:

"I am alone, alone, alone!"